940·5442

ABOUT THE AUTHOR

Joseph Attard was born and educated in Malta and served in the RAF during the war. After a career in the Civil Service he became a freelance journalist and wrote his first English novel in 1968. He has since written three books in English and four in Maltese, in addition to many radio plays and a television serial. He is married and has three children.

THE BATTLE OF MALTA

JOSEPH ATTARD

Hamlyn Paperbacks

THE BATTLE OF MALTA
ISBN 0 600 20548 7

First published in Great Britain 1980
by William Kimber & Co. Limited
Hamlyn Paperbacks edition 1982
Reprinted 1982
Copyright © 1980 by Joseph Attard

Hamlyn Paperbacks are published by
The Hamlyn Publishing Group Ltd,
Astronaut House, Feltham,
Middlesex, England

Printed and bound in Great Britain by
Cox & Wyman Ltd, Reading

Contents

List of Maps

Foreword

The task of writing a true story like that of the Battle of Malta, forty years from the time it took place, must necessarily present the writer with many problems. I could overcome mine because I had intended to write about Malta's ordeal from the very first day of the Italian air onslaught in June 1940. What followed, was then impressed upon me and became throughout the forty years a load to be lifted from my chest, which is what I am doing now. I did not undertake this task before for many reasons. However the passage of time has afforded me the benefit of more recent research, in many instances augmented by explanations and facts which could only now be revealed. The impact of battle on the Maltese people and their behaviour is described from personal experiences and eye-witness accounts, but even here, strange to say, one very often comes across conflicting versions, since what one person may remember clearly may not be similarly recalled by another. So, rather than attempting to reconstruct from different versions, I chose to go for information given by those personally involved, which was confirmed by other sources.

Naturally I have had recourse to several books which directly or indirectly touch on the epic of Malta, and it was here that I had many a time come across inaccuracies, and omissions, which, more than anything else, spurred me on in my endeavours to give to the world the true story of Malta. It may be said as well that I could have included much more material in this history, which I did not. Some of it, I might have considered not to be important for my scope; or maybe I could not find conclusive confirmation of it. Indeed, there might also have been much that I do not know. Even with all the effort I have put in my work, I am convinced that it will take many more writers and attempts to write all there is to be said of the Battle of Malta. All in all, however, I feel that I have managed to give a true picture of what constituted this battle and the siege from 11th June 1940 to 8th September 1943, bringing to the fore the combined efforts of the Three Armed Services (Maltese and British), the Police, the Passive Defences, and last, but certainly not the least, the Maltese people, who with their characteristic heroic forbearance were instrumental in withstanding all and everything, and made it possible for me to be writing today about their victorious epic. It may appear that I have put stress on the religious element in the Maltese character and beliefs, but let it be said that this is true, and has at no time been exaggerated. This was indeed the main factor which made the Maltese act as they did. Even the fact that my story ends, as it begins, with a church service, is neither coincidental nor so planned. It had to be so, since it is the truth.

I would have liked to mention by name and deed all the many Maltese, British, Commonwealth and Allied servicemen and civilians who were decorated for heroic action in Malta during the battle and siege, but this would be a mammoth task which I would not have been able to complete within the limits imposed on me. This omission however is not to be interpreted in any way as any lack of recognition and appreciation of their heroic deeds. It is more than fitting that I should pay tribute to those men and women who gallantly surmounted all the difficulties of enemy superiority, shortages, and human stress, to emerge victorious in whatever battles they were involved in defence of Malta. One of course cannot leave out the rest who fought, even though without official reward for their efforts, which none the less merit admiration. A last special word of praise goes to all those who made the supreme sacrifice and died, so that we could live.

Because this was to be a true story I had to mention persons by their real names, and where it was warranted and possible I obtained their permission to do so. Permission was not sought where the names of the persons involved had become a part of history and could not be left out or disguised without reflecting adversely on the merit of this work. A few persons I mentioned to characterise particular behaviour could not be traced, and it is hoped that if they are still alive they will give me their indulgence. In the very few instances where I made up names it was because I had no particular persons in mind, but the characters depicted under these names existed in abundance.

I wish to record my indebtedness to the publishers who have kindly given me their permission to draw on information and quote from their published works which appear in the Bibliographical list. I am also indebted to the Allied Newspapers Limited of Malta for giving me their permission to use information published in the *Times of Malta* throughout the battle and siege, without missing a single day, and for placing at my disposal their collection of war photographs; to the National War Museum Association of Malta for also affording me the use of photographs from its collection, and to the Acting Director of Information for his prompt co-operation in providing a picture I asked for. My appreciation is also expressed to the British Ministry of Defence (Naval Historical Branch) for assistance rendered by giving me information, and verifying facts whenever this was required. I must mention as well Major Gerald Amato-Gauci, MC, Major Joe A. Agius, MC, Major Joe Micallef Trigona, and Major B.J. Portelli, all of them ex-officers of the Royal Malta Artillery, who favoured me with first hand information on their involvement in the battle. There was also submarine ace and author Alastair Mars DSO, DSC and Bar, who, with his publishers before I knew they were also going to be mine, gave me permission to draw on what he wrote about submarine epics in the Mediterranean and particularly on his Santa Maria exploit. My thanks also go to Mr Victor E Stafrace for placing his painstakingly made up scrap-book at my disposal, to Captain Joe Wismayer for giving me what information he had whenever I asked for it and to my son-in law Mr Costantino Consiglio for drawing the maps. I cannot possibly mention by name the other numerous persons who volunteered information, produced diaries, answered my questions or in some other way helped me out in my task, but to all of them go my grateful thanks.

Malta is no longer a fortress, and visitors from all over the world come to this remarkable island, now an independent republic, to see and sample her homely welcome and cultural heritage. Her people talk of their sun, and their monuments, their homes and their families, and they do it with their well-known gracious smile. But beneath the sunburnt smiling faces of the elders there still lurk the memories of the terrible war years, which can never be erased. To the younger generation the epic of those years may appear to be just another story. But nothing is farther from the truth. Malta went through the three year battle and siege with the pain, anguish, hunger and destruction that will be found in this book, but also with the forbearance and glorious heroism that went with them. This is what constitutes the story I have written, to be added to the island's glorious history.

To those who made it possible, I dedicate this work.

MALTA GC
March, 1980.

Joseph Attard

CHAPTER ONE

The Prelude

Malta is a peaceful land; birds sing and greenery flourishes. The wind is soft, and warm. Only an occasional gusty freak spoils the harmony. True, the summer sun is like a furnace; it boils the blood and cooks the body. But together with the gentle rain it makes trees and flowers grow.

As the sun rises from the east every morning, it strikes Fort St Angelo on its back, shedding its silhouette to frolic across the blue water of Grand Harbour. The water is then like a jewel shimmering with bright light and throwing reflections to mix and die with the golden tide on the bastions of Valletta rising like a fair uplifted bosom.

Beyond the glittering surface of the harbour's main aisle, and past the majestic St Angelo lie the creeks, partly shadowed but flashing reflections of spots of gold light from belfries and cupolas, early risers to the sun. In the background lie more towns and villages still hidden in the misty distance. Nestling in those creeks lie groups of sun-lit buildings, and bastions that form self-contained towns to which the belfries and cupolas belong. The whiteness of the stone in recent extensions contrasts with the grey mellowed by centuries.

One of the towns was all beflagged, and the sound of bells from its belfries reached across the harbour drawing pensive eyes to the church which could be seen rising majestically over the water of the creek, beckoning and inviting all to witness what was taking place inside.

The imposing church was filled to its crimson-draped doors. Men, women and children made a sea of faces, all absorbed and looking towards the high altar splendid with silver, glittering in the light from the big crystal chandeliers. There was also the music, words and tunes from a score of voices and a thirty-strong orchestra in the music balcony over the main door. A cadence in the music, and the air was filled with the murmuring of quiet prayers. The eyes were now all intent on the celebrant at the altar and the canons of the chapter sitting in the handsome choir stalls all in red shoulder capes with snow white cottas over their black

cassocks. Above them loomed a huge canvas by the Calabrian
Mattia Preti, dark and mellowed by time, depicting the martyrdom
of St Lawrence, the titular saint of the church and the patron of
the city of Vittoriosa, or as it was then and is still called today,
Birgu. In the main aisle there was the statue of the saint,
resplendent in the vestments proper to an archdeacon of the
Catholic church in the times of the Roman Emperor Valerian,
complete with red chasuble studded with twentieth-century
precious stones; it stood on its silver pedestal, surrounded with
candles and flowers, drawing looks of admiration from the faithful.
The statue would be taken out of the church in the evening and
carried in procession through the narrow streets of the city, and
the people would play their part in this common Maltese drama
with profound and solemn devoutness.

This was happening at Vittoriosa on 10th August 1939, but it
was only a replica of what had happened and would keep taking
place in every town and village of Malta with different saints, on
other days.

For the rest of the evening and night the people would celebrate
their *festa* by giving themselves to rejoicing wholeheartedly and
necessarily noisily. The local band, supported by bands hired from
other localities would parade the streets and play programmes in
the squares; hawkers would be at their stands erected overnight to
sell nougat, a local and traditional sweet delicacy, and compete
with each other in shouting to attract buyers; the church bells
would clang with no attempt at rhythm, while rockets and Roman
candles would be let off in rapid succession in all directions.
During some rare pause between the bangs one might be lucky to
catch the sound of some band trying to play an air from an opera.
Not that it would matter, because no band would have much hope
of making its output prevail over the general din. As if this would
not be enough, there would be bound to come the end with more
elaborate firework displays and the detonation of bombs and
petards which would resound from end to end of the island.

When the night was quiet again and the streets emptied, the
hawkers would leave, with the lamps of their carts jogging home-
wards winking on the roads as if in a ghostly procession. The thrill
of a guitar might be heard and there might also be a man's voice
raised in plaintive song, expressing satisfaction that another *festa*
had gone by, and, no doubt, thinking of the next one. For the
Maltese calendar contains many such days. When daylight came
for another day, life would return to normal. The women would

put away their voluminous skirts and blouses for another day. Some would put in mothballs their black silk *faldettas* (because they were already going out of use then) and take out their second best which would have to do for the rest of the year. The men, too would do away with their bright shirts, coats and waistcoats which they wear only on feast days. The uncomfortable shoes bought with hard earned pennies were put away for another *festa*, and if by then they became too tight for wearing they could always be handed down to children from year to year.

The men would wear their French cloth trousers and shirts with caps to match, and they would go back to work at the dockyard or some other British establishment, because in those days Maltese economy depended on the British Fleet and the Garrison. They would return to their routine of working their brains and arms out throughout the week to earn a wage of two pounds. On this wage, they maintained their big family and sent their children to school; they would also stake something on the weekly lotto and have a few pints of wine. The wives would also put something away for the rainy day.

Impossible? But that is how Maltese life was in 1939. With sixty per cent of a population of 250,000 illiterate, poverty was rife, but there were also the few who had fortunes and also those with the means to have a better standard of living. They extended their sense of family and filial duty so characteristic of the Maltese, beyond the limits of close relationship, and anyone in the town or village who fell on hard days could turn to them. Rents were low and taxation negligible, and, if wages were fantastically low, so were costs and standards of living. There were of course doctors, lawyers, architects, teachers and civil servants, all products of a university and high schools. There were also numerous priests, monks and nuns, who, besides their holy ministrations, maybe unknowingly but very effectively provided what non-existent social services failed to do. There were deaths, disease and misfortune, but when these occurred they were always the will of God, and the Maltese blamed nothing and no one.

Life was this simple and static. The Maltese lived only for their family and trusted in God. The only two outlets from the daily routine of living were the feast, for which they waited from year to year and gladly contributed to, and their local band club. This was an institution with a far wider significance than the merely musical. After the parish church it was the most important nucleus of the township; the church and club can be said to have bracketed and held each town or village like a pair of book ends. Whatever problem arose to affect the inhabitants, for better or for worse, was bound to be resolved within their portals.

Going back in history one cannot fail to be struck by the comparison of Malta's past with the country of 1939. Going through the long list of periods of occupation by foreign powers, one cannot but think of other eras when the Maltese islands were inhabited by happy kindly beings of more than human wisdom, loving peace when this was allowed to them, and fighting for it when it was denied. There were occupations by the Phoenicians, Carthaginians, Romans, Arabs, Normans, the Angevines and Castilians — a very long list, with each period historically colourful, but when crystallized into definite dates and events it became a lamentable recital of plots and oppression, and restriction of civilisation to breathe and flourish.

The first promising breath of fresh air arrived in 1530 when the Knights of St John came to Malta. They ruled for two and a half centuries until 1798, and these are still looked at by many as Malta's Golden Age. In the island, the Knights found only an arid sparsely peopled rock, with the ancient walled capital of Mdina, and the small tower (where Fort St Elmo was eventually built) at one tip of the Grand Harbour with another fort, that of St Angelo, on the other side. Vittoriosa, the city where we witnessed the *festa* at the beginning of this chapter, was the only other town lying close to St Angelo, but it was in embryonic form. Over and above this there was little else except a number of small unimportant hamlets scattered about the countryside.

During their reign the Knights transformed all this, and today after nearly two centuries one can still see and admire the vast and lovely fortifications which, in the words of Sir Harry Luke in his book *Malta*, are the most impressive monuments in Europe of Western military architecture of the sixteenth, seventeenth and early eighteenth centuries. Cities arose from the rocky dust, like Cospicua and Senglea, which to this day partner Vittoriosa to make the triangle of the Three Cities, as they lurk behind the intricate patterns of curtains, bastions and demi-bastions, cavaliers and counterguards, ravelins, lunettes and gates in the still evocative system of fortifications.

These three cities were endowed with palatial buildings which have survived destructive modernistic trends, and the beautiful *auberges* in Vittoriosa, and the churches, have lived in their haunting splendour throughout the centuries. As if to complete the girdle of magnificence round the Grand Harbour, there was built on its other side the city of Valletta which took the name of the Grand Master who built it, no less sumptuous in its *auberges*, churches, palaces and of course fortifications, and which was made, as it is still today, the island's capital.

With the rapid growth of the population more villages began to rise from the arid areas and from the already existing hamlets. Many of them could not really be called villages, for they were more like compact townships of tall houses and narrow streets built in good Baroque architecture with everything erected round the centrepiece — the church.

The description of this simple way of life may lull one into the belief that the Maltese were in those times a meek people ripe to be held in subjection by any powerful ruler. But nothing is farther from the truth; even in those times democracy and freedom were not mere words for the people of the Maltese islands, and their long history of feudalism was very often sparked with stories in support of their beliefs. This attitude is many a time reflected in their history, such as when they elected their leaders under the Carthaginians and the Romans, in their rebellion against the Arab tyrant whom they succeeded in expelling. Whenever there was cause, Maltese bishops and priests repeatedly led the people in peaceful protests and more than once in armed insurrection, and when circumstances warranted it Grand Masters of the Order were unseated. But more than their belief and love of democracy and freedom history brings out conspicuously the traditional characteristic of the unification of all classes whenever the Maltese were faced by danger or attack. There is no bigger proof of this than the Great Siege of 1565 when the Maltese people rallied together and shoulder to shoulder with their rulers, the Knights of St John, fought the Infidel who had invaded their land; the Maltese endured sickness, hunger and other hardships in bearing the brunt of the enemy's fury for four months. When their resources did not measure up to their aims then they had recourse to assistance which they somehow always obtained.

Just as they had for defence against the Carthaginians called on the Romans and, when these squeezed them, appealed to Caesar, so they called in the Normans to expel Arabs, and Napoleon to destroy the aristocratic Republic of the Sovereign Order. When the French also resorted to oppression, then the Maltese starved their garrison into submission. It was now that they persuaded a reluctant England to accept Malta as a feud of the British Crown.

On 21st March 1800 the Maltese supplicated the Kingdom of Naples to have it transfer their sovereignty to his Britannic Majesty, and on 10th December of the same year Major General Pigot was instructed by Sir Ralph Abercromby, then Commander in Chief of the British Forces in Egypt to take the Maltese Islands under his protection.

Even so, things were not as easy as they appeared because after the departure of the French a storm rose up in Europe about the rightful possession of Malta. The Czar of Russia laid claim to it because of his being elected Grand Master of the Order of St John; France claimed that the French capitulation in Malta had not been authorised and therefore the island was still French; the King of Naples proclaimed himself the original sovereign of Malta since the British had only agreed to protect it on his behalf against the French. This political unrest continued until 1801 when the Treaty of Amiens was initiated which amongst other things laid down that Malta should be restored to the Order of St John under the protection of England, France, Spain and Prussia. However, notwithstanding the fact that a Grand Master was appointed to Malta in 1803, the Maltese continued to press with wit and stratagem until in 1813 they received recognition and confirmation that they belonged to the British Crown, and Sir Thomas Maitland was appointed the first Governor and Commander-in-Chief.

The British found in Malta a land rich in fortifications, palaces, churches, *auberges*, and a hundred other cultural embellishments, but lacking in administration and similarly important functions. It therefore needed a truculent and combatant man like Maitland to set the ball rolling. Even as far as that time, Italian, as the language of the nearest country on the continent of Europe, was much spoken and it might have been a mistake on the part of the British when they directed Maitland to issue his proclamation in English and Italian in the hope that after a few years the latter would be disused. Maitland set about his task of bringing the required organisation to Malta and began with overhauling the legal system. He took education in hand, and also negotiated with the Vatican on matters affecting the Church. But he died in Malta in 1824. His work was continued by other governors who followed.

Looking at the many innovations carried out in Malta under British rule one immediately realizes that many of them lacked the international approach of those of the Knights; they were more of a domestic nature for they were the way of converting Malta into a fortress and a base to serve British commitments in the Mediterranean. The naval military hospital of Bighi was built, while the Grand Harbour was extended to Marsa in an effort to afford more protection to storm-battered ships. The naval dockyard which will play a large part in this story owes its birth to this period, and so does the magnificent break-water which made of Malta's harbour the desired haven for the British Fleet. As if to balance all this there were of course the Valletta Market, which was built and still stands today, and the beautiful Royal Opera House which was constructed on a design by E.A. Barry, the architect responsible for the similar edifice in Covent Garden in London.

A modern water supply system was built; deep underground galleries were dug and water found in abundance. Electricity was introduced too, and these two commodities together with the improvement and asphalting of roads no doubt benefited the military side as much as the civilian population. The beginning and development of modern Maltese politics and the growth of systematic education can be traced to this period, which also witnessed the ever present language question. This persistent problem divided the people. Some of them presented a picture of feudal Latin upper class, who could talk and write Italian, jumping at any occasion to use it, and of course looking with benign eyes on Italy as a more fit ruler for their people. The rest talked a concocted Maltese and pidgin English, appearing the under-privileged lower class. The British had already erred in bringing this about, and persisted in their error when they accepted Italian as the official language of the courts and similar high institutions. Now they acquiesced in the situation. Temporary disruption and solution of the problem came with the advent of the First World War in 1914 when in their characteristic way the Maltese joined hands in moments of danger and forgot differences. About 20,000 joined the British forces and saw service in various theatres of operations during that war, while more than 25,000 beds were made available in Malta where the sick and wounded troops were brought for care.

With the war over and won, however, there followed a slump. With the British fleet and garrison depleted, employment went down. Even the boatmen who earned their living ferrying ships' crews across the harbour felt the pinch. So did the barmaids in their bars. It had become more obvious than ever that Malta's lot was tied up with crisis and belligerency.

The giving of a self-governing Constitution in 1921 looked like infusing new-found life, but the difficulties and hectic confrontation this brought between the political parties, were not to everybody's taste. The ever-present language question however was settled, bringing in the Maltese language instead of Italian. There was also the emergence of the Church as the strong power to be contended with in the local political arena, and this might have been instrumental in consolidating the Maltese. Church, work (when this was available), family and *festa* became more than ever before the cardinal points of the Maltese compass. So much so that even when the Abyssinian crisis in 1935 brought the fleet back in strength, and there was work again and money for everyone, it did not swerve the people from their old ways.

When the crisis was over and Mussolini's star was in descent, Hitler's began to rise. In 1936 he moved to re-occupy the demilitarized zone of the Rhineland and the world knew this was no insignificant move and was bound to be followed by more. The red warning found its way into Maltese newspapers as well but any feelings it might have raised were subdued by the clanging of church bells and fireworks. Nobody cared. Even when the airfield at Hal Far was put into operation it failed to raise more than a slight interest in the Swordfish aircraft which could then be seen in the Maltese skies together with the Italian Ala Littoria flying boats which were using Marsaxlokk Bay as a base.

When in 1938 the Germans moved into Austria the British intensified their preparations in Malta. The papers were more often carrying notices of firing practice by the Fleet, the dark night skies began to be scanned by searchlights, and platoons of troops and marines route-marching all over the island became a frequent spectacle to be watched by old and young alike with different feelings. Old coastal forts which had lain dormant supervised by watchmen and maintenance personnel were now becoming alive, and St Elmo and Ricasoli lying astride the harbour entrance, with Tigne and Campbell to the west and St Rocco and Delimara to the east, had new big guns sprouting from their embrasures. Hundreds of recruits to the Royal Malta Artillery flocked to these newly found homes to drill every morning, polish their brass and learn all about their new big toys. Even proud St Angelo in the centre of the harbour which until then had only boasted of a small saluting battery was now showing a second battery of four inch guns guarding the entrance to the harbour.

Could any enemy force approach Malta in face of those guns?

Everyone was asking this same question. And as if to find confirmation eyes wandered to the warships which every day filled the port. The battleships of those days, *Barham, Warspite, Royal Oak, Royal Sovereign, Queen Elizabeth, Renown* and *Ramillies* spelt power even in friendly eyes as they lay at anchor; the cruisers and destroyers at their berths in the creeks. The aircraft carriers *Glorious, Furious, Courageous* and *Eagle* took their turn in harbour and added to the powerful glamour, with their flying decks rising as if in competition with the Valletta bastions. It was a similar story at Lazaretto, in Marsamxetto Harbour with the sleek grey submarines and their supply ships. It was a magnificent armada which strengthened the heart of anyone with warlike thoughts, and spelt immunity from sea attack. But what about the air? News was already coming from Germany, England and Italy of the new types of aircraft that were being produced, but when Maltese eyes roved all over the skies they failed to see any of them. Everyone looked around with fear and eagerness and all one could see were the 4.5 guns being placed in the few batteries that were sprouting up in the countryside. But what could such guns do? They might shoot down aircraft, but they would not keep away the bombs. And bombs there would be, because there were already appearing in the papers details of how one could protect oneself against them or mitigate their effects.

One comforting bit of information was that Malta stone was highly resistant to high explosive while it was virtually immune to incendiary bombs. But there was also danger from the lately developed weapon of poisonous gas which the Italians had only just used in Abyssinia, and this danger was a real one. argued the people, since they were all being told how to fit an anti-gas room in the house with blocked windows and blankets to cover doorways, which were to be sprinkled with water when in use. All heard the rantings of Mussolini who had passed the word on radio that the Maltese belonged to the Italian race and Malta was by right closer to Italy in its ties than to Britain. If it came to the worst he claimed, and the Italians had to attack Malta, they would do it with flowers and not with bombs. The word was quickly taken up by the few pro-Italians as a diversion, no doubt, in their fight for the Italian language. But nobody believed them. They did not even believe it themselves.

Italy was at that time still sitting on the fence, but this did not delude anyone when assessing intentions, and it was realised that if there ever were to be an attack on Malta it would come from the

Italian side, with the airfields in Sicily only some sixty miles away. Whether it would be by bombs or flowers would remain to be seen; and it was not yet certain whether Italy would join the war. After all England was not even at war yet, and from the look of things Neville Chamberlain, the British Prime Minister, was doing his damnedest to avoid it. Even after Czechoslovakia had been taken, on 10th March 1939 Chamberlain expressed the view that the prospects for peace were better than ever before.

So why worry? The Maltese continued with their own life. The masons chipped the white Malta stone in a blazing sun, the herdsmen milked their goats from door to door and the hawkers plied their wares to the appraising haggling housewives. The men toiled at the dockyard and the boatmen traded in swill from the warships in the harbour, which they would take to the shops in the evening, where they would share and eat it with others and wash it down with pungent red wine. They had never stopped doing this, and they would keep on doing it for all the days to come leaving everything else to God's will utterly in which they trusted.

The 11th August 1939, was such a day, and the people of Vittoriosa still tired and listless from their feast were no different. But there was puzzlement and perplexity in the faces of the men who met at the band club in the evening; there was fresh news in the air which was suddenly causing stir and bustle. Some were reading the evening editions, sharing them with those who leant across their shoulders, and on the scanning faces and in bewildered eyes there seemed to be the same question which was soon translated into words to ask whether after all they would be celebrating their *festa* the following year.

They had their reply barely three weeks later when on Friday 1st September, the German armies invaded Poland, and on the following Sunday the British Government declared war on Germany.

*

I was then not yet fifteen — a son of a country that had taken so many centuries to forge itself into a peace-loving nation and looked like being thwarted now when it was seeing the end of the road. I was one of the many boys on which Malta was basing its hopes for a new type of life — well-educated, disciplined and loyal. What we knew of war then came only from the books and newspapers we read which told us what was going on in the rest of the world. It was little, but enough to infuse in me, however young, an insight into what might be expected. With a war on, which was threatening suffering and annihilation, I was suddenly burning to serve my country and my people in whatever capacity presented itself. Yet what could a boy of fourteen do?

The clarity of those days in Malta and the others that followed have remained with me throughout these forty years and it was this that made me write about them today with sureness of description and expression as if they had only happened yesterday.

On that morning of 3rd September 1939, the square and streets of Vittoriosa were full of people as they always were on Sundays, but now there were silent crowds looking askance as if waiting for answers to the silent questions in their eyes which never came. Those were all people who had built the simple Maltese life which was threatened with disruption, now that the country was at war, and the only forlorn hope that emerged from their conversation, when they spoke at all rested on the fact of Malta being distant from the main theatre of operations. We were, however, soon to know.

With the imminence of war Malta was denuded of most naval forces. This was obviously done because of mobilisation and deployment. The Grand Harbour looked so empty and futile without the familiar warships, and there were days when the only ship that could be seen was the *Westgate* which controlled the anti-submarine boom in the entrance of the harbour, now looking like an empty house, silent after the children had left. But the names of those children remained on everyone's lips and in Maltese hearts, which would leap with pleasure on hearing them mentioned on the radio or read about them in the newspapers.

Hearts did not leap however, when on 17th September news reached Malta of the sinking of the aircraft carrier *Courageous* by a German submarine. As well as the connection the ship had with Malta there were the Maltese seamen who were lost with it. Hardly had the sorrow subsided when the battleship *Royal Oak* a well-known ship at Malta, was sunk at Scapa Flow with a higher death toll of Maltese seamen. These were the first two painful blows for the local population even if they were not directly connected with Malta.

There were others to follow, but there was also much activity going on in Malta itself which obviously received more attention.

Mobilisation continued at a steady pace, and recruiting was causing a steady flow of able-bodied men to swell the Royal Malta Artillery and the King's Own Malta Regiment. There were men for the Royal Army Service Corps, the Medical Corps, the Royal Engineers, the Royal Navy and of course the Royal Air Force. Those who because of age or some other reason could not join up, could give their services as a Special Constable or an Air Raid Warden. There wasn't much to do for these last two in the way of action, but there was great scope to learn in anticipation of what might be expected of them later on.

Paraphernalia and accoutrements of war began flowing swiftly into the island and the civilian population was soon being issued with gas masks which was a job for Air Raid Wardens and Special Constables. It was a foregone conclusion that should Malta be attacked from the air the dockyard and harbour would be the obvious targets, and Valletta and the Three Cities of Vittoriosa, Cospicua and Senglea would be bound to be hit being so close. It was therefore decided to evacuate the civilian population from these cities and a scheme was put into operation whereby all families were encouraged to evacuate to some safer place, but those who had nowhere to go or could not be bothered to find somewhere were allocated accommodation in outlying villages. As one would have expected, such accommodation was in most cases not what one desired and many of those registered to evacuate decided against it and to stay where they were. There was also the question of air raid shelters to be seen to, and the first resort was for cellars and buildings with arched roofs; where these were found, and there were many, the authorities provided wooden buttressing to the arches. Churches with their arched and pillared aisles were also declared to be safer than ordinary rooms. Where such buildings were not available shelters were constructed by digging trenches and roofing them with earth and rubble. These however became quagmires with the first heavy rains and were hardly ever used. With these preparations there was also the training in air raid precautions for the population. Black-outs, sounding of sirens, and enforced wearing of gas masks for short periods became the order of the day.

One would have expected that all this should not have diverted anyone's attention from the bad times that were approaching, but there was one such important diversion. With the onset of war and expected shortage of supplies everybody started hoarding what foodstuffs that could be found and many resorted to buying clandestinely; this brought the black market to Malta for the first time. All this became Maltese everyday life, leaving no time for thinking about what was happening in other places. When the phrase of 'Phoney War' was coined by the American press for the period from the collapse of Poland in September 1939, until Hitler's Western offensive in the following spring, it could aptly be applied to Malta as well. The difference was that while the English and French faced the Germans on the Western Front, each side knew where to expect the attack from and were convinced that it would materialise, while Malta, and of course England as the planner of her defence, knew that any attack that would be aimed at eliminating Malta would have to come from Italy; as Italy was not yet in the war however they could not know if and when it would come. The British were convinced Italy would enter the war against them, and this was evident from their preparations in Malta. When they considered the time ripe, they even took in custody those Maltese who were self-declared pro-Italian and thought dangerous. But despite such measures the people remained as always hoping and praying that nothing would disturb the Phoney War that was not harming them except through the tension of not knowing what was going to happen. With each month that went past they became less wary and more hopeful until in their characteristic way they began slipping back into the easy going, day-to-day existence although hemmed in by the restrictions that were unavoidably imposed and the preparations for war that had become a routine of life. There were days when these war preparations lost their ghastly purpose and were considered as something to be looked at as some new experience or a pastime.

Then on the evening of 10th June 1940 Italy declared war on England, and the Maltese knew that whether they liked it or not they would have to face what was in store for them. Anyone who knew something about armament statistics and the balance of power was convinced of the holocaust that could be expected to hit Malta. What nobody could say was how easy-going and docile Malta would react.

That is going to be my story.

CHAPTER TWO

Baptism of Fire

Soon after the Italian declaration of war on 10th June, the governor of Malta, Lieutenant General William Dobbie, spoke to the people. In contrast with Mussolini's bombastic ranting from Palazzo Venezia in Rome the British General was calm and measured. Briefly and to the point he told his people that Italy was at war with England and therefore with Malta, and that this meant that hard times were ahead. Then expressing his hope in divine aid to help him and the Maltese to maintain the security of their country, he appealed to everyone to seek such aid and rely on God to help him do his duty unflinchingly.

This brought tears to many eyes. They were tears of sympathy for their governor, who would share with them whatever turmoils they would have to face; of anguish from the women whose men were away on the guns for the coming night; and of agitation from those few who left their homes there and then to get out of the target area. There were also the tears of relief of those who felt easier now that they knew where they stood, and what to expect. But there were also the looks of determination in the eyes of those who had long expected this, and now wanted to see it through.

In Valletta where the evening crowds were more cosmopolitan with the influx of young men and women from the villages, the reaction was different. Crowds assembled at various points, but the biggest one was certainly that opposite the Police Station in Kingsway to watch members of the Italian Colony in Malta being brought there after being rounded up for detention in an internment camp. Every time the Italians were brought over patriotic shouts were heard rising from the crowd, which then broke into singing the *Marseillaise*. Those who left their homes that evening carrying blankets and pillows flocked to the newly opened tunnels in the bastions of Valletta and the Three Cities, emulating the ancient Christians who had to escape the wrath of the Roman emperors in the time of persecution. The people of Valletta and Floriana found a ready-made shelter in the old disused railway tunnel which joined the two cities. By the time all movement had ceased, there wasn't a soul to be seen in the streets except some over-zealous policeman or Air Raid Warden making sure there were no visible lights. Those who decided to remain in their homes joined up with other relatives as if in numbers they found strength to face whatever the night would bring, and Malta became a silent island of darkness.

Excitement must have kept many from sleeping that night. I was one of them, and was up by six the following morning. My first realisation was that after all the night had not brought anything and my next thought was to look out of the window on the first morning of war, not knowing what to expect to see. There were the usual dockyard people walking to their work, and groups of women chattering and gesticulating as they walked to church. But there were others, men, women and children carrying bags and baskets full of clothing and personal needs walking to the bus terminus obviously to leave town. There were cars and carts carrying people and belongings. They must have been those who had overnight decided to leave. Special Constables and Air Raid Wardens were helping all and sundry with instructions.

For half an hour I remained at the window watching the exodus gathering momentum. It appeared to me then that the hundreds of people who had ignored the evacuation plan laid down for them, had suddenly changed their minds and wanted to go. The sad truth was that those people had never believed such a situation would materialise. Theirs was not an isolated problem, and, as I thought then and confirmed later, the same thing was happening in Cospicua, Senglea, Marsa, Valletta and Floriana, all of them being close to the harbour and the dockyard. Even at that time the roads leading out of these places were full of people, walking in a hurry lest something happened before they reached their destination. The buses that were available could certainly not cope with those crowds, and neither could the transport that the authorities provided.

There were of course those who remained in their homes, and, either because they were at a loss for what to do, or because of altruistic determination, tried to carry on with their normal life as if nothing abnormal had happened. The men went as usual to their place of work, and the women to the church. Maybe some of them took their children with them having decided there would be no school on that day. The priests and the monks carried on with their usual services. They would never dream of deserting their flock.

I went on the roof from where I could get a better view of what was going on. My eyes wandered to the empty harbour looking so forlorn and helpless. There had only been three ships on the previous day, the monitor *Terror*, and the gunboats *Aphis* and *Ladybird*. Now they were no longer there. Apart from the noise of moving humanity which still reached me from the streets there was no other sound. No bells, no hawkers, no ships' whistles. Nothing. Not even the sound of machinery from the dockyard which was always heard so clearly at that time of day. Even the clocks seemed to have stopped. Stretched out beneath me stood the sombre city of the Knights lying, I thought, as it must have done on that fateful day of 1565, waiting for the Turkish assault. But then there had been the Knights, marshalled by their bold Grand Master La Valette, whose hat and sword are still kept to this day in the small church where he had left them when he was called to the bastions on the approach of the Turkish Infidel. There had been 9,000 Maltese soldiers better armed with their faith and determination than with the weapons they were bearing, and they had all been ready and anxious to withstand the weight of the Turkish navy and army.

I could however see nothing like that now. Beneath me there was a conglomeration of palaces, *auberges*, churches, monasteries, convents, bastions and narrow streets, a disorganised jumble of sacred and secular buildings; a complex of functions as fortress, sanctuary and a city; a blend of civilization and archaic barbarism, whose living members were either closed in their houses and churches or running away to save their heads. I looked for the heroes that I expected to see as a part of the epic drama I was waiting to see beginning like many others. But I saw none. Was this therefore going to be the destruction of what history had built of the Maltese nation?

I found myself looking at the clock tower in Victory Square, from where La Valette had watched the Infidels and directed his forces, and the clock was showing the time to be fifteen minutes to seven. Suddenly I was wishing the clock hands would run, not once round the dial but hundreds and thousands of times as if to take me away from that moment of sad recollection. As the minutes crawled I heard my heartbeats, stronger than I had ever heard them before, and not even the noise from the streets could drown them. Two minutes flashed by in what seemed as many seconds. Then I began to look forward to hearing the chiming of the clock bell at seven o'clock. It would at least raise my spirits to feel that not all that was representative of the valour that was

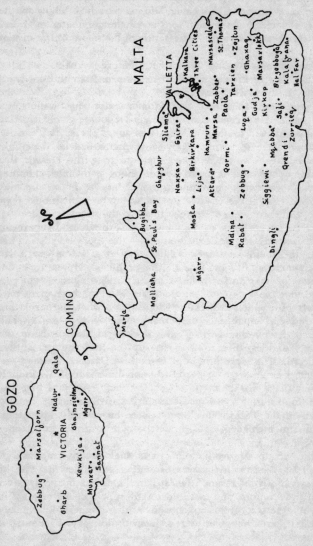

Map of Malta, Gozo and Comino

Maltese was keeping silent. Another minute went by, and the expectancy became like a game. I found myself watching for the slight movement of the hand for the remaining minutes and found my heart beating faster in anticipation of the sound of the striking bell.

Then the sound came. Ten minutes before I expected it. But it was not that of the clock bell striking seven. It came from sirens wailing the first Air Raid Warning.

I was never to forget that moment, nor that wailing, the shouting and pandemonium that was let loose in the streets. I stood transfixed looking at what was going on beneath me not knowing what to think. Then some dozen Special Constables appeared from nowhere and began herding the crowds into whatever cover was at hand. Houses, shops, bandclubs, churches, all had their doors open, and the multitude of noisy humanity dissolved as if at the wave of a magic wand. No more shouting, no panic, and there was nothing else to see in the streets.

My eyes went back to the harbour. There was nothing moving there. But no. On one of the bastions in the dockyard where I had some days before watched soldiers mount a Bofors gun, I saw movement, and the sun's rays glinting on the barrel were reflecting splinters of light on the helmets of the men sitting round the gun. They were workers from the dockyard who had been given anti-aircraft guns which they learned to use, and when the enemy had declared his intentions, they had donned blue clean overalls instead of their clumsy dirty ones, exchanged their caps for steel helmets, and left their tools to take up the guns and defend their dockyard. This was how the Dockyard Defence Battery was formed. I could see a six-barrelled pom-pom manned by similarly blue-clad men at the far end of Senglea where Fort St Michael had once stood during the Siege of 1565. It had been one of the forts to fall to the Turks. Now three and a half centuries later, these handful of men seemed to be determined not to let this happen again.

Those groups of men huddling round their deadly weapons were the first to raise my low spirits. I found myself saying that after all not everybody had submitted to the imminent intruder, and a silent prayer went out to the deserted streets below me as if to entreat others to come out and join those gunners. But no one came out, and nobody answered. Silence still reigned in the streets of Birgu.

There was then a soft rhythmic grumbling sound in the sky and my heart missed a beat as I looked up searching the innocent-looking blue expanse. The sound deepened, and from the corner of my eye I caught a movement on the bastion where I had seen the gun. It was now rising slowly to an angle of 45 degrees. My eyes ran feverishly to a point in the sky at where the gun seemed to point. Then I saw them. Ten planes with the sun glittering on their aluminium bodies. A formation of seven followed by a smaller one of three, flying very high. But from pictures I had seen I knew them for Italian Savoia Marchetti three-engined bombers. They must have been flying at a height of some 20,000 feet. Then as I could not take my eyes off them I saw the glistening moving dots higher up like stars in the morning. They were escorting fighters — nine Macchi 200.

Four white smoke puffs suddenly appeared beneath the planes, as I had so often seen round the target, planes used to tow. There were four simultaneous bangs. Four more puffs appeared in front followed by another four, and then followed the roar of eight guns. I felt like clapping at the defiant gunners behind those guns, but my enthusiasm was shortlived when I heard for the first time the whining of falling bombs. The explosions followed, and the roof beneath my feet was jerking in shuddering waves of shock. More guns were firing and more bombs fell, to be followed by explosions, rising clouds of debris from buildings and water spouts in the harbour. Then as if to outdo this crescendo there was an ear-splitting explosion which must have reached all over the island. For a second I covered by eyes fearing that one of the bombs had found an ammunition dump, but when I opened my eyes again to be greeted by a second similar explosion I was struck dumb as I realised that those were naval anti-aircraft guns from *Terror* and the other gunboats now lying at Marsamxett Harbour. Salvo after salvo followed from the ships adding the tell-tale white puffs to the blue space around and amongst the planes. At that moment I certainly did not envy the airmen inside them.

Strangely enough this defiant retaliation from Malta's defenders — soldiers of the Royal Malta Artillery and British Seamen filled me with such enthusiasm as I had never felt before. Rather than taking cover I wanted to shout and point to others what was happening in the sky. But there was nobody I could shout to. My father was at the dockyard, and my mother at the church. I suddenly realised that she had been in church when the sirens sounded, and must have stayed there. Thinking of how terrified she must have been I ran out and rushed to the church.

There were two big churches in Birgu, the Conventual one which had belonged to the Knights, and which was, as it is still today, the parish church of that city, and another one run by Dominican monks. It was to this latter I ran since I knew that my mother had gone there. I was met with a different and moving picture. The church was full of people and a mass was about to end. The air was full of voices raised in prayer, but rising in crescendo to every explosion that was heard from outside immaterial whether it was that of exploding bombs or firing guns. The service was not so much a hearing of mass as a linked succession of prayers, drawing unbelievable power from the surging voices. Someone had taken up a chant, and others taking up the cue were following with their voices now raised in unison shouting more than chanting the words which everybody learned and liked:

Gesu, Guzeppi, Marija
Itfghu l-bombi fil-hamrija

which was an invocation meaning Jesus, Mary and Joseph, make the bombs drop in soil.

The looks on the hundreds of faces varied, but if one had to see what eyes were hiding inside, the common factor would have certainly been fear. This was evident not only in the obvious looks and movement of unrest but also in the glances continually thrown at the roof and the pillars holding the arches, as if to assess whether they would hold if the church was hit. Some had indeed left on hearing the sirens, but the majority had stayed and continued with the mass when the raid began. This was what in fact had kept them there. The monk who happened to be saying mass when the sirens sounded, continued with the service as if nothing had happened. Not that he was not afraid of bombs and what they could bring, but because for him and for the faithful in the church, the mass, as every religious service, offered the extremes of emotion which brought courage from fear and ecstasy from gloom. Had he run for shelter, everyone in that church would have done the same, but he stayed, and with him stayed the flock. It was a good omen which was bound to find strength for the Maltese to bear what burdens that would be coming to them.

Suddenly, after the mass was ended, there were no more noises from outside. It seemed as if bombs had stopped and guns had ceased firing. A word went round that the raid might have ended even though no one had heard the sirens sounding the 'Raiders Passed'. Mastering their fear some of the men went for the door and looked outside. Smiles broke on their faces when they found everything was still as they had left it. What's more, there were people in the streets and the sound of raised voices. More men and even women went outside, and I went with them. People were in groups in the streets and in the square, and Special Constables were having a hard time persuading them that the raid was not yet over and asking them to go back indoors. But like the man who has his throat released from the choking grip of an assailant, the people wanted to remain there and breathe the fresh air in ease as if to make sure they were still alive, and that nothing had changed.

It was only when the sound of planes was heard that some of them relented and heeded the constables' words. There were even those who laughed away their admonitions, saying that the planes must be British. But when the planes flew overhead and everyone raised his eyes to the sky, we saw that they were the same Savoia Marchetti that had some time before rained death and terror. This time however they had lost the precisely set formation in which they had come in; they were dispersed as if each plane was on his own.

'There they are,' Shouted a few in a chorus of excitement.

'The bastards,' shouted another.

'But why are they being left alone without being fired at?' I asked myself.

The answer came soon after with the renewed sound of engines, this time heavier and more awkward. A Gladiator fighter went by, and another followed in his wake.

'They are ours!' shouted the men who knew them.

'Chase the bastards to hell!' went up a shout in chorus. As if in reply there was the sound of machine gun fire.

A little while later the sirens wailed the straight note for Raider Passed, bringing back life in the streets, and a respite for reflection

*

When the sound of sirens had died away and was followed by church bells for the All Clear, it brought an ironic sense of peace. I say ironic because it had now become just a signal for the population silently and timidly to emerge from under cover, and to walk and run with more vigour, intent on leaving home for places where the bombs were not likely to reach them. Those who

had decided against moving were beset by a different problem as
they watched with a certain bewilderment their friends and
neighbours striding about, busy on making their departure as if
this had suddenly become of some national importance. In those
urgent moments few seemed to be giving thought to the fresh
problems that might arise if they were caught on the open road by
an air-raid. Indeed, those who were thus caught in the previous
raid had quickly left the road to seek shelter in houses, and when
there were none there, they had to resort to hiding under trees or
in the shadow of rubble walls, as if bombs would strike only those
that were exposed. When planes came close, then the refugees
would drop themselves prostrate on the ground as they had been
told to do if caught without shelter.

Those who lived away from the target areas did not have these
problems, though they were of course in the same boat as far as
the war was concerned. They heard the sirens and knew what they
meant. They also heard the gunfire and exploding bombs, very
likely associating them with the petards of their *festa* which they
would not be celebrating for a long time. But a new unexpected
worry began when they saw the influx of people into their town
or villages asking for shelter in their homes. But shelter for how
long? For the duration of the war? And when would the war end?
There were sudden problems arising over the supply of food,
clothing, sanitary facilities, cooking and bedding, apart from the
small and very limited accommodation the reception areas could
offer to the people from the cities accustomed to bigger houses.
These were problems to be faced also by the authorities, who had
foreseen something like this might happen, and had appointed
Protection Officers to cope with it. But what had now happened
was that while these officers had worked on statistics to get to
know the people they had to care for, by ensuring food supplies
and accommodation, all of a sudden their preparations which had
taken them months to make had gone awry. Those in the target
areas had found themselves with a lot of statistics and supplies but
no people, while those in the reception areas found many more
people than they could handle with neither statistics nor supplies.

Only God knew of the purpose for which tunnels in the
bastions were made by the Knights. They had certainly not been
dug for human habitation, and for centuries they had housed only
rats and vermin. Now, after the first night of war and the first raid
they had found unexpected patronage, from those who stayed
there. They had thick roofs and walls, affording shelter both from

elements of nature and from war. So they suddenly became established as places to live and sleep in. Even tunnels on the surface open at both ends, whose only purpose had been for the passage of traffic from one side to another, were quickly utilized by refugees who sat down with their belongings and made them their homes. Evacuees also moved into Ghar Dalam Caves in Birzebbugia, a very important museum from prehistoric times, but certainly not ideal for twentieth-century habitation.

There were a few people who did not move at all, and even after the raid, carried on with their normal life as indeed the monk had carried on with his mass. What seemed to matter to these and to others not in any way involved in the sudden mass migration of the population, was that in the first air attack Malta had suffered, the guns had fired back and the fighter planes (with no one knowing there were only three) had flown to meet the raiders and drove them back. When the news came that the Maltese gunners had made the sign of the cross, sung 'God Save the King', and blazed away with their guns, they were filled with patriotic excitement which broke out into lunatic exhibitions when it was learned that the guns had shot down one plane and damaged another one, while the fighters got another probable.

There was only time for sober meditation when they knew of the other side of the balance sheet. Bombs had fallen at Hal Far and Kalafrana, as well as between Benghaiza and Birzebbugia, all of them military installations which suffered no serious damage. But a bomb which fell near Portes des Bombes outside Floriana had killed two workmen, while bombs which fell on the newly built hospital of St Luke's had killed a man and his wife in a nearby house. At Fort St Elmo, too, six soldiers were killed and another English soldier was killed at French creek. These, besides the number of those injured by splinters. Luckily bombs dropped at Pieta caused no casualties except a motor boat which was sunk. At Gzira, a cinema was hit. So there had been Maltese blood shed as well in this first raid; and people were soon asking whether the three hit planes were considered a good score, and if this score justified the casualties. It was a question which could have many different answers.

On the whole it was not a bad outcome and augured well for the future. What the people and defenders of Malta did not know was that the island had already been written off by Britain as untenable, and that therefore whatever the future might hold in store would take it nearer to collapse and surrender.

There wasn't even time for all the answers to be given, however, because barely an hour after the first raid, the sirens wailed their warning again. This time one of the enemy planes which came in tried to carry out a low flying attack on Fort St Elmo. The gunners went into action. As the plane bypassed the fort, the gunners of the Dockyard Defence Battery, frustrated as they were from their inability to fire at the high-flying planes during the previous raid, now got the chance to make up for it with fervour. All the same they were disappointed when they had to stop as the plane quickly turned tail in the face of their barrage.

There were five more raids until sunset, but all of them were light, some abortive, and this made it possible for the still moving streams of refugees fleeing from the man-made terror of bombs to reach their destinations. The authorities tried to interfere with a view to putting some organisation into this suddenly increased exodus, but it had become humanly impossible to stem the tide of men, women, and children carrying household goods and pushing prams and wheelbarrows overflowing with bedding, toys, clocks and pictures. Rather than abating tension, the abortive raids had the contrary effect of increasing panic and offered desperate relief in flight. It was only as evening approached that the roads were clear, not because the problem was solved, but because it had then shifted itself on to the reception towns and villages which the refugees had reached and were searching for accommodation which they wanted at any price, and in any condition.

When the sun set on that first fateful day, and the gloomy twilight was tossing its last shadows, there seemed to be no more problems. Even for the few stalwarts who had remained in the target cities and were now hurrying home exhaustedly, there was a blanket of silence on the streets they walked in, more like a deathlike spell that one could not live with. It was as abnormal as the war that had engulfed them, and it looked more like the lull before the big storm. But if a whole day with seven air-raids had been endured, there was no chance of one getting rattled now, at the end of it. But what would the morrow bring? It seemed that not even those who were ready to compromise with the abnormal situation could find peace. Something seemed to hint that the end had not come for that day.

It was in fact so. Half an hour later the sirens began to wail. With the silent hope for an abortive raid like the others many remained in their homes, but there were those who took shelter with others, more for company than for protection. In my case I went with my family to some neighbours and went down into a cellar beneath the house. We had hardly reached it when pandemonium was let loose.

Twenty-five Italian planes came in formations of five, converging from different directions dropping bombs on the way, but all intent on a final appointment over the Dockyard. The heavy batteries engaged them when they could see them in the falling darkness, but the moment they reached Grand Harbour, they found the part-timers of the Dockyard Defence Battery who blazed away at them to their hearts' content, even where they could not reach them. Those planes that sought protection in height were lunged at by the heavy guns from the forts and HMS *Terror*, while those who ventured close to their objective were swept by the Bofors and Pom-poms of the Dockyard workers. It seemed as if unknowingly and without any premeditation the Maltese defenders were having a dress rehearsal of the box barrage that later became the terror of both Italian and German pilots.

In the houses and cellars trembling under bomb explosions people howled, wept and shouted hysterically, window panes broke and glass flew like rose petals in a wind. Monks and priests who had sought refuge with different families in the neighbourhood were reciting prayers, but their voices could not outdo those raised in hysteria. It seemed as if the end of the world had come, and the fearful clamour did not look like stopping except with extinction.

Yet an end did come, and with the same suddenness as the raid had begun. When the raiders had had enough, in a much shorter time than they had bargained for, they left. And when they left, the guns ceased firing, and the women stopped crying. The ARP people went out to tend to the casualties, and the fire engines rushed to put out the fires. In this raid substantial damage was caused in various localities, but except for superficial damage at Fort Ricasoli, military objectives were untouched. There were however 30 civilians killed and 120 wounded. Three planes were said to have been shot down over Grand Harbour, but God and the Italians knew how many more of the rest failed to reach their base. When the three elements so hotly engaged in that fighting triangle retired to lick their wounds, the three of them went to sleep with a new determination.

The people in the target areas decided it was no place for them and to evacuate as the others had done; the gunners became confident and more determined to shoot out the Italians every time they appeared in the Malta sky; and the Italians too found respect for the Maltese defences.

Nicola Malizia in his *Inferno su Malta* described Malta's first anti-aircraft gunfire on that first day of the war as violent and abundant but not accurate in its aim. He mentioned how firing increased until the whole sky was full of exploding shells. Mention was also made of the British fighters which went for the Italian planes, and opened fire on them, and praise for their courageous pilots was not lacking. In contrast with this he criticized the Italian pilots who reported that they were attacked by something like twenty fighters, when it was known that there were only three. He claimed that all attacking planes had returned to their base, but six of them were hit. From his reports emerges the fact that Italian attacks were mainly directed against Hal Far Airport, the seaplane base at Kalafrana, the Dockyard, and the Torpedo Depot at Msida. In reality Hal Far hosted only the three Gladiators which were in the air in almost every raid, Kalafrana had no seaplanes, while the Torpedo Depot had no torpedoes or indeed anything worth bombing. This makes it evident that the Italian Air Force, was resting on information that might have been given to it by the fliers of their Ala Littoria seaplanes based at Marsaxlokk before the war, because it was then that these three installations were potential military targets. In June 1940 there was only the Dockyard which was worth the bombs it received. If there had been any truth in what this Italian writer said that they had also intended to silence anti-aircraft defences, then it can be said that they failed, because not a single anti-aircraft gun was silenced. The truth is that the six artillery soldiers killed at St Elmo did not belong to any gun crew, as alleged by Malizia and indeed as was also very often stated by English and Maltese writers. These soldiers were bandsmen belonging to the 1st Coast Regiment, and they were killed while acting as observers on the cavalier at St Elmo, as Harbour Fire Control.

So ended the first day of the war with Italy, and as if in confirmation of their resolution, on the following morning of 12th June, all those in the target areas who had not found room in a tunnel, left their home for somewhere else; the gunners were called to action stations at 8.30 in the morning by a sole plane coming obviously to reconnoitre the damage done in the previous night and, as they had resolved, the gunners shot it down. The Italians too kept their promise, as in the days that followed they maintained their height.

CHAPTER THREE

The Recoil

When Italy entered the war it possessed greatly superior forces in numbers and fire power than Britain could muster in the Mediterranean. It had a vast array of warships and numerous squadrons of the latest types of aircraft which logically one expected to see pulverizing Malta. Moreover, with the island some one thousand miles distant from the nearest British bases at Gibraltar and Alexandria it was considered impracticable, if not impossible, to get the regular supplies and reinforcements that would be required to maintain her in fighting condition. Added to this there was the lack of proper airfields, as both Luqa and Hal Far were considered to be inadequate. These were the main factors that had weighed in Britain's momentous assumption that Malta could not be held in the face of a belligerent Italy.

This was without a doubt what led Britain to base the British Mediterranean Fleet at Alexandria, thus denuding Malta of all naval forces that had for several years succoured her. It is to be said that this move must have been made at a sacrifice since there were no refit facilities at Alexandria, but someone must have reasoned that it was preferable to go without this and save ships, than to have them like sitting ducks in a harbour only 60-odd miles from the biggest hostile air force in the Mediterranean. Whoever was behind such reasoning must have patted himself for a sound decision when in their first patrols of the Mediterranean war the three British submarines *Grampus, Odin* and *Orpheus* were sunk by Italian warships in as many days.

In the air however it was a different matter, and during the eight Italian air attacks of the first day the anti-aircraft defences and, in addition to them, the civilian population had come out with flying colours. If any indication was required of the spirit with which the Maltese people were imbued in this onslaught it could doubtlessly be found in the gunners and particularly the amateurs and part-timers of the Dockyard Defence Battery who faced the Italian planes without giving an inch, and, as the aftermath showed, emerged from the confrontation with full honours.

What the guns could not do because of the enemy's tactics of
flying out of range then, there were the three Gladiators to do, the
Gladiators which at that time constituted the whole of Malta's
fighter defence. What those three fighters did has gone down as an
outstanding page in history, but no less spectacular was the way in
which those machines had found themselves as the main, and
indeed the only, flying force to face the much vaunted Regia
Aeronautica. It had never been anyone's intention to have any
fighting planes in Malta in June of 1940, and until only a few
weeks before the fateful day there had indeed been none. The
Gladiators had found themselves in the island only as boxed spares
which were left behind by an aircraft carrier. The need of the
moment and the presence of mind of the Air Officer Commanding
of the time, Air Commodore Maynard, were instrumental in
assembling the parts together, thus giving birth to the three planes.

The few who knew about this matter must have wondered how
long it would be before this fact would be known by the Maltese
and the enemy. It might have registered when the three planes
were christened 'Faith', 'Hope' and 'Charity', the three virtues on
which the Catholic religion is based, and the comparison between
the three planes on which the aerial defence rested and the religion
which was the salient point in the people's perseverance in the
fight can be realised now, as it must have been then. The Italians
did not give themselves the chance to realise this, because from the
second day of the conflict they seemed to be busier avoiding
contact with the defences than in facing or assessing them. The
raid by one reconnaissance aircraft on the second day of the
conflict has already been mentioned when the aircraft was shot
down by the guns. On 13th June there were four warnings. In two
of these the enemy planes did not approach the island. In the
other two they flew over Kalafrana, dropped their bombs which
killed two people and injured four, and flew out again. They came
in again at 4.45 p.m. flying high above the clouds and out of range
of the guns, but when the Gladiators tried to engage them they
turned tail and hurried away after releasing their bombs on
Mellieha, some of which fell in fields and the rest in the sea.

The old owner of the field where the bombs fell was ploughing
his field when the planes flew over chased by the Gladiators. He
obeyed the instructions given and having nowhere to take shelter
laid himself prostrate on the ground. The explosions harmed neither
him nor the mule that was pulling his plough, but when Air Raid
Wardens reached him they found him seeing red with anger.

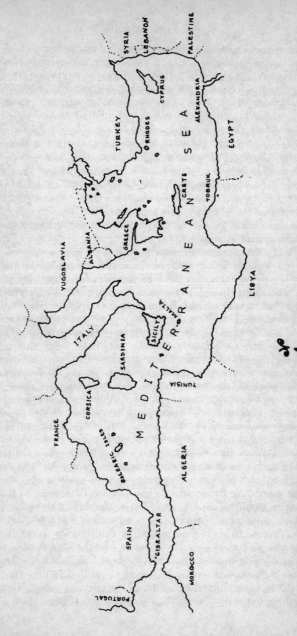

Map of the Mediterranean Sea

'But there is nothing to be angry about, ' one of them said.

'Of course, there is,' replied the farmer. ' I spent the whole morning watering this patch of tomatoes and I broke my back doing it, only to have it spoilt now by those bastards.'

On Friday, 14th June there was another raid at 8.35 in the morning, and on being engaged by anti-aircraft batteries the two bombers that flew over dropped their bombs on Grand Harbour, Fort St Angelo and Pieta, and flew away. For a few days this behaviour by the Italians looked like developing into a game, and when on Sunday 16th June there were two raids and the Savoia Marchetti bombers flew in, heavily accompanied by Macchi 200 fighters, there were many Maltese who kept away from cover, anxious and ready to see the British fighters come to grips with the Italians. But they were disappointed as the enemy dispersed before he could be engaged.

It was becoming astonishingly clear that the enemy did not welcome confrontation with the guns and the three fighters, but when the newspapers and the local newscasters began saying that the Italians were dropping bombs haphazardly in their hurry to get out, no one could believe them. Then, as if to justify what was being said, on 21st June the Italians came in on four raids, and bombs were dropped only on Marfa and the sister island of Gozo which certainly contained no military targets.

Whatever was the reason for the less frequent and shorter attacks, there was now granted a much needed breathing space which could be used to provide what was considered to have priority where defence was concerned. Volunteers began to swell the ranks of the Royal Malta Artillery and a second infantry battalion was added to the King's Own Malta Regiment. Those who because of age could not serve, were enticed into the newly formed Malta Volunteer Defence Force, a hotch-potch collection formed mainly of those who possessed shot guns, who were drilled and given identification arm-bands and steel helmets, and of course cartridges for their shot guns. They were given to believe that they would be expected to fight alongside British and Maltese regular regiments if the country was invaded. But what did they care? They were given free cartridges for shooting practice, and there was plenty of game to shoot at. Beaches began now to be desecrated with hideous concrete pill-boxes, and barbed wire, and the beautiful coastal roads lost their virginity to tank-traps and minefields. Invasion seemed to be a foregone conclusion. This was something undreamt of with the British navy at hand. But where was the British fleet? When it was based at Alexandria it was allocated as its first immediate object to disrupt enemy seaborne communication to North Africa, and this necessarily kept it away from Maltese ports. There were only submarines which called for refuelling and refit. It appeared that Malta had to rely only on what British service units happened to be there when Italy had declared war, and of course on the Maltese themselves who had overnight found themselves in their first baptism of fire.

Now that fortunately there was time to do it, the most immediate objective from the civilian point of view was to bring back the population to its proper senses. It is true that all the evacuees had found some sort of roof under which to shelter, and a bed to sleep in, but most of them had made only temporary and sometimes makeshift arrangements. This was one problem that had to be solved. Another one that followed was to ensure knowing who was staying where, and apart from the less important changes in postal arrangements, police control, transport facilities and similar requirements, there was the question of the distribution of foodstuffs which was already receiving top priority since there had been no replenishment since the outbreak of war with Italy.

This competence belonged to Protection Officers who were appointed for various localities. Now Assistant District Commissioners were also appointed, with a handful of District Commissioners to whom to refer their unsolved problems. Between them they tried to bring some order but it was a mammoth task. There were those who obeyed orders and gave the information that was requested, but there were others who couldn't care less. Everyone made sure of being issued with a ration card as this had become a passport for food when this would be short, but when certain items disappeared overnight, there were always those willing to barter, or the farmer who gladly milked his goats out for the few extra pennies. When kerosene was not delivered there was resort to the *kenur*, the old open stone cooker which could also be carried with one's belongings. The sister island of Gozo was the least affected with these problems since its only involvement was in accommodating the evacuees that crossed over. As for food there were plenty of eggs, soft cheeses, and vegetables for the Gozitans and also to be sold to paying Maltese.

Another headache that assailed the authorities was that of shelters. What had been made available in the target areas, and that was where there had been the emphasis, had become superfluous with the evacuation while the places which had received evacuees did not have enough. The shelter problem had never been forgotten, and even where these were available mostly in the way of buttressed cellars the authorities had kept investigations going and had even gone as far as to study and observe the effects of bombs being dropped in order to assess the grading of shelters that had to be built with the progress of war. Even though the bombs used by the Italians were mostly of the 100-kg size these were causing much more damage than had been anticipated, and there was agreement to improve in the kind of shelter being built. This reappraisement of the situation provided the right opportunity. If there were more shelters constructed it would be better to make them good ones. It might have been to produce shelters quicker rather than to make them safer that it was decided to dig rather than construct. The tough but easily cut rock in which Malta abounded provided the answer; pickaxes and the expert people, of which there were many, could do the rest. There had never been a more splendid idea. It paid big dividends later on.

Another man with a big problem was the Air Officer Commanding. With constant air attacks, there was going to come a time when he would have to do something in the way of defence. The three Gladiators could not remain for ever. There had already been occasions when one or even two of them could not fly, and the three of them had already been patched up to the extent of looking hefty and grotesque. If he was to prevent a day when the Italians would be free to roam in the Maltese skies unopposed, something had to be done. In the same way as he had procured the Gladiators he thought of something else. With the situation in North Africa already building up, Britain was sending Hurricane fighter aircraft to that theatre, and these had to break their flight somewhere on their way to Mersa Matruh. Where better than in Malta? Four of them came here. The right word was said in the right place, and with Malta's record now riding the waves in Whitehall it wasn't difficult for permission to be granted to retain two of the fighters here.

The Hawker Hurricane was the fighter which formed the bulk of Britain's fighter force at the time. It was powered by a Rolls Royce engine which gave it a speed of 325 miles per hour. It was armed with eight Browning machine-guns fixed forward in the wings, and together with the Spitfire was to bear the brunt of aerial combats in the Battle of Britain. When later it was considered that the German Messerschmitt 109 was better armed with two 20 mm cannons, first the Spitfire and then the Hurricane were similarly armed. The Hurricane with four 20 mm Hispano (Oerlikon) cannon came into use later.

On 23rd June when the Italians flew their 39th raid there were not only the Gladiators to meet them but also two Hurricanes. The bombers dropped their bombs and flew back hurriedly, but the escorting fighters were engaged in a dog fight, losing one plane watched by a cheering population.

Everyone now began to realise that Italian bombing prowess must have been over-estimated, and this provided the necessary pep for an effort to try and bring life back to as near to normal as possible. The lulls in between raids were not spent in idleness. Now that the evacuees seemed to have settled themselves and the trek from the towns had ceased, schools were reopened where they were most convenient, the law courts changed venue from Valletta to Rabat, hospitals were moved, and the bus services improved. Cinemas reopened and Valletta began to have a daily influx of people. The population was after all learning to live with the air raids.

The Hawker Hurricanes, even though only two in number, were seen and commented upon by everybody, except of course the newspapers which for the sake of security kept referring to the planes as fighters without distinguishing between Gladiators and Hurricanes. However the Italians certainly knew of them, and began reporting on them as in fact can now be evidenced by Nicola Malizia, a serious Italian writer on the subject in whose writings I found confirmation for much of what I am writing. Maybe a more imposing and apparent effect was expected in the Malta skies following the arrival of the Hurricanes, but there were only two of them. Even so, one could attribute the successes of July to the presence and use of this fighter. After the last raids of 27th June when one other plane was shot down, the number of air raids up to 23rd July reached 80, during which 12 Italian planes were shot down over the island. One should lay emphasis on this fact that in many of the raids it was very often mentioned that planes were so seriously damaged that possibly they were unable to reach their base. This was true then and has since been confirmed by the Italians themselves. To quote one example I can take the raids on 10th July, when besides shooting down three planes the Malta defences claimed two more as damaged. Malizia states very clearly that on that day there were ten planes which had reached Sicily in a damaged condition, and one of them had to make a forced landing. During this time, to be exact, on the 16th there was the first British aircraft to be shot down in an air battle. So the score of downed planes stood 12 − 1.

The month of July was outstanding in more ways than one however. The population had by now become so confident and at home with air raids that whenever a plane was shot down on land people in the neighbourhood would rush to it as if it had been something from another world. There would be not only the trophy hunters, but also those who would go to grin and show on their faces the determination that was in their hearts. On one occasion, 10th July, a crowd was watching a dog fight and the onlookers saw an Italian fighter being hit and gliding down with the tell-tale trail of smoke streaming from its tail. The pilot baled out but his parachute also caught fire. When the crowd followed the plane to where it was seen to be dropping it was shaken by the explosion that followed as the plane exploded to smithereens which could have harmed them had it exploded a minute later. Another crowd was on the bastions watching the same dog fight and cheering the shooting down of another plane when the enemy in flight turned back and dropped bombs which killed one and injured three.

This was now happening with every air raid as if the people felt they had to give this kind of support to the fighting that was going on. So much so that it was at this time that the authorities laid stress on the fact that people should not leave their shelters on hearing the 'Raiders Passed' signal, but only when they heard the church bells ringing the All Clear. This was the drill from the very beginning — warbling note by the siren for Air Raid Warning, straight note for Raiders Passed, and church bells for All Clear. Rediffusion, the local broadcast relay service, which was popular and common to houses and public places, began to give the warnings, and, as programmes were interrupted, listeners came to expect the warning *'Sinjal ta' l-Attakki mill-Ajru'* (Air Raid Warning), and later, *'L-Ajruplani ta' l-Ghadu ghaddew'* (Raiders Passed).

There were those who still did not understand what was happening. Manwela, a mother with eleven children was concerned about her husband who was away from Malta on a Fleet Auxiliary ship, the name of which she did not even know. Until the war started she had only thought of him when she received his letters which her children read for her, and his monthly pay cheque. Now she could hazily comprehend that his ship must be where the fleet and inherent danger was. Her eldest son was away in a dockyard at Suez, while two others had joined the Navy and were somewhere with their ships. She could not read, and the news on Redifussion contained such words and details she did not understand that she could make neither head nor tail of what to think or believe. She ran to the door every time the postman called with the mail dreading the worst. Then someone told her that what she feared would be brought to her by a telegram and not a letter. She soon realised that what was happening in Malta did not directly affect her husband and sons, but when there were sighs of relief and prayers in thanksgiving after a raid she would still be worried. She worried more about her husband and sons than about what was happening to her. And there were many others like her.

There were those also, who had read and knew about war and its effects, and they realised they were only experiencing what had already happened in Spain, France and other countries. To them, however crude, this was another adventure which had to be seen through. No amount of warning would deter them, and they were the ones who reflected the same undaunted spirit that had always prevailed, when there was sufficient cause.

During one of the raids a splinter from a bomb pierced the wall of a small derelict church at a place called Fgura. The splinter also hit a statue of Christ and decapitated it. Someone, probably with good intentions, took up the decapitated head and placed it to rest in the aperture left by the splinter in the wall. The result was that from outside the face of Christ could be seen looking with sad eyes at the sky in the direction of Grand Harbour. The word spread round and thousands of people went to visit the shrine where this supposed miracle had occurred, leaving money and oil for the oil lamp.

Even under the everyday threat of death and destruction the simple and honest characteristic Maltese streak prevailed when there was place for it.

During those days too there were two more soldiers killed and ten civilians, with another twenty wounded, but this did not keep the people from celebrating when it was learned that on 9th July the British Fleet under Admiral Sir Andrew Cunningham encountered the Italians off Calabria and repulsed them. It was the first positive news for the Maltese about the fighting Navy which had never ceased to be their darling. As if to add to local felicitations a convoy of five ships arrived on 15th July, bringing amongst other things more guns and ammunition.

At this stage the Air Officer Commanding had repeated his stratagem to obtain more fighters, and by keeping two more back had raised the number of Hurricanes to five, not counting the one that was shot down on the 16th. It wasn't the ideal time to obtain aircraft and armaments from Great Britain, for it was only a little over a month since the debacle of Dunkirk from where despite all the difficulties involved 338,000 British and Allied troops defeated on the French front were evacuated to Britain, most of them without their arms. Moreover there were already indications of German plans to invade Britain. (It was learned later that Operation Sealion as the invasion plan was called, was at that time scheduled to be put into operation by mid-August 1940) and Air Chief Marshal Dowding Commander-in-Chief of Fighter Command, was husbanding his resources during that month of July. Indeed, the invasion did not materialise, but there was later the Battle of Britain, instead.

It can therefore be appreciated with what sacrifice Britain parted with the Hurricane fighters that were conceded to Malta. On 2nd August the whole of Malta was shaken by the sudden roar of low flying aircraft. Everyone must have rushed out of doors, thinking the worst — that the enemy had managed to fly on Malta undetected by the island's radar system. But the thrilled Maltese hearts jumped with pleasure, and there could not have been one who didn't clap, raise a hand in salute or in some other gesture showed his relief as the aircraft were recognised as Hawker Hurricane fighters — twelve brand new planes which were flown from the aircraft carrier *Argus* which had carried them as far as 12 miles from Malta.

They had arrived as if to show British appreciation for the sincere and heroic stand Malta was taking in front of the Italian onslaught. But there was a more significant meaning in the arrival of those planes. It was obvious that the belief that Malta was untenable had disappeared, and that Britain had realised that the island should be given what it had lacked until then. There is no doubt that this change could have been brought about by the Maltese themselves when with their attitude and behaviour they had changed what was expected to be destruction and defeat by a much stronger enemy, into a brave and unexpected resistance. Never before had Malta shown so clearly how its characteristic qualities had been misjudged and underestimated. And this change was reflected in the people, and more than before, seemed to infuse them with more will and determination to get in the fray. But what more could they do? The convoys had brought more guns, and they were mounting them to add to the already terrific and efficient barrage; they were seeing their houses destroyed for which they shed human tears only to wipe them with a determined hand; they had to tend their wounded and bury their dead, and this did not deter them at all. They were gladly enduring the pangs of want, and seeing their palaces and *auberges*, a heritage of a superior civilisation being destroyed by a wanton enemy. What could they do more? But if they could do nothing more, even at the price of death, they could at least live. They could ignore the shackling and restrictions brought about by bombing and continue on their road to bring life nearer to normality. In this way they would not only be meeting the challenge being thrown at them, but they would be throwing it back into the enemy's face.

These were of course only symbolic thoughts. But they could have actually been reflected in the attitude that became so evident as that summer of 1940 had set in with its hot golden sun. The evacuees, who were in fact displaced persons, had somehow fitted themselves in the villages. They were there in limited space, and living without furniture and essential commodities, but they had mixed well with their hosts. They shared with them their hours of rest and leisure, and the time they spent in the crammed shelters when these were available. When they weren't they just sat together underneath tables or under arched ceilings during air attacks. In certain cases they even shared the cooking. They joined families, and many a boy met girl and later finished by getting married. The city-bred learned to live with the country people, and by this time only the clipped speech differentiated between them. But at the end of every day the evacuees had always the same thoughts and desires . . . to go back to their homes if these were still standing. It is no wonder then that when all of them began stepping into their day-to-day existence, hemmed in by the thoughts of any possible disrupting air raid there were those of them who decided to have a look at their homes. Even if it had to be for a short time. And they went back.

First it was a trickle. There were the housewives and children looking round the streets they knew so well, and trying to give a clean up to the houses they had had to leave. They met the few who had remained in the tunnels, and experiences were exchanged. Then the siren would sound and they would take shelter. On 10th August, the feast of St Lawrence, the patron saint of the beleaguered city of Vittoriosa, was celebrated in the Conventual church. There were more evacuees who had purposely gone down from the villages than locals from the tunnels. And when I was there on that day I could see how those people were spending their lives. They lived in their houses during the day and went to the tunnel during air raids. But they slept there during the nights. I could not help strolling down the narrow streets where only a few doors were open, and some buildings were damaged. There were mounds of debris I had to cross over where houses were demolished, but they weren't much, considering what that area had gone through in two months. When I sauntered back to the main square I could see the band club still standing, as were the beautiful bars I knew so well. But they were now all closed up and silent. The church of St Dominic where my mother used to seek shelter was still intact too, and La Valette's clock tower; but the clock was not working, and its hands had stopped at an abnormal hour as if despondent and knowing that there were no longer the faces to be lifted towards it and eyes to look at its dial.

Not everything had the air of despondency however. A hawker had spread out a tarpaulin on the ground and on it were displayed old clocks, lamps, lengths of bright silk, dolls and wrought handicraft in wood and stone. There was a crowd looking on but no one seemed to be buying. Then when people were sauntering away, an icecream seller came on the scene and he was soon doing brisk business. Like many others I had my last icecream for a long time, for six days later on 16th August the manufacture of ice-cream was stopped.

In the insecurity of those times everyone who had gone to Vittoriosa on that day seemed to have enjoyed the interlude, knowing it for what it really was, a temporary armistice with fate. It must have been the same with those who had on other days gone to the other cities of Cospicua, Senglea and Valletta. There were meetings between friends who had separated on that first day of 11th June, and reminiscences exchanged, but it was good to see faces that had been without laughter for almost two months laughing again. Although beneath that laughter, one could not help noticing the depth of thought and experience.

The lull in the raids was no doubt one of the features of these conversations. It was in fact the reason or excuse that had pushed them to come back to their homes, maybe with some hesitation at first, but now that they saw the same old streets, and the buildings still standing and sampled again the comforts of their home they had missed so much for the last two months, there was scope for reflection. Hadn't they after all wanted to throw back the challenge into the enemy's face by taking up normal life again? And they had done this by settling down in their village of adoption. They could now fulfil this wish by returning home, now that the incidence of air attacks and bombs had become so insignificant.

This must have been the thinking that in the latter half of August began bringing the first families back from their exile. Little did they know that what they were doing seemed to be reflected in the more intricate decisions that motivated the British Mediterranean Fleet.

Admiral Sir Andrew Cunningham had at this time left Alexandria leading an array of naval might and a number of merchant ships laden with provisions. At the same time Admiral Somerville left Gibraltar with a similar force, Force H, but which also included the battleship *Valiant* and the aircraft carrier *Illustrious* and two destroyers carrying guns munitions and troops. The venue of both forces was Malta. The fleet had after all returned to Malta even if only to leave again. But its stay, however brief, was enough to give scope to the population lining the bastions round Grand Harbour on 3rd September to cheer them in and showing that their old feelings were still there, and stronger than ever. The local authority seemed to approve of the relaxation that had obviously come about, and they signified this by a relaxation from their part in Curfew time.

The only interruption to this period of calm came on 5th September when five single-engined aircraft which did not look like bombers, escorted by a squadron of 10 Fiat CR42 and another of 10 Macchi 200 flew over Grand Harbour, then proceeded to Delimara and Kalafrana where bombs were dropped. It was now that the unfamiliar-looking aircraft were identified as German Junkers 87 (Stukas) but they had Italian markings. They were in fact Junkers 87 handed over to Italians, who gave them the name of Picchiatelli dive-bombers. A dog fight soon developed and one of the Italian fighters was shot down before the rest flew away.

Picchiatellis were used again on 17th September. There were 12 of them, heavily escorted by fighters, and they delivered a dive-bombing attack on Hal Far airfield. Sergeant A. Stevens, a Royal Malta Artillery territorial of 22nd Light Anti-Aircraft Battery, was commander of a gun detachment at the airfield. As the dive bombers dropped their bombs two of his gun crew became casualties leaving him with only four men and himself to man the gun. After dropping their bombs the enemy aircraft went down again to machine-gun the airfield and Sergeant Stevens and his remaining crew were under constant machine-gun fire. Notwithstanding this he continued firing his gun and brought down an enemy plane.

There was however another danger coming from unexploded time bombs which dropped round the gun emplacement threatening to explode any minute and blow the gun with its crew and ammunition to blazes. Sergeant Stevens, with the aid of only his four men moved the gun and ammunition to a new position, and was back in action within half an hour. For his deed Sergeant Stevens was awarded the Medal of Order of the British Empire.

When another attack was made on the same airfield two days later, the guns brought down one plane while Hurricanes destroyed three.

By this time there were already other awards made in recognition of meritorious service in the face of the enemy and these appropriately comprised the two other sectors of the combined front that was so splendidly facing the onslaught. Flight Lieutenant George Burgess, the pilot of one of the three Gladiators, had already on 14th July been awarded the Distinguished Flying Cross for gallantry and devotion to duty in the air defence of Malta. The Civilian Sector was represented by R.J. Lewis and Frank Mallia, two chargemen at the Dockyard, who were awarded the George Medal for exceptional meritorious and devoted service rendered in the face of enemy air attacks at Malta during June 1940.

By the end of September all the signs were that Italy could not press further with air attacks. They had dwindled in numbers, frequency and intensity and this gave scope for what was to be done in Malta. I am now not referring to the return of evacuees to their homes in Valletta and the Three Cities, because these had been flowing in, and resuming their old life; they were not given any guidance nor did they ask for it. This was the second move of its kind and it presented no problems. The authorities had other things on their hands as they were not deluded into thinking that Italian decline was going to leave Malta on velvet, and if there were to be any new measures to reduce and restrict the use of essential supplies now was the time to do it.

They first clamped down on petrol. It was placed under strict control, and the bus service was given an alternative and more economical time table while taxis were stopped altogether. The second problem was that of shelters. Until then there had been constructed 110 slit shelters on public roads, 2,509 domestic shelters, and 850 adapted ones mostly in business and private premises. But the need for more 'bomb proof' shelters in rock had already been felt and work had started. Now, it was accelerated, not only in target areas but also in outlying villages. This official attitude gave ideas to many individual families and it wasn't long before some began digging their own private shelters in some selected public place, not strictly for use during attacks but to live and sleep in throughout day and night. Now that people had learned what bombing was like, they preferred to have their one room in the safety of rock, clinging to its relative comfort and privacy to the similarly meagre accommodation they might have to find should the situation change again.

The people of Vittoriosa began to dig in Coronation Garden which was a planted ditch between bastions running from Vittoriosa to Calcara, the small seaside town at the innermost point of one of the creeks in Grand Harbour. In Cospicua similar shelters began to appear in the bastions of St John Elemosiniere, in Senglea too the foundations of bastions were being dug to provide individual and private cubicles. In the approaches to Floriana and Valletta the shelter cubicles that were dug in the bastions can be still seen today. Besides these, there were the big tunnels which remained occupied by those who had gone in them. This move was bound to ease the problem of public shelters should the worst ever happen and therefore the authorities did not only agree to them but gave help where this was required. But the people who had taken over Ghar Dalam Museum Caves in Birzebbugia were now evicted because these caves were required for storage of aviation spirit, which was required in bigger quantities for the increased number of aircraft in the island.

The Royal Air Force had swollen to respectable proportions. There was a whole squadron of Hawker Hurricanes at Hal Far — No 261 Squadron. Work was also being hurriedly carried out in the development of Ta' Qali Airfield beneath the stalwart bastions of the old city of Mdina, and this was intended to take fighters. On being vacated, Hal Far was handed over to the Fleet Air Arm and the first Swordfish torpedo bombers soon made it their home. In November, Malta had its first bomber squadron, and the honour went to No 37 Squadron composed of Wellingtons, which went to Luqa Airfield.

Everyone sensed the change but no one knew what it was going to bring. When on 8th October there was an alarm sounded at night everyone thought the worst, and left their homes to run to the nearest shelter. But they were only two Italian bombers which provided diversion to the searchlights. The white silvery tentacles were soon scanning the dark skies as they had done so many times in practice, and they didn't take long to get one of the raiders in their beams. Try as he would to escape them, they did not let him go. Those watching the spectacle expected to hear the AA guns go into action, but the gunners seemed to take pity on the population and did not fire at that time of night. Instead, an unseen Hurricane fighter pounced on the raider and pumping a burst of red tracers into it shot it down. The second raider soon disappeared from the scene. When there was a repetition on the following night, there were less people rushing for shelter, and everything proceeded as before, with one raider being shot down in the same way, bringing the total of enemy aircraft destroyed to 25. The local defences had lost three fighters and two pilots.

Casualties are not always directly attributable to the enemy, and in the early morning of 4th November Malta had to witness an unexpected accident which caused the death of two civilians and four members of a plane's crew. Inhabitants of the village of Qormi were awakened by the strange loud drone of an aircraft, and, expecting to see some enemy bomber, many rushed into the streets and were able to witness the tragedy. It was a British aircraft they saw, however, with sparks bursting from his engines and losing height. It became obvious that the plane was crashing and the pilot was trying to clear the village. But he didn't make it, and crashed on a house where the parents and their five children were trapped beneath falling masonry and debris. When the aircraft burst in two, half of it fell into a 40-foot shaft taking with it a still living member of the crew.

As expected, assistance was soon forthcoming from the Passive Defence, Police, Civilians from the area and also soldiers from the Royal West Kent Regiment stationed in the vicinity. For their part in rescuing the five children from the burning house, Captain Anthony J.M. Flint and 2nd Lieutenant Richard H. Lavington, both of the Royal West Kent, were awarded the Medal of the British Empire, while Police Constable Carmel Camilleri of the Malta Police who went down the shaft and was instrumental in saving the airman that had fallen down there, was awarded the George Medal.

It was a case of coordinated action with British servicemen risking their lives to save Maltese civilians and a Maltese doing the same to save an English airman. Although under such pitiful circumstances, it was an action that was a good omen.

On 17th November, through a misjudgement on the part of whoever was responsible for launching them, ten precious Hurricanes were lost to Malta. The aircraft carrier *Argus* was delivering fourteen of the Hurricanes, when for some reason it launched them 400 miles away from the island. Some of them might have lost direction and missed Malta, and on wanting to adjust their route found they had not enough petrol. Only four reached Hal Far, and they just made it. The rest were lost. The anti-aircraft batteries on the island had now been increased considerably, and each one was allotted a name which was to earn glory that is still spoken of today. They were spread all over the island, but there was a ring of them from coast to coast surrounding the Harbour and the Dockyard and we used to refer to them with much respect. Some of them had 4.5 guns reaching up to 43,000 feet to provide a ceiling for a box barrage. Within that ring there were others with the 3.7's, and then sprinkled all over the place were the Bofors, singles or in batteries.

A splendid array. But greater than the guns there was the determination of the men behind them. They had already shown the enemy what they were worth, and they were convinced that they would do it again if and when it was called for. As in fact they did, and made name with friend and foe alike.

New guns had occasion to go into action between the night of 27th and the morning of 28th November when two convoys of six ships reached Malta, and Italian aircraft attempted to attack them no less than eight times. But once the ships hugged the coast and came under the protective umbrella of AA firing, the planes could not face the fire. Two of them were shot down.

Submarines of the Mediterranean Fleet kept coming to Malta for replenishments and refits, but now with the obvious ascendancy of the British Fleet in the Mediterranean and the victorious emergence of Malta from its first ordeal everything possible was being made to make her a tenable base. There were problems to be overcome like the lack of torpedoes and spare gear, and this necessitated the over-loading of submarines arriving from Gibraltar restricting operations until they were unloaded. There were also old destroyer torpedoes to be converted for submarine use. But all this would be remedied in time, as long as the naval situation in the area was maintained. As if in confirmation of British intentions in this respect, on 11th November the Fleet Air Arm brilliantly attacked Taranto harbour in moonlight, sinking the pride of the Italian navy, the battleship *Cavour*, and seriously damaging two other battleships, *Littorio* and *Caio Diulio*.

Together with the submarines, bigger elements of the fleet began to call at Malta again but only for a short and limited time, between spells of searching for the Italian Fleet, which because of its rare appearances began to be called the 'Phantom Fleet'. But even the short stays in port were enough to renew acquaintances with the Maltese — the Dockyard people who carried out quick and efficient repairs, the girl friends that had not been seen for months, and even the *dghajsa* men, and the barmaids in the bars seamen frequented.

So the Malta scene took a turn for the better, and the people could respire again unfettered. The churches began to be full and shops reopened. Band clubs in Valletta and the Three Cities were opened for their members again (those in villages had never closed), but somebody looked like having taken over their job when British regimental bands began to render musical programmes in various localities. This of course was a godsend, as no local club could muster a band with the many bandsmen in the services.

It would be wrong to assume that life had returned to what it had been before 11th June, because it had not. There were the demolished buildings which could not be rebuilt, and the dead who could not be brought back, the wounded still in hospital, and those maimed for life who would never smile again. There were the shortages of food and commodities, the sleepless nights and the crowding in shelters or in places where they could be reached in time, with the ever-prevailing thought that the morning would bring the usual call for work and duty. All this the people had endured together in silence, never threatening revenge or vowing everlasting hatred. There was only the conviction that the bombing and the destruction of churches and the houses that had nothing to do with any military target, stemmed from decadence in the enemy's character, and because of this the enemy was doomed. And what was happening outside Malta seemed to confirm that this was so.

On the North African front, a numerically superior and better

equipped Italian army under Marshal Graziani had been defeated
and was running away from a scanty British and Commonwealth
force under General Wavell, and what had already been taken in
Italian prisoners was more than the British and Commonwealth
forces together. After invading Greece on the 28th October the
Italian army was not only repulsed but also had to retreat into
Albania from where it had attacked. It looked as if the local
conviction was accurate. Indeed this was the Italian explanation
for the lull in the raids on Malta, because, they said, they had to
transfer planes to other theatres of war. But the real reason was, as
circumstances were showing, that Italian forces whether on land,
sea or in the air were impotent as a war machine. But if this were
so why were the authorities still building up defences and
measures of protection from air attack? As Nicola Malizia
admitted in his writings that 'in December Malta was full of
Hurricanes, and was like a burning cauldron of guns and shells, and
the Italian airmen had been wasted in vain' there was no likelihood
of any further Italian threat. So what was the threat being
anticipated which was reflected in the breathless preparations?
These were the questions being asked in Malta in December 1940.
But there were no answers. Only the unspoken feeling that
something was in the air.

The answer could have been found with Hitler, the man who
was pulling all the strings of the Axis puppets. Obsessed though he
was with other fronts he did not forget North Africa, and he could
not afford to do so with the plans he had for the Eastern
Mediterranean. His generals von Brauchitsch, Halder and von
Thoma were all against sending German troops to help the Italians,
even though they made quite clear their feelings about Italians'
inability to fight. But even they had never expected Wavell's
success. So with Graziani utterly defeated, Hitler acted and
expressed his determination to do everything in his power to
prevent Italy from losing North Africa. As he had occasion to
express himself, he feared that with the loss of North Africa,
Britain would hold a pistol at Italy's head and could make her
change sides with the obvious results. So ignoring previous Italian
rejections of his help Hitler ordered German help for Italy in that
theatre of operations, and the first step in this direction was the
moving of the Luftwaffe to assist the Italians from Sicily. The
order of operations given by Hitler to his Army Staff at a domestic
meeting mentioned amongst other things that the Luftwaffe,
which had already been ordered to assist the Italians, must

intervene still more actively with Stukas and fighters, and must strike a blow against the British troops in Cyrenaica using the heaviest bombs. It must work in co-operation with the Italian Air Force to protect and to disrupt British supplies by land and sea and to combat the British fleet. But first of all attempts must be made to subdue the air base of Malta.

This was a more serious threat from a vastly different enemy.

CHAPTER FOUR

The *Illustrious* – Sojourn of Defiance

On 10th January 1941 the British fleet under Admiral Sir Andrew Cunningham was in the process of completing a repetition of the Operation Hats of the previous September by bringing two convoys from the East and West, one of which was destined for Malta. The combined convoys consisted of fourteen ships, and they were escorted by one of the biggest British naval forces that had so far appeared in the Mediterranean. Admiral Somerville, leading Forces H and F from Gibraltar and flying his flag on the battleship *Renown*, had with him the battleship *Malaya*, the aircraft carrier *Ark Royal*, the cruiser *Bonaventure* and no less than eleven destroyers. From Alexandria Admiral Cunningham had proceeded to meet him in his flagship *Warspite*, and with him he had the battleships *Valiant* and *Barham*, the aircraft carriers *Eagle* and *Illustrious*, the cruisers *Orion*, *York*, *Ajax*, *Perth*, *Calcutta*, *Gloucester* and *Southampton*, together with sixteen destroyers. To patrol the area where the two forces were to meet there were the submarines *Triumph, Upholder* and *Pandora*.

The British admirals were hoping to engage the Italian Fleet. But this did not make an appearance, and there was only the Luftwaffe in Sicily to be tickled into action. It was an occasion that Fliegerkorps X of the Luftwaffe had been waiting for to implement the Führer's orders. It had been following the progress of the convoy, and struck when it was at the desired spot, past Pantellaria and only some 80 miles from Malta. The attack was pressed home, but their fury was unleashed on the aircraft carrier *Illustrious* which was hit by several heavy bombs and badly crippled. Such an attack would have spelled death to any other ship, but, like the felled gladiator who rises up again and transfers his weapon from the stricken and useless hand to the remaining good one, the *Illustrious* met a second onslaught as she continued her way towards Malta with what guns she could still fire at the attacking bombers. Hers were not the last movements of a dying ship fighting it out to the end, but of fierce determination to reach her destination which was Malta, not only as the protector of the convoy, but to land the Swordfish and Fulmar aircraft destined for Hal Far. Most of these were destroyed with the first attack but a squadron of Fulmars had managed to take off in time and fight in defence of their ship. When their fuel got low they flew to Malta, refuelled and re-armed and went back to fight in the second attack. Hit again the *Illustrious* still did not sink and continued with what little power left to her, maintaining her course with difficulty. The sound of gunfire at sea was heard all over Malta, and everyone was speaking of some naval battle at sea, not far away from the island.

It appeared now as if the Luftwaffe's malevolence was directed solely towards *Illustrious* because when the third attack was delivered it was again directed against her. It could have been the stubborn German reaction to the ship's fantastic resistance, but if it was, then *Illustrious* met this third attack with the same determined fortitude even though it made this once fine ship a twisted, limping, but miraculously still floating, shambles.

This was how *Illustrious* reached Malta during the night of 10th January 1941; before her arrived the laden ships which would succour Malta and for which she had suffered martyrdom. Even the way they had arrived before her accompanied by the destroyer *Gallant* with her bows blown off seemed to illustrate the story of a mother facing the wolf until her children could run away to safety.

On the morning of the 11th *Illustrious* was no longer alone. From the first moment during the previous night that she had been towed to Parlatorio Wharf in French Creek and gangways came down, hordes of people stormed the ship — firemen with hoses to put out the still burning fires, doctors and ambulance men to attend to the wounded, stretcher bearers to carry them, seamen from other ships, surveyors to see to the first needs of an impossible task of making the ship seaworthy, and others who in one way or another had a job to do. All of them worked their way in a forest of twisted, torn and blackened steel. At first light on the morning of the 11th the Maltese dockyard workers took over. Their specific orders were not to deal with the smashed deck and twisted alleyways, or anything else above the waterline, but to attend only to the bare essentials that would make it possible for the ship to go out to sea and quickly. Divers went down to examine the bottom, the fitters invaded the engine room, and the welders began to take out the wooden pegs in her punctured hull and to weld holes. In the meantime the island's defences maintained the alert they had been put on after the ship's arrival.

The dockyard workers worked like ants until late and only left when others came to take their places. That morning the news had flashed all over the island and onlookers began to appear over the bastions and in boats outside the creek to see the fantastic ship that had withstood so much, so that Malta could have her convoy.

I also wanted to see her, but I couldn't bring myself to go near enough until Thursday the 16th. My father, who himself was working on the *Illustrious*, had asked me to collect a cap for him from a hosiery in Cospicua, and close to the shop there was the bastion of St John Elemosiniere standing high over No 3 and 4 docks at the inner end of French Creek where the *Illustrious* lay, at the outer end. At half past one I reached the hosiery and found it closed. Very convenient, I thought. Until it was time for the shop to open I could walk to the bastions and have a good look at the fabulous aircraft-carrier. And so I did.

It was a dull afternoon with grey skies promising rain. From the place where I stood, the dockyard lay spread out below me. Workers were all over the place busily engaged on some job, and in their movements there appeared to be an element of urgency that had not been there before. My father had mentioned that it had been like that for the last four days. Everybody was talking about what the *Illustrious* had been through.

I gazed at the ship, now unrecognizable, festooned as she was with scaffolding and other repair accoutrements. Against her blackened hull there were the flashes of acetylene from the welders at work. Two men were at the wheel of an air pump maintaining a diver and the tell-tale bubbles indicated where he was working. There were people on the bastions of Senglea, as they had been for the last four days, looking at the dwarfed ship which looked like a beehive with Maltese workers as the bees. They must have all been thinking how long it would take to repair her.

The rest of their unspoken thoughts were no doubt tinged with fear that as the Germans had persecuted her on the high seas they might decide to come for her where she was. Hadn't after all Hitler himself said that the harbour of Malta would be her grave? But after the long raidless spell we had had, it felt almost silly to think of air raids again.

I was wrong. The air raid sirens began wailing that very minute.

I stood where I was, transfixed and unable to believe that an alarm was being sounded on a day and at a time when everyone was thinking about the Germans. The workmen in the dockyard were suddenly running to their shelters, while those working on the *Illustrious* were going down the gangways to take shelter too. The diver was being brought up, and, as the ship seemed to have emptied, my thoughts went to its crew. At least, I thought, if this attack was aimed at them they could now rely on the safety of rock shelters which were close to the ship. But there was no need to think about her men as I saw them then. At least some of them were quickly removing tarpaulins from a couple of places, and from the uncovered points began to rise anti-aircraft guns, and pom-poms. So even if there was to be a further battle, the stricken ship meant to have her share. And at that time my heart was full as it had never been before.

In the silence that seemed to have suddenly fallen over the dockyard and harbour, and possibly the whole of Malta I thought that this raid, coming after a lull, was going to be something special. If it were going to be the first German raid on Malta and to be aimed at the *Illustrious* then it would probably add a new page in history. There was also the excitement and anxiety borne from stories of prowess of the Luftwaffe which had never as yet appeared in Malta, and it would be interesting to see how the Germans would react to the new Maltese barrage reinforced with many new guns which had never until then been in a heavy action. There was above all the thrilling knowledge that, if this was going to be the raid many had spoken with awe about, I was there at vantage point to witness it as I had witnessed the first air raids by the Italians.

And at that moment I heard the noise of approaching aircraft. I looked up at the sky, and with the sun being hidden behind the high grey clouds it wasn't difficult to scan the grey expanse. Then I saw them. A multitude of tiny dots like a swarm of flies, coming over Grand Harbour from the direction of Fort Ricasoli and Kalkara. But they must be flying high, I thought. Surely they were not Italians. Those had never come in such force. There seemed to be more than a hundred of them. Straining my eyes I saw that there were others above them, escorting fighters, no doubt, and amongst these there was the occasional glint of sun on aluminium. So some of those were after all Italians. But the bombers beneath them were not. Then I knew why they appeared higher than they must have actually been. Because most of them were Stukas — Junkers 87 — which looked smaller. The whole force consisted of 44 Stukas Junkers 87, 17 Junkers 88, 10 Messerschmitt 110, 10 Italian Fiat CR 42 fighters and a number of Macchi 200.

Immediately it seemed as if hell was let loose. The guns from the batteries ringing the harbour opened rapid fire, and the grey sky became a blazing inferno. The noise was so shattering that even from that height it felt as if it was going to rupture my ear drums. I stood where I was, intent on the straight-moving formations, as I had never seen anything like it and I was wondering how long those planes could endure the steel and explosive that was going up at them. I became curious to see how they would react. And they reacted well.

First one, then the rest of the Stukas one at a time, peeled off from the formations and dived straight on to the Dockyard below, and with the first indication of their intention a second noise broke in from the guns which began firing to meet them half way. It takes a brave heart to dive from an inferno such as they had been in, straight into another one. But the Stukas did not falter and kept to their dive notwithstanding the one or two that were hit and exploded in mid-air. When they were past the second barrage of murderous fire they went straight into the third barrage put up by the Bofors and Pom Poms. But after that there was the whistling of bombs and the whining planes pulled out of the dives, followed by tremendous explosions.

I still think that on that day I learned what hell is like. The shattering noise of what I have seen described as the world's heaviest barrage is something difficult to describe, and from where I stood, the harbour and dockyard looked a terrific sight. Every ship that was there began firing, and I had to run and take cover myself from the rain of shrapnel that began falling around me. When I reached the shelter entrance I tried to look back, and at that moment a formation of aircraft was diving in our direction, so I ran in as I heard the whistling bombs. There were then explosions and the shaking of the shelter as bombs were hitting the Dockyard part which was beneath the bastion where the shelter stood, only fifty yards away. I felt the strong wave of blast in the shelter and pressed myself to the wall in the first cavity I found. Women and men alike, screaming prayers, were toppled on each other, and they screamed more than before, this time with no mind for holy words. Children began to cry while the shattering noises from outside continued, with more diving, whistling bombs, explosions, blocks of concrete that were lifted from the dockyard below and smashed against the face of the shelter, and of course the never ending gunfire. It looked as if the world had come to an end and no one would live.

The firing continued, and in those acute moments I registered that the gunners were still there and fighting. But so must have been the German airmen in their still diving planes and behind the dropping bombs. Then as part of the barrage fell silent there was the new welcome sound of different engines I had come to know so well and as I ran out of the shelter I was just in time to see the British Hurricanes, going in amongst the enemy formations like devils with guns blazing. It is hard to believe that there were only fifteen of them going into that enemy mass. I could not help the tears of emotion that came to my eyes as slogging minutes behind the Hurricanes, I saw two heavy Gladiators. They were there as well and flying into the fray notwithstanding the odds in numbers, armament and speed. But no human eye could remain averted from the scene that was visible from where I stood. Vittoriosa, Cospicua and Senglea were covered with a thin mist-like haze. I thought it was a smoke screen because there had been rumours of putting out such smoke screens during air attacks. But I realised immediately the thought occurred that what I was seeing was not of a chemical nature. There was the persistent smell of cordite, and dust in the air which stuck to one's nostrils and I knew then that the haze was caused by suspended dust from demolished buildings. There were fires burning in the Dockyard, reflecting dancing colours in the misty surroundings; palls of smoke were rising from what I took to be Senglea and Cospicua. The road where I stood was littered with chunks of concrete which had been lifted from the Dockyard wharfs hundreds of yards away. I remember one man saying that the Germans must have used bombs made of concrete for lack of steel. Of course it was nothing of the sort, but I could not even find the time to tell him so, engrossed as I was in trying to look through the haze at the far end of the creek as if to confirm what I was expecting to see.

A small crowd had emerged from the shelter and joined me, and eyes forming silent questions must have all been looking in the direction of the now fast drifting haze. But it seemed as if even that small momentary curiosity was being deprived us. There were fresh noises of aircraft and, having heard them so shortly before, we knew they were Germans. It was impossible to believe that having met such a murderous reception they would return only fifteen minutes later. This was of course a second wave, which had not yet sampled the barrage. The Stukas began to dive this time from all directions as the guns still hot from the first phase went into action again. The heavens seemed to split with exploding

shells as the gunners, like men possessed, put up a rapid fire, and
again there was the whining of the Stukas rising to shrieks like
those of lost souls followed by the whistling and explosion of
bombs. Added to this pandemonium there was the droning of the
Junkers 88 which were releasing bombs from their racks over the
Dockyard and where the *Illustrious* should have been. As it was
hidden to me after the first phase with the dust clouds that had
now thickened again, so it could have been to them.

No one believed the Maltese gunners who later said how they
saw the German pilots waving at them as they dived as low as 100
or 200 feet in line with their gun positions, but it was true as
coming out of their dive, the Stukas flew out very low over the
water of Grand Harbour, safe from guns which could not be
depressed to fire at them from the bastions.

As the battle increased, and the Dockyard waters were rising in
a hundred spouts, the Three Cities shuddered to the continuous
impact of bombs. But the Germans kept coming on, and no-one
can deny the courage of the men in those planes. But greater
praise later went to the Maltese and British gunners, and
particularly to the part-timers of the Dockyard Defence Battery
who stuck to their guns in face of the devilish fury of the Junkers.
Lieutenant Francis W. Angle, the officer in charge of the multiple
pom-pom on St Michael's Bastion, barely 200 yards from the
Illustrious retained his composure amidst the flying planes and
bombs exploding around him, and by his excellent example and
coolness in front of the heavy attack encouraged his men, all
Dockyard part-time gunners to keep firing with telling effect. He
was later awarded the Military Cross.

No less brave was Sergeant Leone Apap, a dockyard worker
turned part-time soldier during the war, who was deputising for
his officer and took charge of another multiple pom-pom. Any
other person would have panicked and ran when the pom-pom
jammed and stopped firing during the attack. But not Leone.
Calmly he kept three of his crew with him and the rest he sent to
take cover. Then he traced the fault and repaired it. Without losing
his calm, after doing all this under continuous fire, he reassembled
his crew and began firing again with considerable effect. He was
awarded the Military Medal. Bombardier Gerald Balzan was
another dockyard worker and part-timer of the Dockyard Defence
Battery who was manning a Bofors. A brace of bombs fell close to
his gun injuring two members of his crew. Gerald reorganised the
set up and with only the remaining three he continued firing his

gun until the raid was over. Then he attended to his injured men. This deed earned him the Military Medal.

There were however no medals for the many gunners who under the heat of attack had to improvise and act as they thought best. With Lieutenant Micallef Trigona, a territorial officer of the 3rd Light Anti Aircraft Regiment, it was more a case of frustration and desperation. He commanded a Bofors positioned on the ravelin of Lower Barracca Gardens overlooking Grand Harbour, giving him a front seat position for the attack. He pumped shells at the diving planes, but as the Stukas pulled out of their dive they were flying out of Grand Harbour, past him, but lower than his position. As he could not depress his gun barrel because of a depression rail meant to prevent him firing at the level of buildings, the Lieutenant could only look at the pilots grinning at him from their cockpit as they flew past. But when the second formation came in, he could endure it no longer, and had his men remove the depression rail. As the Germans were flying out he ordered the men to depress the gun barrel, and the grin on the pilots' faces disappeared as they met the Bofors spitting fire at them, and saw its commander standing on the ravelin crossing his right arm over his left transmitting the vulgar Maltese message which they understood. Shells which missed the planes hit the bastion of Fort St Angelo and one of the lighthouses on the breakwater of Grand Harbour, blowing half of it away, which is still missing today.

When the noise of planes and the gunfire had died away into nothingness I emerged out of the shelter where I had taken cover when it became too hot, and looked at the dockyard. There was again the tell-tale dust haze as before. But as it drifted slowly across French Creek the wharves which had been the beehive of dockyard activity for years stood out in a stark macabre picture. They were pockmarked by craters and laced by twisted girders of ruined sheds. Where there had been warehouses there were now only mounds of rubble, and in the great desolation of smashed stone and tortured steel nothing moved but the eddying dust. There was no time to linger on that devastation; my eyes were following the drifting dust moving away as if in conformity with my wish to find out what had brought all this about. One palpitating minute, in which I saw yet more destruction, then out of the mist loomed the shape of what I was looking for. The *Illustrious* was there. What tarpaulins and scaffolding there had been before the raid were all blown away, lines of smoke were trailing out of a couple of places, and the ship was listing slightly

on one side. Its sides were gashed and holed where splinters from
near misses must have struck, and her flying deck was a field of
devastation. But she was still moored to the wharf, and somehow
floating.

All those who looked at her breathed a sigh of relief; and there
were eyes only for her. The other warships, the convoy ships she
had escorted herself meant nothing at that moment. Not even the
Essex which was not far away. But there would have been more
significant signs had it been known then that the ship was carrying
400 tons of ammunition. She was hit by a bomb during the attack
which went straight to the engine room, killing 15 and injuring 23
of the crew. Had it touched any of the magazines holding the
ammunition it would have been blown the whole harbour to
blazes.

Across the tormented harbour the sirens began wailing the All
Clear, and fire parties began to emerge from their cover in the
dockyard hurrying towards the blazing beacons. Dockyard
workers and sailors from other ships where their presence was not
required hurried too, first individually, then in groups, and they
were all making a beeline towards the ship which had been the
protagonist of the drama and where their help was obviously
required.

In the street where I was, nothing moved, and what people had
left their shelter at the sound of the sirens stood in crowds near
the entrance and were not going to depart until the church bells
gave the All Clear. The thought of the return of the raiders seemed
to be in everyone's mind. A policeman on a bicycle came in my
direction making his way round the concrete chunks that littered
the street. He was warning everybody to stay near the shelters, and
trying to answer some of the hundreds of questions that were
being shot at him. The Three Cities, had suffered badly, he told
everybody, and two churches had been hit. There were many
killed.

At his words my thoughts flew to my mother whom I had left
at home and who still against my advice preferred to take shelter
in St Dominic's church in Vittoriosa. When I asked the policeman
which were the churches hit he could not say. All the same his
words of doom were like a premonition and I immediately rushed
there in case I might be of help.

I heard the bells of fire engines approaching fast, and at that
moment they appeared to be the quickest means of transportation.
They had to slow down when they reached us because of the

concrete and boulders in the street. I took out the ARP armlet which I always carried with me in those days, even after ARP personnel had been constituted into a full time corps, and putting it on my arm I reached to the nearest engine and asked for a lift to Vittoriosa. The police sergeant looked at me and the armlet and told me to jump on, and after the crew had cleared a way through the concrete litter, the fire engine proceeded on its way.

As we went through the heart of Cospicua I could see that whole blocks of buildings were gone, and the streets were littered with stone, wood, and smashed contents from the houses that had been there. But the magnificent church, though marked and chipped by splinters, was still standing, looking more opulent with the buildings that had crowded it, now razed to the ground. It was a welcome sight for me, but if the Church of Cospicua was still standing, then the two which were hit must have been in Senglea and Vittoriosa I reasoned. And if there was only one big church in Senglea then one of the stricken ones must be in Vittoriosa. In fact, as we left Cospicua and proceeded to Vittoriosa the Senglea Church on the other side of Dockyard Creek came into view and I could see that it was badly hit. But its damage was minimised by that of the whole neighbourhood which had vanished, and the residential quarter that had been there lay in a vast rubble of stones as if that area had been passed over by some giant bulldozer. One hundred yards away then there was the Couvre Porte entrance through the bastions to Vittoriosa, and as my eyes roamed over the battlements on the left I was met with a sombre and strange sight. The cupolas and steeples of the two churches of Vittoriosa were still standing. Was it possible that the policeman had been wrong? The answer came a few hundred yards and five minutes later as the fire engine was boarded by a local policeman to direct it to the fires. In answer to my question he said that it was the Coventual Parish Church of St Lawrence which was hit, and that there were many dead.

There were in fact forty people killed. Some were locals who had taken shelter in the sacristy, and others who had just landed at St Lawrence steps from the ferry which still ran trips from Valletta and Senglea in those days. The church had been the nearest shelter to turn to. Someone who had taken shelter in the bell tower escaped unhurt since it was not touched. But besides the people in the sacristy there were also the church records and priceless treasures from Byzantine times and the Order of St John, which were destroyed. All the stainless glass windows in the church were smashed. But there had also been the beautiful chandeliers of Belgian crystal which shone and twinkled their splendour on every feast. They will now shine no more. The magnificent cupola, with its famous Cali' frescoes of the Great Siege of 1565 was gashed and shaken, but remained standing. My mother had, as I expected, taken shelter in the other church of St Dominic which was untouched. But for her and for everybody else there was going to be no more sheltering in churches. It became obvious that the new enemy would allow no quarter, and the only protection from his bombs would from now onwards have to be that of solid rock.

As I worked with the ARP people, in the stricken area, news began to filter through of other damage and casualties caused in the other two cities and also the dockyard. The enemy had failed to sink the *Illustrious* but it had extended its vengeance to the three cities that sheltered her.

After the church bells had peeled the All Clear some of those who had foolishly returned from the villages decided to go back. The rest went for the nearest rock shelter with the firm intention of making their home there. The tunnels in the bastions of the Three Cities were filled with men, women and children all carrying their essential belongings and pushing their way in even just for that coming night, intending to see what was to be done in the morning. The old railway tunnel joining Valletta to Floriana housed 5,000 people that night, and that was how it remained for a long time to come.

This situation which had arisen so suddenly affected the villages as well since as the evening approached the refugees who had again left the hit cities began to flow into them. Terrified people who had left their homes, many of them indeed homeless from the German raid, were everywhere—along roads, in village squares, and in the open. Some did find shelter for the night but others had to be provided for even if only as a temporary measure. The authorities made schools available to them, and convents and monasteries opened their doors to all. As night approached there was not a single person to be seen in the streets of the stricken areas, which were only for windowless roofless buildings gaping at the rising moon. From wherever the people lay they waited for the attack that they felt must come during the night. But this did not come. It was on Saturday 18th January that the Germans came again with a heavy attack on the airfields. 51 Junkers 87, 12 Junkers 88, 17 Messerschmitts 110 and a number of Macchi

200 took part in this attack. There was considerable damage caused and there were casualties in villages close to the airfield.

In Mosta, 13 people were killed and 15 injured while 2 persons were just not found.

A gun detachment at Hal Far under Sergeant Arthur Kitney of the 3rd Battalion the King's Own Malta Regiment was dive-bombed during this raid, and the sergeant was wounded when the building where his post was situated received several direct hits. But though wounded Sergeant Kitney maintained his guns in action. For his bravery he was awarded the Military Medal.

When during this raid a Fulmar aircraft was shot down in the rough sea at Marsaxlokk the pilot found himself in difficulties. Sapper Spiru Zammit of the Royal Engineers (T) dived into the water and reaching the pilot held him up until rescued by a speed boat. Sapper Zammit who was instrumental in saving the pilot's life was awarded the Medal of the Order of the British Empire.

Attacks were pressed home again on the following day, Sunday the 19th, this time back on the harbour and the *Illustrious*. There were two attacks, one in the morning and another in the afternoon, both as harsh as that on the previous Thursday. There was again a heavy number of Stukas, Junkers 88s and Messerschmitt 110s involved, together with Italian fighters. There was also the same response by Malta with a curtain of steel from the guns and outstanding interception by fighters, this time supplemented by Fairey Fulmars previously belonging to the *Illustrious* but now operating from Hal Far.

There was again very serious damage in the Three Cities with Senglea's parish church being hit again and the church of St Dominic in Vittoriosa razed to the ground. Looking at the vast wilderness of devastation with the streets of three cities that had been the pride of Malta now passable only along pitted trails that snaked through mounds of rubble, one would have been right to wonder how life could exist in those areas. The voices of those buried in the debris of St Lawrence Church on Thursday, were heard by ARP workers until Friday, as they dug for them. But then rain had brought down more masonry over them, and they too became a prey to the silence that fell in the city.

Those were three days of woe for the Three Cities, and the defences were again superb with a Military Medal being awarded to Sergeant John W. Quennel of the Royal Artillery for his brave behaviour with his Bofors gun during this attack. There were however two major consolations; one being that the enemy had not been left unscathed, as during those three days the defences shot down 39 aircraft and damaged and probably destroyed 14 with the loss of 2 British planes, while the *Illustrious* was still floating and carrying on with repairs.

Some interesting points mentioned by Nicola Malizia in connection with these attacks throw more light on the outcome. It is noticeable from what he says that he tries to avoid saying how many German aircraft were shot down. Regarding Thursday's raid he wrote that he had no information (strange to read this in an otherwise well-researched work). Then for Sunday's raids, after saying that the Germans said that they lost ten planes, he goes on to say in no uncertain way that many German aircraft were ditched, beyond the coast of Malta while many others had reached their base in a damaged condition and their crews seriously injured or dead. This is confirmed from two reports: namely, one referring to the Cant Z 506 Seaplane with the Red Cross marks which patrolled the sea channel between Malta and Sicily obviously looking for survivors from the crews of the ditched aircraft, and confirmed by the Malta Defences which had the plane on their radar. Malizia says that this Red Cross plane was shot down by British fighters. The other report came from a different Italian source which mentioned the funerals which were held in Sicily for dead German aircraft crews.

Another point mentioned by Malizia gives the lie to the composed behaviour of the German crews in front of the Maltese defences. They were so lost and excited that, according to him, the German Messerschmitt 110s fired on escorting Italian fighters, and shot down one of them.

The prior of the Dominican friary in Vittoriosa was beset by grief and despair. For seven months since the beginning of the war with Italy he had stuck to his post with a handful of monks to run normal church services, and during raids the team dispersed to places where people were taking shelter and gave comfort in prayers and companionship. Now his church was destroyed and his friary deserted. There was nowhere to stay and he would have to leave with the others for some other Dominican friary. Maybe to the provincial one in Valletta, but probably it would be the one at Rabat, away from the dockyard but close to Ta' Qali Airfield. There would be more people to tend to over there since the village had received many evacuees. But wherever they might go they would be far and away from Vittoriosa, where their shattered church would remain derelict, exposed to sun and rain.

The Archpriest had felt the same way about the Conventual Parish Church of St Lawrence after it was hit during the second round of the attack on the *Illustrious* on Thursday. During the raid he had taken shelter in the steeple only twenty yards away from the sacristy which had collapsed on forty people. The heart-rending whistling of the bombs that hit the sacristy had terrified him, and the explosions had deafened him. The blast shook the steeple like a pack of cards and it looked as if it was toppling down. The priest covered his face with his hands and prayed shaking with fear. When the explosions died down and the rumble of falling masonry quietened he rushed out of the steeple, with pale face and his black cassock now white with dust, and ran to the mound of masonry and debris that was still emitting smoke. But what could he do in the face of that catastrophic mountain that had once been a part of his beautiful church? He heard pitiful whimpering from some of those buried beneath those big boulders calling for assistance, but the only assistance he could give was spiritual, and shocked as he was he managed to find enough strength to shout the same words of absolution as he must have done so many times before to those same people.

It was only then that he could spare a look at the remains of his church where the high altar and aisles had remained intact. But they now lay wide open to the weather from the side that was blown off and the cupola looked ready to crumple down any moment. He walked on the marble floor now covered by soot and shards of glass to the door leading to the sacristy from the church as he had done since his childhood, but now for the first time in thirty years he found it closed to him, blocked by debris and fallen masonry. He stood there looking in silence with tears in his eyes, as if he knew that in that door beneath those tons of debris there was his beloved sexton who was caught by the avalanche of stone as he ran to the church from the sacristy which was no more.

Amongst the dead there were also a seaman and his wife. Only a few weeks before he had returned to Malta shocked and shaken up but safe after a terrifying ordeal at sea with a convoy. He had prayed to St Lawrence during those terrible moments for deliverance. And he had remembered his vow to pray again in thanksgiving on that day of 16th January, so he went to the church in Vittoriosa to complete his vow. That was when the sirens sounded and he and his wife took shelter in the sacristy.

Another woman, normally a resident of Vittoriosa but now an

evacuee at Zurrieq, had on that day decided to go to collect some clothes from her house in Vittoriosa. She took her two small children with her. When the sirens sounded she went to take shelter in the sacristy. An elder daughter escaped death after missing the bus from Zurrieq when she decided to follow her mother.

Another dockyard worker had left the yard to go to a dentist when the sirens sounded and he took shelter in the sacristy where he was killed with the rest.

More than with sorrow for the dead, the living were faced with their immediate problems. The first was that facing the Archpriest. It was bigger than that which beset the dignitaries of Cospicua and Senglea. The church in one city was still standing while in the other, there was a substitute church to take over. In Vittoriosa he made use of the second church on Sunday the 19th, as on that same afternoon this was also destroyed.

That same evening he began to make arrangements to use the small chapel at the police station at Couvre Porte as his substitute church, so that on the morrow he could administer religious services from the chapel to the crowds which would have to assemble in the open.

Even though the dead and mutilated had all been removed from the debris where the sacristy had once stood, he could not help feeling the pangs of sorrow as he passed by so many times in his errands to salvage what little he could from the stricken church before the cupola and maybe the whole ceiling collapsed. Perhaps the worst thing about it was that this was only the beginning; no one could see the end of it, if there was going to be an end. Even if most of his flock had run away to other pastures there was still that part of it who had crept into the bastion tunnels like ancient cave dwellers and those who had dug in rock and squirmed themselves in like snails running away from rain. They were living victims of this modern man-made tragedy who were still to suffer, and God only knew what more suffering lay in store for them. He knew that he would suffer with them. This much he would have to endure by virtue of his being their archpriest and shepherd. They would attempt to endure this difficult life, but there would still be the need for masses to be said, confessions heard, and holy communion administered. There would be marriages, and births would not cease, requiring baptisms. The incidence of death had increased considerably with the threat of more violent air attacks, but there would still be natural deaths requiring assistance and encouragement before the exit to eternity. All this his flock had required and enjoyed when times were normal and there were other priests to help him do it. Now that he was alone, he would give it to them just the same. Alone. No matter what it would cost him in danger and fear. Or the sorrow he would not be able to help feeling at the lot that had become theirs. His mission would be the right antidote.

The several priests and monks who had assumed chaplainship of Maltese regiments were now faced with a similar situation. It had been normal for them in the first days of war to administer services in set chapels uninterrupted by air attacks. Now, they would have to attend to the soldiers in their flock dispersed in outlying gun positions with gun platforms as their altars and a tent or even the blue sky for their roof. But none of them shirked their duties, and under attack or not they were always close to the soldiers to sustain them, and attend to their needs.

A different problem had assailed Dun Luret, the parish priest of a small village still in the slow-moving process of absorbing an additional five hundred immigrants from the cities within its already expanded community. The village Domus, which had hosted a few score of children every evening for their classes in catechism, had overnight been turned into a hostel for two hundred people, men, women and children, who had to live and sleep there. He was struck dumb on his first visit to see how things were going. He was met by grumbling, shouting, children's crying and even a quarrel or two over the best rooms. It was impossible to believe that these were the brethren of the same quiet and submissive rural flock which he had attended since taking holy orders. He walked along the corridors in silence, trying to make the best entrance he could, darting looks at the strange types he had never dreamed of seeing in his beloved village. Families whose lot fell for the main hall which had during its existence been used as a chapel or conference hall were now busily hanging sheets and blankets from ropes strung out from wall to wall in an attempt to provide some sort of privacy for themselves and their families. There were two women however who were not bothering about such privations, and were already changing without any hesitation, exhibiting thick white thighs and faces grinning with the smoke going into their eyes from cigarettes firmly held between their red painted lips. In his mind he suddenly stamped them as prostitutes. He did not know why he had thus concluded because he had never met any, but he seemed to associate their looks, behaviour and the disparity between their little clothing and much flesh with what he had been given to understand about women in this profession. He crossed himself on such a thought, but as he walked on he could not help feeling that these and their type had also a right to live. But he also knew he had a right to defend the morals of his village.

Monday was relatively a quiet day. There were indications of alarms, but the raiders that appeared on radar never crossed the coast.

"It looks as if the battle has been given back to the Italians," said one.

"Don't be so sure," was the obvious reply he received. "The Germans may be licking their wounds, but the *Illustrious* is still here, and while she is here we will not be left alone."

True, the *Illustrious* was still there, but there had been an additional day's work done on her. Twenty-four hours of day and night shifts without stopping, not even when the sirens sounded. One particular Maltese diver elected to stay at his work beneath the ship even during alarms. It seemed as if a race was now on. Never in the history of the dockyard had the workers worked so fast.

For others it was a day to wait and see whether after all it was a fluke and the Germans would come again on the morrow or whether there was something else which kept them away. It was different in the villages where the evacuees continued with their efforts in settling down, the shops were open as usual, and cinemas held their usual shows, schools continued in their new locations. In the stricken cities round the harbour the busiest people were the men of the Demolition Squads who were trying to bring some order to the devastated streets by clearing main thoroughfares and pulling down dangerous buildings. Those who left their shelters did so with some purpose and made sure they would not go far. But with the husbands away for work the women made hay in the sun by taking out their bedding in this same sun after four days of continuous dampness in the tunnels and shelters. There was a treat for the people of Vittoriosa that morning when Pawlu, nicknamed Il-Bazari, a typical character more than a part-time fisherman, went to the bastions where the women were airing their bedding, pushing a hand-cart laden with fish. Never had those women seen so much fish in one place, and Pawlu was soon doing brisk business. With cleared cart and bulging pockets he soon made a beeline for the nearest wine shop which was where he spent most of his time. The women wondered where all that fish had come from. It was a godsend, but strange. That evening a strong smell of fish wafted along the tunnels in the bastions, and everyone ate with gusto. Husbands nodded at their wives as if to say, 'That was good. Let's have it again.'

There were those who tasted the sour smell of TNT in the fish. But they ate it all the same. They would still have eaten it had they seen Pawlu collecting the dead fish that had been brought to the surface by bomb explosions after the Sunday afternoon raid.

The following day Malta was thrilled at Churchill's message which was splashed in the *Times of Malta* and its Maltese counterpart *Il-Berqa*, and repeatedly broadcast on Rediffusion. 'I send you, on behalf of the War Cabinet', ran the message, 'heartfelt congratulations upon the magnificent and ever memorable defence which your heroic garrison and citizens, assisted by the Navy and above all, by the Royal Air Force, are making against the Italian and German attacks'. But it seemed that there was something else which had become contagious. There was easy talk, but beneath it one could detect the tension as if now the question everybody was trying to put as why the Germans had allowed another day of grace. This tension reflected itself in the workers still labouring in the race to repair the *Illustrious*. Hearing people talk in those days would have made one think they might have been sorry to be left alone. There continued to be alarms which either did not materialise or produced a single plane, probably to reconnoitre for some purpose. It must have been the *Illustrious* which was still festooned with planking and repair accoutrements on Wednesday 22nd January. But, was it? That night the climax was reached when everyone was woken up by the sound of bombers flying overhead. It was the first sound of its kind that had been heard in Malta since the war began, heavy and throbbing, and there were many who went out of doors to look up at the sky and try to see what was going on. One or two shadows across the moon was all they could see. Everyone went back to sleep with a thrill in his heart too beset by memories of the hard times he had endured to be optimistic about what this incident could mean. But when the radio gave the news on the morrow that 23 British bombers had bombed Cermisso and the airfields at Augusta and Catania in Sicily, there was much rejoicing and patting of shoulders. Everyone knew without being told that it must have been the Wellingtons from 37 Squadron that had carried out the bombing, and that they had flown from Malta. More than the fact in itself that the Italians were given a taste of their own medicine there was the feeling that Malta had taken the offensive. It is satisfying to know that one can defend himself, but more gratifying to be able even under duress to hit hard at the enemy. Then, as if this was not enough, on the morning of the 24th there were more smiles of happiness in the Three Cities, and people were running to the bastions. I ran with them too, and looked at where eyes were focussed and fingers pointing. There was shouting and clapping as we looked at Parlatorio Wharf in the Dockyard and saw the empty mooring place where until the previous night the *Illustrious* had lain. Now it was no longer there. The race had been won.

The aircraft carrier had left for Alexandria during the early hours of the night of 23rd January, escorted by the Australian cruiser *Perth* which had accompanied her like a shadow since that fateful day of thirteen days before, and had even stayed in Malta with her to help with her guns during air attacks. Now she was completing her mission by seeing her safely to Alexandria. This mission was in fact completed safely. The *Illustrious* went on to be repaired in the United States and was then back in the fight.

CHAPTER FIVE

Herald to a Siege

The bright sun shone from a blue sky on the morning of 24th January, and when it struck St Angelo there was a different silhouette to frolic across the blue water of Grand Harbour as its rays spread across the chunks that had been bitten off the mighty fort, and lay crumbled below. The bastions of Valletta were there rising as always, but beyond them could be seen the newly charred skeletons of buildings. The creeks too were there, still in the shade, this time as if ashamed to show the black devastation that was in them. Where there had been the victualling yards, machine shops and warehouses along the shore line, there were now only soot-covered, jagged remains running thinner into nothingness towards Parlatorio Wharf where the ship which had brought this destruction had been moored.

Now she was no longer there, and behind her she had left her dead and wounded as a contribution towards the big sacrifice, and her Swordfish and Fulmar aircraft now housed at Hal Far in recompense for her departure. They would increase both the defensive and offensive roles of the island. But one could not forget that such increases necessitated more supplies in replenishment of stores, spares and ammunition which were definitely going to command bigger allocations in the holds and on the decks of the few ships that managed to get through. This obviously meant less foodstuffs and ancillary commodities for the population, unless there were to be more frequent and bigger convoys. But the practicability of such quick and obvious solutions must be seen against the background of the international situation prevailing at the time and one has to appreciate the position of Malta in the chess game that was then being played in the Mediterranean.

While the island was wintering in expectation of the arrival of the Germans, on 3rd January 1941 the British forces in North Africa attacked Bardia, which collapsed after three days with the surrender of its 45,000 strong garrison, 462 guns, and 129 tanks. Tobruk was attacked on 21st January and also fell the next day yielding a further bag of 30,000 prisoners, 236 guns and 87 tanks. It would have been sensible for the British army to have kept pursuing the now routed troops of Marshal Graziani, but the expected and obvious encouragement did not materialise, as Churchill was now chasing a different hare. Encouraged by the success of the Greek army against the Italians he was pressing Greece to accept British tank and artillery units to be landed at Salonika and had gone as far as ordering General Wavell to make immediate preparations to despatch them from his already weakened forces.

It was General Metaxas, then head of the Greek Government, who opposed the proposal saying that it might provoke a German invasion. But Churchill continued to cherish this Balkan project and when General Metaxas died suddenly on 29th January 1941, Churchill prevailed over a less formidable Greek Government and it was agreed to proceed with the move. In the meantime the Germans could not understand why the British had not pressed their advantage in North Africa, because as General Warlimont, a leading member of Hitler's staff, said, there was nothing to check them from pushing on to Tripoli. The few Italian troops who remained were panic-stricken, and expected British tanks to appear any moment.

What's in a coincidence? A lot. Wavell on superior orders dilly-dallied in his push and continued mopping up isolated pockets. Beda Fomm was one of these, and on 6th February 3,000 British troops wiped out all Italian resistance there taking 20,000 prisoners, 216 guns and 120 tanks. On that same day in Germany, Hitler summoned General Erwin Rommel and ordered him to go to North Africa with two divisions, the 5th Light and 15th Panzer. The move necessitated transport of troops and equipment to Tripoli and this entailed the assurance of a clear road of transportation from Sicily to Tripoli. In the middle of this stood Malta, with her Wellingtons, Swordfish torpedo bombers, destroyers and submarines which were now already spending a longer time in its harbours. It was therefore obvious why the Luftwaffe again turned its attention to Malta.

The first raid to break the quiet spell came on 2nd February, and it was a fighter attack on Luqa airfield. There were fifteen aircraft in three formations with one of them breaking the formation and remaining aloof to protect the attackers from above. The anti-aircraft barrage wiped it out with the first salvo. The remaining planes continued with their attack, but as they came out of their dive they found the Hurricanes waiting for them. An aerial battle ensued and as the roar of diving planes and the sound of machine-gun fire were heard people began to leave their shelters to watch the battle and cheer the British fighters. On that morning, it is recorded, the shelters of Valletta became almost empty, and the squares and bastions were filled with people ignoring danger from bombs or any stray machine-gun fire. The police and special constables intervened and tried to send the people back under cover. But nothing would make the madly cheering crowds budge from their places of vantage. Many of them had their names taken by the police for breaking regulations, but nothing would make them miss the spectacle which ended with four further enemy planes being shot down, to the even greater joy of the crowds.

There were three further alerts that day. Two of them did not materialise. In the last one three Italian bomber formations flew on the island and were met with the intense barrage. One plane dropped a single bomb, and then they all turned for home. Amazing, but true.

A different pattern of behaviour was shown by the Germans, who began to come with sporadic attacks which wrought havoc to buildings and caused many casualties. For the first time the Germans began using the parachute mine. These mines were dropped with a parachute, playing with the wind, and were likely to drop anywhere within a wide radius. They provided another job for the gunners who fired at them to explode them in mid-air, but many reached the ground and caused very heavy damage and casualties.

I remember these attacks with such mines. One in February is typical. The planes came in early in the morning. Anti-aircraft guns opened their usual heavy fire and exploded one mine in the air but the rest reached the ground in Valletta. As there was only a ten minute interval between the alarm and the arrival of the planes many people were still in bed when the guns opened fire, and it was their noise which made them rush to the shelters. This was what had prevented more casualties, because apart from the three who were killed and eight injured, there were 200 houses destroyed in Valletta, and their inhabitants found themselves homeless on coming out of the shelter after the raid. The homeless were temporarily accommodated in a Franciscan monastery and given refreshments until alternative accommodation was found for them. A historical church in Valletta was hit and badly damaged together with the adjacent convent. Fortunately the nuns were in the shelter.

These mines are not to be confused with the magnetic mines which were also being dropped by parachute in the harbours and the sea in the proximity of the island. Those dropped on buildings were land mines and their main force was in blast effect. On exploding they normally opened a crater some 25 feet across but only 5 feet deep, and their blast spread out with phenomenal results. One man was in his bathroom when one of these mines dropped nearby. He was on the verge of looking out of his window when he was thrown to the floor with the blast, and as he was looking up he saw the ceiling flying away from the room, as if it had been pushed away by some giant hand. Thinking that after all he had a lucky escape this man gingerly felt for the bath behind him, as if thinking that he could still carry on with what he intended to do. But the bath was no longer there. It had disappeared with the ceiling.

Another victim of the blast from a mine was blown into a cupboard, where he was found by ARP people. A row of houses had the roofs sliced off like the top of an egg, leaving the walls and the rest comparatively intact.

I was personally involved in two incidents with these parachute mines which might have proved disastrous, and which I feel I should relate as they throw further light on the healthy way in which the people were taking it even during this dark part of the siege. One day the word went round in Vittoriosa that a parachutist had dropped at the Jews Sallyport called '*It-Toqba*' and, as always happened, people were running there to see him (there were many who were doing roaring business from parachutes which sold well to be turned into bed sheets). As I reached the Sallyport myself people were saying that the plane's tank had also dropped there. When I reached the place I found a policeman keeping a crowd away from what looked like a steel coffin with half of it on land and the other half in water. I asked the policeman where the parachutist was, but he corrected the rumour and said that there had only been a parachute which a local fisherman had dived for and collected. I had by then recognised that the coffin-like object was not a tank at all, but a magnetic mine, and what was said about the parachute confirmed that it had been attached to it. I told the policeman what I thought and he quickly cleared the crowd away and called the Bomb Disposal Squad who confirmed that the 'tank' was in fact a magnetic mine, intended for the sea.

In the other occasion what began as a joke might have finished as a disaster. I was with a group of ARP personnel, during a night raid, and we were all cracking jokes. We were later joined by another one from whom they used to take the mickey. As he was always expressing his wish to meet a German pilot face to face, his friends jokingly asked him to stay with us in case a plane was shot down in the vicinity. At that moment a searchlight caught a parachute mine in its beam, and the men turned jokingly to their friend and told him that there was the pilot he wanted. He looked at it, and rushed in the direction where it would be dropping, shouting what he would do to the ruddy airman.

I told his friends that was a parachute mine and not a parachutist. They were flabbergasted, but when they realised what they had done and tried to call their friend back, he had already disappeared. When the explosion came we were all thinking the worst. But a few moments later their friend came back bruised and shaken, but none the worse for his experience. The mine had fortunately exploded before he had reached it, and the blast had only thrown him away.

In those first days of mine-dropping, even military people were mistaking parachute mines dropped at night for airmen from shot-down planes. Lieutenant Joe Agius, then stationed at Fort Ricasoli, mentions occasions when he had his men looking for what appeared to be dropping parachutists in the night only to find out later that they were mines destined for the sea. When it was realised how Grand Harbour was slowly being mined, Lieutenant Agius with his men was ordered to mount a 24-hour watch to note and report the mines.

Air attacks continued without interruption throughout February, and apart from those with parachute mines which were obviously meant to cause damage, create casualties and destroy morale, they were mostly directed towards airfields in an attempt to keep away British aircraft from interfering with the transportation of German forces to North Africa. As attacks were in most cases carried out by the Luftwaffe they were pressed home effectively and of course taking more punishment. One heavy attack on Luqa Airfield was carried out by a large formation of Junkers 88s, Dorniers and Messerschmitt 109s. There was the usual reception by anti-aircraft fire which shot down nine of the enemy planes. When the fighters took over they shot down a further seven and damaged five, with the loss of one Hurricane. The defences were by now collaborating beautifully, letting the barrage take toll of the enemy first, then the fighters would go in to chase him out. As recorded in the Luftwaffe War Diaries, failure of German aircraft to return to base continued day after day, and week after week. To Marshal Deichmann, the Chief of Staff of Fliegerkorps II, the losses over Malta seemed incomprehensible.

It had by now become obvious that Malta was in for a long and heavy siege. Even though the bigger part of the then population of 260,000 was somehow accommodated in villages they came under fire, as well. Maybe not so much and so often as those in Valletta, and the Three Cities, but they were similarily exposed because of the military installations which had necessarily sprung up in the vicinity. There were three active airfields, Hal Far, Luqa and Ta' Qali, one of which Luqa was extended to incorporate dispersal strips close to the villages of Safi, Mqabba, and Qrendi, the three of them full of evacuees. There were the troop encampments to house the various British regiments that had by now been brought to the island and for whom there could not possibly be adequate barracks. Therefore many of them were housed in camps or houses taken over for the purpose. Apart from the fact that these troop dispersals made likely targets of otherwise simply rural areas they also deprived evacuees of badly needed accommodation. It is true that these had somehow settled down by now, but with heavy damaging attacks on the increase there were always houses being hit and made uninhabitable and very often, on coming out of their shelter after a raid whole families were being faced with finding alternative accommodation for themselves and what remained of their furniture. Therefore, even though a family was housed and settled there was no assurance that it would not have to begin on a quest for a new home after an attack. In the streets and roads it became a familiar sight to see nomad families on the move in search of accommodation. Horse-driven carts, loaded with furniture and household belongings, trudging along the roads, became the order of the day, and it was not unusual to see lots of furniture and belongings dumped in the streets near damaged buildings awaiting collection, though no one was sure when this would happen. Added to this there were families who because of circumstances other than damage by bombs had to change accommodation, and the whole of rural Malta became like a colony of always moving prospectors. But instead of gold everyone was looking for a roof under which to shelter from the rain and sun, as now everyone was convinced that protection from bombs could only be found in rock.

Fortunately enough, the drive for more bomb-proof shelters which was begun by the authorities months before had already borne fruit. Every available pick and jack-hammer had been put to use, and where government or service diggers and drillers were not readily available, the people dug shelters themselves. It was not unusual to find men who after a tiring day at the dockyard or a gruelling vigil in some gun position would spend their would-be hours of rest digging a shelter for their family. And in this job women and even children helped too. It was because of this concerted effort that in February 1941 there was accommodation in rock or under concrete for 170,500 persons which included sleeping accommodation for about 10,000.

Efforts neither slackened nor stopped, and it was hoped that in a short time there would be shelter space for 230,000 persons. Malta's soft limestone seemed to be repeating its service to history, and as it had enabled the Knights of St John four hundred years before to dig ditches and construct invincible bastions against the invaders, it was now affording the same protection to the people of the Maltese islands.

There was, however, besides the question of shelters the problem of shortages of supplies. The passage of convoys was being made more difficult, apart from the fact that ships had now a bigger variation in stores that had to be brought, with the expansion and increase in armaments and aircraft. The air force for example had become bigger with the arrival of more Hurricanes, and Glenn Martin reconnaissance aircraft and there was also the slow flowing in of Blenheim medium bombers. There was so much activity that Air Commodore Maynard was on 24th February promoted to Air Vice-Marshal, a rank more in line with his upgraded command. The first step towards a restriction in supplies was the control of condensed milk which was placed on rationing. Laundry soap too was controlled by being issued against coupons to ensure fair distribution.

The situation in the island of Gozo was different. Being as it was a virgin island and denuded of big military installations Gozo had not attracted serious enemy attention. Those who had evacuated to this sister island, and there were many, were not subjected to the daily gruelling moments as those in Malta. The people in Gozo could follow every day what was going on in Malta through a spectacular view of the anti-aircraft barrage in action, and the dogfights in the air which sometimes took the planes over there, but there had as yet not been any direct attack on that island. There were the occasional sporadic aircraft which chose, maybe in a weak or desperate moment, to attack Gozo.

Particularly to suffer from such attacks were the picturesque Gozo fishing boats which in face of the existing peril continued with their fishing and plying between the two islands, and were many a time caught exposed in the Malta channel during an air raid without any chance of shelter. One German bomber, flying low after being crippled by the Malta guns, met some of these craft during a raid and lost no time in machine-gunning them. Aircraft returning from the same raid dropped a remaining bomb on the island on that occasion as if to remind the Gozitans that they were also in the war. Another potential danger to Gozitan fishing boats came from mines. The sea around Malta was rife with minefields, both British and Italian, which were laid by submarines and special motor boats adapted with an additional electric motor to enable them to come closer to the shore silently under the darkness of night. There were occasions when such boats were engaged by coastal artillery, firing only by radar direction. A Gozo boat struck one of these mines and sank on 26th February. Two of the crew were killed while the rest were picked up and landed in Malta, one of them seriously injured.

Against all expectations there was no shelter problem in the beleagured cities of Cospicua, Senglea, Vittoriosa, Valletta and also Floriana. All those who had remained behind had either found a place in the tunnels or dug their own shelter which they used for daily habitation. Where such shelters were dug there came to grow small communities like Coronation Garden in Vittoriosa, St John's Bastion in Cospicua or St James Ravelin outside Floriana; despite the circumstances under which such communities were born they quickly offered scope to enterprise.

Fredu Schembri, a well-built, active man just into his fifties had run a grocery shop in Vittoriosa for many years. Not that anyone believed that Fredu lived on his grocery business, because everyone knew that he was well off. In fact when he was not behind his counter he was doing something more profitable like lending money at high interest. If anyone wanted something which was not readily available he could probably get it from Fredu at a price. He had kept his shop open whilst there were the few people who still ran the gauntlet from their tunnels and shelters to get the sparsely available commodities and perhaps that something extra beneath the counter. Then one fine day emerging from the shelter after a raid Fredu found only a mound of stones where his house and grocery had stood an hour before. In his case this was no catastrophe. His money was safely in the bank or on loan to others, and his wife had carried all her jewels with her to the shelter. What he lost in furniture and household goods wasn't worth worrying about. As for habitation he could now use the shelter he had dug in Coronation Garden, and spend his time doing something else. He could join the local Passive Defence Force maybe and that would give him the right of going about even during air raids. It would give him back the sense of importance he always felt he had in life. But after a few days in Coronation Garden hearing people lamenting and dreading to walk long distances for groceries, his business mind overwhelmed his patriotic spirit, and he thought of reopening his grocery in the Gardens. It was easy to erect a wooden stall outside his shelter, and when he did, all the owners of the shelters in those gardens became his clients. This time however he was an important person, because, he felt, he had done something for those people. After all no one else had thought of it before him. On the strength of this he could talk as much as he wanted and tell his clients how many planes had been shot down during raids, and how many people were killed, and when the war would end. And the people believed him, they did not know he could not even write his name.

Following in Fredu's footsteps, came Belin with his wine shop where he did roaring business with the police and passive defence personnel in the area, while Censu, a house whitewasher from Cospicua, thought of a better idea and dug a shelter to be hired as a delivery room. Even under fire, childbirth in Malta retained its usual levels. Pawlu Bazari too, now had a more lucrative outlet for his bombed fish, and he could even charge a higher price for that which was collected after mine explosions. Because this did not taste of TNT.

It was either that others had the same ideas or maybe because the word went round that similar arrangements were made where groups of families were to be found. One would know the location of such shops by the people waiting to be served. There were queues everywhere these days whether in town or village — for the grocer, the baker and the kerosene vendor in the streets, even for water when the mains were hit. More and more since the turn of the tide on 16th January all became tired and tense, but now people began to appear pre-occupied. They talked about the war; not that they knew what to say, but it was the only subject at hand. Now there was a new threat which seemed to be in everybody's mind, perhaps unspoken, but there for all to sense in the looks and quiet innuendoes. Invasion. In one of his first speeches Mussolini had said that he would subdue Malta by siege and when he did not succeed there had come the Germans who also looked like failing. There would obviously have to be the last resort of invasion if Malta were to be silenced. The imposition of a curfew from 9 p.m. to 6.30 a.m. seemed to point to this. Those who knew what invasion meant watched for signs that helped them from losing heart. Notwithstanding the barbed wire on the coast, and the machine-gun nests, the pill-boxes on the beaches and in the countryside, the roads were still open. There were no road blocks or tank traps on the main streets, no specific instructions other than those relating to vehicles to be immobilised by the removal of the rotor arm when left in the streets during raids, which had been issued from the very beginning. Anyway, no one had obeyed them. On the other hand there was comfort taken from the number of British regiments that were already in the island. But would they be enough? As if to answer this question Conscription Law was legislated on 22nd February 1941 which made it lawful for the authorities to call up all able-bodied men between the ages of 18 and 56 years for military service.

The last time that Malta's able-bodied manpower was called up in the country's defence had been in 1792 when levies were called upon to maintain the siege of Valletta where Napoleon's forces under General Vaubois had taken refuge. Then, they had besieged the enemy hiding behind the bastions and fortifications. Now it was the Maltese that were being besieged, and these same fortifications that had once afforded protection to their enemies were now being slowly demolished and depriving them of similar protection in a new kind of siege.

As on that other occasion there was a very good response to the call and on 3rd March when enrolment began, hundreds of youths were already queueing up at the recruiting offices laughing and chattering about which unit they would opt for and impatient to be called in and become soldiers. They were all between 20 and 21 and it was no wonder that they were looking at that historical moment through their young adventurous eyes. They had all tasted war with their elders during the previous months, indeed there were those amongst them who had reason to mourn the loss of some parent, relative or friend through enemy action, but this for them had already become a part of life as if they had been born and educated to make a career out of death and destruction. In fact soldiering was going to be their first job, and they would have to bear arms until victory over their enemy could be achieved. But when would this be? To their question there was no answer. They only knew that their elders had been called to fight and now it was their turn to join them or replace those who had fallen in defence of their country. And they would do it well, in the best of Maltese tradition, as in fact their elders had done and were still doing. Hadn't they listened as well to the Governor, General Dobbie, in his broadcast on 4th February describing how the civilian population and the three services were all four square in their fight? And there had been Winston Churchill himself when he spoke to the nation five days later, and paid tribute to the Maltese defenders and the Dockyard workers. A burden feels lighter when it is thus acknowledged and appreciated as if it is being shared.

Later, when other classes were called, there were those for whom military service raised problems. The news about conscription had been a blow to Anglu Fenech. He stared incredulously at his sister Sarah when she told him.

'Are you sure?' he asked her. "Are you quite sure?"

Sarah nodded. 'I've heard the news on Rediffussion. There is no doubt about it.'

Brother and sister looked at each other in silence. For the last fifteen years they had lived so closely together that they had become one, and they had managed to get through the last months of difficulties as they were sustained by the conviction that even under fire they could remain together. Now, it appeared as if they would have to part. Who would help Sarah in the shop they had run together for these last years, if he were to be away with his regiment? And who would help her to go down into shelter during raids, crippled as she was. There had been time to drag herself slowly for cover during Italian raids, but with the Germans it was different. Planes arrived sooner after the siren and went straight into attack giving one no chance. There had been occasions when he had carried her down the shelter steps in his arms like a baby. Now there would be no one to do it when he was away.

When his clients had decreased following the evacuation of Valletta, and the raids began to make him close his shop for longer periods, Anglu had perforce to think of alternative means of living, and joining the army might have provided a ready employment. But there had always been this question of his sister which took priority. Now it seemed that he was not going to have any choice.

Carmelo Vella was a good carpenter and worked at the dockyard.

He also played the saxophone for his village band at Zabbar. It was this musical vent which occasionally sparked an iota of activity in his otherwise timid character. Away from the band club he would not speak until he was spoken to, and he blushed every time he looked at a girl. When he received his conscription papers he stared at them without knowing what to think. It was his father who patted him on the back and told him not to worry.

'This may after all provide the tonic you have always needed and never found,' he told him meaningly.

'But what is going to happen to my plans?' said Carmelo.

'I've always wanted to leave the dockyard and make a carpentry business of my own after the war, and get married maybe, and raise a family?'

'If the war is not won, there will be no business to go to, my son,' said the father. 'Neither will there by any future, nor a girl.'

Carmelo did not reply, but lowered his head in thought, and blushed at the mention of a girl.

John and Mary wandered off together in the countryside which had been their haunt since they had fallen in love. There was silence as their thoughts kept returning to the subject that loomed over them which could easily make this their last walk together for a time. They followed a path that led across lawns and trees.

'When will you be reporting for conscription?' asked Mary in a subdued voice.

'Tomorrow.' said John, 'and I will join the Royal Malta Artillery.'

He was slightly taller than Mary, and the sun glinted metallically on his fair hair. She looked at him and mentally saw him, looking slim and younger than his twenty years in his khaki uniform. When she didn't say another word John began speaking himself. He explained to her that he did not mind it in the least that he was interrupting his studies to become a teacher in order to join up. It had to be done and he was doing it gladly. The only snag would be that he would not be able to see her as often as before. That would be the only difference, because he would still love her. His cheerful smiling face radiated light to those dark moments, and Mary knew that rather than doubting her future feelings for him in uniform she would love him more for it. If she could not don a uniform herself and take up a rifle, she could at least do this.

Many others also had problems, every one according to his

character, temperament or situation. But who did not have problems in those days? At this time indeed a problem which had irked official minds for some time came to light. The supply situation had been appearing to them like a big fist ready to crack down on Malta. With convoys not getting closer in arrival, and with their passage not becoming easier further restrictions on food consumption became imperative if there was not to be a shortage that would bring the wonderful resolutions being made all toppling down. As far back as 19th February a system of coupons to obtain tinned milk had been introduced, and there was a similar arrangement for laundry soap. But now there was the need for more control, and, leaving untouched bread and olive oil, which then formed the main diet of the population, the authorities introduced rationing of sugar, milk, lard, margarine, matches, coffee, tea and rice. It became an open secret that stocks of these commodities would in the future only be brought in quantities that would leave enough space on the ships for more essential items like flour, olive oil, ammunition and petrol.

As if in confirmation of the good sense of this measure it was on the day of its imposition, 14th March, that the news was flashed of the bestowing on the Governor, General William Dobbie with a knighthood as Knight Commander of the Most Honourable Order of the Bath. On that day too, Malta had its 400th air raid.

The enemy, too, had a problem: despite the terrible hammering, how was small and insignificant Malta not only still resisting but even increasing its offensive action. Attacks had not ceased and although there were not any repetitions of the *Illustrious* raids there had been continuous day and night attacks with bombs and mines. In some German and Italian reports this was attributed to the fact that during this time they had again to pay attention to other fronts, and there were the mercurial movements of the battle in North Africa, and of course the Italo-Greek war. But the most likely reason was that attacks had become too costly for the enemy, and if any fresh indication of this was required it came on 26th February when as if in despair the Luftwaffe delivered an attack on the airfields which resembled that on the *Illustrious* in intensity. Thirteen aircraft were either shot down or seriously damaged. Then as if not to be outdone the Luftwaffe came again with a similar attack on 6th March. This time sixteen were shot down with the loss of one British plane.

All these details about losses can today be verified from Nicola Malizia's accounts in his book *Inferno su Malta*, but more than these accounts it may be worthwhile recording here how this author described the raiding flights to Malta which German and Italian fliers were being sent on. Malizia wrote as follows: *'La rotta della morte, come fu definito tra la Sicilia e Malta, registrava ogni giorno la perdita di uomini e mezzi.'* This means in English that the route of death, as has been called the route from Sicily to Malta, was registering every day loss of men and means.

What the above writer did not say was how the people of Malta, whom he had described as running away in panic in the first Italian raids, had in true Maltese style managed to surmount fears and preoccupations and resume normal living under raids. Then when the Germans came with their deadly attacks, they had again gone underground only to come out again and make the best of life. They had not only beaten the enemy's efforts to subdue them, but they had even impressed the local authorities with their sensible way of adjusting their life to their present conditions. This became evident when the Employers (Discontinuation of Service) Emergency Regulations of 1940 were in March 1941 repealed. These regulations had been enacted to safeguard the interests of employers when constant air attacks induced employers to shut down their business. Now that the people had shown that they could discipline themselves to take cover during raids; it was being left to them to take cover only when there was imminent danger.

No one can deny that there was guidance from the authorities for the population in those days of turmoil. It has however always been my feeling that it was more a case of the population guiding the authorities.

In that March of 1941 there seemed to be an air of optimism all round, and this rose higher when on the 24th a convoy of four ships came in. But it wasn't the convoy as such that raised spirits all round; when the Germans came in to sink the ships in port after they had eluded them on the high seas, the defences as usual rose to the occasion and shot down thirteen planes in the process, to the delight of the many who were watching.

To rub salt on the enemy's wounds, ships of the British Mediterranean fleet which the Maltese knew and loved so well, engaged the Italian Navy at Cape Matapan on 30th March and scored a resounding success which sent all Malta hysterical with joy.

British convoys were throughout the month transporting some 60,000 troops from North Africa to Greece, where Churchill wanted a foothold. This provided a golden opportunity for Admiral

Cunningham for he had accurate intelligence that the Italian navy would attempt to intercept. He made the necessary dispositions and the Italian Admiral Iachino went for the bait with most of his fleet. The British force which was waiting to meet him was composed of the battleships *Warspite, Barham* and *Valiant*, the aircraft carrier *Formidable*, four cruisers and nine destroyers. As the Italians approached, torpedo bombers from *Formidable* attacked and hit with torpedoes the battleship *Vittorio Veneto*. In a second attack other torpedo bombers hit the Italian heavy cruiser *Pola* and forced her to stop. The Italian fleet broke the action and retreated, but unaware that the rest of the British fleet was near, the Italian Admiral sent the heavy cruisers *Zara* and *Fiume* to assist *Pola*, and that was when Admiral Cunningham reappeared on the scene and engaged them with his battleships destroying the three cruisers at almost point-blank range.

Nor was that all for throughout the action the Italian destroyers *Vincenzo Gioberti* and *Maestrale* were also sunk.

*

Despite the constant air raids, and the limited rations in foodstuffs and other commodities Malta still carried on. Whether in shelters or houses housewives made their purchases when they found them and cooked for their families when there was something to cook. When there wasn't any kerosene for their cooking, firewood collected by the husbands or children from destroyed buildings came in handy for the *kenur* or stone cooker of a century before which had by now come back into use. To substantiate their diets children were soon foraging for carobs from trees that were still not destroyed in the countryside. It started as a childish idea, but the youngsters were soon taking carobs to their homes. Farmers began selling their carobs and even vintners decided to use it for their wine. Apart from the abnormal food and clothing situation, and allowing for the continual interruptions from air raids and their results, the population continued in its attempts to enforce some sort of normality in its life. Cinemas kept going and churches held their normal functions; Services shows were sometimes given for civilians, while regimental band programmes were not interrupted. Even football matches were carried on, which featured mostly regimental teams. All this filled up the void left by the war — except that in the stomach. Public transport ran for limited hours, and in this sector old horse-drawn contraptions were taken out to substantiate services. This was where the old omnibus made a reappearance.

On the offensive side there was also an identical situation. Rather than reducing their activities the two offensive services increased their efforts. The Royal Air Force continued with its bombing raids on Sicily and Italy, and with torpedo bombers on the convoys that were continually trying to cross over with forces and equipment for Rommel in North Africa. The navy too had at this time began building up a basic force. There were four destroyers stationed in Malta, the *Janus, Jervis, Nubian* and *Mohawk*, while in February there had already assembled a small flotilla of eight 'U' class submarines: *Upright, Utmost, Unique, Urge, Ursula, Upholder, Union* and *Usk*. So with a surface striking force and the submarines, together with the aircraft Malta was looking forward to a more active, offensive role as March turned into April.

The effect this increasingly offensive activity had on the enemy can be gauged from the following comparison taken from official Italian records. Between June and November 1940 there had been only four Italian ships sunk while on their way to North Africa, with a total of 11,104 tons. From December 1940 to March 1941 there were thirty sunk with a total of 109,089 tons.

On 6th April the Germans attacked Greece and Jugoslavia. This was a surprise move, except perhaps to the British, since they had already transferred an army of 60,000 men to Greece, and had already been anticipated in such a move by the late General Metaxas. But the effect of the situation in Malta was different. Apart from the feelings that were evident about the dive-bombing of Belgrade, it was obvious that the occupation of Greece and Jugoslavia by the Germans would expand the German hold in the Mediterranean, and this particularly to countries which were close. The fact that at that time Rommel had occupied the whole of North Africa and was soon to be knocking at the gates of Egypt made the situation more bleak since Malta was now alone in the Central Mediterranean and isolated from the nearest British forces which were in Gibraltar and Alexandria. But this did not immediately affect the situation. The raids continued as before and offensive operations against Italian and German shipping were continued. The destroyers and submarines had to put an extra effort since every available warship of the Mediterranean fleet was soon standing by to evacuate British forces from Greece, as things had gone wrong from the very beginning.

Everyone was looking with different eyes at the new situation
as if it was unbelievable that the new battle fronts would no
affect Malta. But there was no significant conclusion. Maybe thi
was because of the local tragedy which occurred on 8th Apri
when the mooring ship *Moore* struck a mine inside Grand Harbou
(obviously one that was dropped by German aircraft), and sank
with only one survivor. All the members of the crew were Maltese

Looking at a diary of a young girl of those days I could not help
seeing the contrast of one with a light heart to the silent probing
that must have been going on in adult and heavy minds: '10 April
Carried out visits of Holy Sepulchre.'

So ran the entry for that Maundy Thursday of 1941, and as can
be seen the people were still carrying out the religious devotion of
visiting seven Holy Sepulchres in their home town or village. The
Visits of the Seven Churches, as this function is called, is still
practised now as it was then. In 1941 it could of course not be
carried out properly in Vittoriosa and Senglea, as their churches
were destroyed, but the substitute church in Senglea and the
police chapel in Vittoriosa were nonetheless the venue of the
inhabitants of those cities. The following day was Good Friday
and the entry against this date went to say that it was the first
time that bells were rung on Good Friday. Even today church bells
do not ring on Good Friday, but in 1941 they had to ring for the
All Clear signal after a raid. Because, as the entry went, there were
five raids on that day during which five persons were killed and
seven injured. One Junkers 87 was shot down.

On Saturday, the following day, the Germans obligingly kept
away. Maybe they were more interested in the British convoy that
was then near Malta on its way to North Africa. Little did they
know that the aircraft carrier *Ark Royal* with her flight deck
packed with fifty Hurricanes Mark II flew off twenty of them for
Malta to join the depleted 261 Squadron.

On Easter Sunday, the 13th, there were still more raids, and
bombs were dropped at the old city of Mdina. If there was a virgin
city without any military installations Mdina was certainly the
one. Yet it was bombed. Some reasoned that it was too close to
Ta' Qali Airfield, but the distance was such as not to deceive
German pilots who were low fliers. Could it have been an error of
judgement? Maybe. On that day Jugoslavia was as good as
conquered by the Germans, only one week after its invasion, and
Maltese minds were still probing for that elusive point that was
now radiating more awful anticipatory warnings that could be fel

without being seen or understood.

Even the Germans seemed to want to give time to all to think about that elusive something because they refrained from raids for three days. But if there was any time being lost in thinking about such matters it wasn't by the Royal Air Force. A Glenn Martin was on its usual reconnaissance on the 16th when it located a convoy of five Italian ships escorted by three Italian destroyers. A quick look showed the ships to be laden with troops, tanks and vehicles, probably German Panzers heading for Rommel. Its message to Malta was brief, and the *Janus, Jervis, Nubian* and *Mohawk* were out of harbour in a flash. Three hours later they intercepted the convoy and engaged the three Italian destroyers, *Tarigo, Lampo* and *Baleno* in battle. The five laden ships were sunk together with the three escorts, but before sinking the *Tarigo* managed to hit the *Mohawk* with torpedoes and sank her.

The lull in raids for some reason remained till the 27th, then as if to celebrate their victory in Greece the Germans returned to Malta, this time with a vengeance.

A heavy raid on the night of the 28th was followed by an obvious rundown attack on the following night which was directed at Valletta using both bombs and mines. Heavy damage was caused also hitting St John's Cathedral. The capital was again the target of a raid on the following day, with a similar result and destruction of a church, hotel and cinema.

This was the last action for men of the Dockyard Defence Battery which was disbanded on the following day — 28th April, 1941 after one year and 283 days of service in the defence of the dockyard. They were given the option of joining as regular soldiers in the Royal Malta Artillery which took over the guns. Their patriotic deeds, particularly in those first crucial days of the siege, certainly merit the emphasis placed on them in this book, and their account should be recorded for ever in the annals of history to serve as a shining example to others.

These raids were similar in type to some of the raids the Germans made on England which Field Marshal Kesselring described in his Memoirs as reprisal raids, but without entering into the merits or reasons for such reprisal action on England, I would ask in reprisal for what were such raids delivered on Malta? Had this question been put in those days of 1941 there would have probably been some concocted reason, but today thirty-nine years after the event all concerned had time to verify facts and know that bombers from Malta had restricted themselves purely to known military targets. Maybe they were only desperate reprisals for what was being done to the convoys that were trying to cross to North Africa only to be sunk by Malta-based units. If it was so, it could be seen even then that such reprisals had the opposite effect to that intended since these attacks increased, and so did the sinkings.

For me the Siege of Malta had become far too personal a thing to let it pass without watching, examining and deliberating in my own simple way all that was going on. I was at this time only a youngster of sixteen but with great powers of observation and reasoning. So I began to notice the intensification of certain defensive measures that had not received the same kind of attention since they had been laid down. Coastal infantry patrols were increased but this could have been due to the new men that had been taken into the forces by conscription; in fields and open spaces in the countryside were being erected obstacles as if to prevent the landing of aircraft, pill boxes and other defensive positions were being constructed further inland than the ones which had been lining the coast; extended training and patrols by British Infantry. Then there was the reorganisation of the Malta Volunteer Defence Force into a more compact unit which was renamed Home Guard. There were fresh and younger men roped into it, who were given good weapons and trained in their use. Even I, not yet seventeen, was allowed to join. To me every step, and every precaution pointed at the possibility of invasion, and with this feeling flashed the sensation of preoccupation that had been felt by everyone without being explained. Even another convoy which came into the harbour on 9th May failed to raise the usual excitement, and when the Germans attacked the ships in harbour I and others watched the attack in silence as if feeling that it was no ordinary attack as the others before it, but a prelude to something else. The planes which were shot down on that day failed to raise our spirits.

Even the fact that following the arrival of the twenty Hurricanes in April, and some more unassembled in boxes on 8th May, there was to be a reorganisation of the RAF defences might have had something to do with the impending peril. Indeed, 261 Squadron was disbanded then and from its remaining Hurricanes and the new ones that were brought in three squadrons were formed — 185 Squadron which was stationed at Hal Far, 126 and 249 Squadrons which were sent to Ta' Qali. Luqa retained the bomber squadrons which this month were strengthened by 82

Squadron of Blenheims. With the expansion of the Command, Air Vice-Marshal Maynard was replaced by Air Vice-Marshal Hugh P. Lloyd.

There was then another attack on the 12th and finally a heavier one on the 20th which hit two churches in Valletta and caused many casualties. On that same day the news was flashed that German parachute troops had landed on the island of Crete.

This news hit the people like a bombshell, and stunned everyone into silence. Then a tongue wagged and others followed. Crete had like Malta been defended by the Royal Navy which was confident of preventing an invasion by sea. And so it did, at very heavy expense. But the Germans had gone in from the air with gliders and paratroops. So could they do in Malta. The hurried preparations that had been going on lately then all fell into perspective, and it was realised that what everyone was thinking had already been anticipated by the people in the know. This was a consolation but it was also confirmation of what everyone had been suspecting without being able to put a name to it. Notwithstanding the heavy coastal defences, and the Navy, the Germans could after all invade Malta successfully. And the invasion of Crete might have been the dress rehearsal.

CHAPTER SIX

Seaborne Attack

Not only will we not give up Malta, but we have no intention of allowing it to be taken from us, whether by the Germans or the Italians. We have to face the possibility of invasion. Malta is immeasurably more capable of resisting attacks than was Crete. This opinion is fully shared by responsible officers, and I am saying this with the quiet confidence that I consider the circumstances justify. I know that Malta will rise to the occasion whatever is required of it. The Government and fighting services are leaving no stone unturned to ensure that Malta shall give a good account of itself and make its present history more splendid even than its past.

With God's help I am confident that we shall succeed in so doing.

This was Lieutenant-General Sir William Dobbie, the Governor, speaking to the people of Malta in the beginning of July 1941.

Crete was invaded by the Germans on 20th May. It surrendered on 1st June. The progress of fighting in that island was followed by everyone in Malta since everyone was convinced that the same could happen to Malta. After it was all over what happened during the month of June had no significance. The nuisance raids continued, but there was occasion for rejoicing on 11th June, the anniversary of the first attacks on the island, when ironically, or maybe intentionally, the Italians flew over, and one of them was shot down. But nothing could divert attention from the one thought that was burning Maltese minds. It had blacked out thought of other sensational news, like the sinking of the battle-cruiser *Hood* with one salvo on the 24th from the German battleship *Bismarck*, which was itself sunk three days later. Even the news of the sinking of the monitor *Terror*, and the gunboat *Ladybird* which helped so much in the first raids on Malta was missed, on the 13th. Air raids seemed to have lost the excitement they had brought to the island until then, even though the air raids on that first anniversary registered a tally of 694 with 155 enemy aircraft shot down and 60 probables. There was now only the invasion to think about, and, if there had been any doubt about its coming, the Governor had removed it.

What happened at Crete seemed to have hypnotized everyone in thinking that there was no way out. But was an invasion really such a foregone conclusion?

In Britain the war lords were convinced of the sequence of events that would be undertaken by the Germans after the fall of Crete, not necessarily in the stated order — a pounce upon Cyprus, Syria, Suez or Malta. But what did the Germans think?

The possibility of invading Malta had been put to Hitler as far back as 3rd February in that same year, but after then, when Rommel was biding his time, before his advance in North Africa and foresaw his future requirements for a drive against Suez, he expressed himself that nothing could be done about guaranteeing his supplies without an invasion of Malta. Now, after what had happened in Crete he went as far as to inform the German High Command that he could take Malta with smoke and airborne troops. But his appeal seemed to fall on deaf ears. Hitler had something else on his mind.

Neither the Maltese nor the British had reason to know this, and Crete dominated all their planning and actions. Pros and cons were weighed up and the situation seemed to have returned to those days before June 1940 when no one knew what Italy would be doing. All that had happened in Crete became like a series of pictures on film being run again and again and hammering all into acceptance. It would therefore not be out of place to record here the events of that catastrophe not only for historical record but also for consideration of its effect on what was to happen to Malta.

The invasion of Crete was astonishingly and audaciously delivered by air, and it was certainly the most striking airborne operation of the war. It is to be said that Hitler was reluctant to risk it, but General Student, the mastermind behind it, managed to persuade him. It was started by some 3,000 German parachute troops which were dropped from the sky. Considering the fact that Crete was on that day held by 28,600 British, Australian and New Zealand troops, along with two Greek divisions amounting to almost as many in numbers one would have expected the first German onslaught to be easily contained. But by the evening of that first day of onslaught the Germans were reinforced with further drops to more than double. Further reinforcements were sent by gliders and troop-carriers which occupied the one and only

airfield of Malem even while it was still under the defenders' fire.
The number of German troops reached 22,000, and it was
thought, indeed confidence was expressed, both by the
experienced General Freyberg VC and the British Cabinet, that the
numerically superior defence would win the day. Strangely
enough, on the seventh day of fighting the Allied position was
considered to be untenable and troops began to be evacuated. A
total of 16,500 troops were taken out, including 2,000 Greeks but
the rest were left dead or after having been taken prisoners. More
than the Army, it was the Navy that suffered, losing three cruisers
and six destroyers to German aerial bombardment, besides damage
caused to two battleships and one aircraft carrier. 2,000 sailors
were killed. German losses were 4,000 killed and half as many
wounded.

No military tactician could have foreseen such an outcome. The
Allied troops, particularly the Australians and New Zealanders
were all seasoned soldiers, and outnumbered the Germans. They
were also commanded by a brave and experienced man. What had
gone wrong then?

The first and foremost cause was the lack of anti-aircraft guns,
which were described as scanty. Another weakness was the lack of
air support. These two weaknesses made it possible for the
German bombers to hammer the defences, and for the transports
and gliders to fly in and land as and how they wanted. There was
also a tendency on the part of the defence to be more concerned
about a possible seaborne invasion, and a good part of the
defending force was left awaiting a seaborne attack which never
came. The Germans confessed that they did not have any sea
transport, and the heavy arms artillery and some tanks together
with two battalions of the 5th Mountain Division had to be
transported by Greek caiques from nearby Greece.

It here becomes apparent that the advantages the Germans had
in the invasion of Crete would not exist in Malta, and this might
have been what, as was said by the Governor, made local
responsible officers share the view that invasion would be beaten
off. But the people did not know this. Therefore they remained
highly aware and tense as they went about their chores of life
from day to day, dreading the morrow.

Fredu Schembri had become the king of Coronation Gardens in
Vittoriosa, but with the newly introduced strict rationing while he
earned the respect of the minority who could patronise his black
market goods, he became unpopular with the majority who could

not meet his terms. With his rationed commodities being taken up immediately they were available, and unrationed stuff becoming virtually non-existent he began to find more spare time on his hands then he bargained for. So this was the time, he thought, when he could contribute to some patriotic activity, particularly with an invasion in the offing. With his never diminishing ambition to become the important man of the moment he joined the newly-reorganised Home Guard. He was given an arm band (as there wasn't a uniform to fit him) a rifle, and a steel-helmet.

Anglu Fenech had decided to try to avoid his calling up by applying to the Hardship Committee and tried for an exemption because of his sister's plight. But there was then an unexpected development in the form of Concetta, an orphaned girl of his own age whom he had many a time seen in the shelter during raids. She had answered his questions when he talked to her, and she had also accepted his oil lamp when hers had run out of kerosene. But she did not encourage further advances. She had however suddenly struck up a friendship with his sister Sarah and gladly volunteered to step into the breach and keep her company when she learned of his problem. He accepted her kind offer, and thought that if he could still get round the Hardship Committee he might get time to care for two women instead of one. Then he realised that no one could reach where his sister stood in his affections, although she could not provide what Concetta could give — if she was willing. Apparently she was not, and so he decided to join up. After all he was not a coward, and there was talk of an invasion.

Carmelo Vella took the short road. It seemed he was destined to spend a part of his life soldiering, but he could always opt for something that would allow him to exercise his trade. So he joined up in the Royal Engineers, and told the recruiting officers of his carpentry talent. It must have been the longest speech he had made in his life. They listened and accepted him, nodding at all his suggestions. But he had to do some recruit training first which he did with pleasure since it was going to take him to a carpentry shop. He even offered to take his own tools. They politely told him there was no need, and instead gave him a rifle to play with. The tools would come later. When he could march, drill and use his rifle, he was posted to a searchlight platoon, because that was where he was required.

John looked so manly in his brand-new uniform, and Mary loved him the more for it. He did not see her once during his first six weeks recruit training. Then they met once, and he kissed her as he had never done before. He also gave her the bars of plain chocolate and the tin of boiled sweets he had saved for her from his rations. She was delighted, as they were not available to civilians. But she never told him she had also received some from Bob, a British soldier she had once met in a shelter and who had forced his attentions on her. After his first fortnight spell at Salina Battery where he was posted John told her of his work on the guns. It was a pity he disliked his sergeant who was a bully and a slave driver. Who knows, maybe, he'd make the grade for a commission some day, and then he'd have his own troops.

Censu the whitewasher, saw the Hardship Committee and was somehow exempted, but Pawlu Bazari was taken on. He told them of his competence with boats and water and also of his knowledge of explosives. He thought he might be able to wangle his way to use his recently found profession as a side line after all. After his training he began to handle both explosive and fish, when he alternated his fatigues on a gun position and the cook house. His professional ability was doomed to be lost, as his fish were lost to the tunnel people at Vittoriosa for the duration.

Spring had merged into summer promising relief from dampness, dripping roofs and wet walls in shelters, where everyone was beginning to think he might have to spend the rest of his life. With the coming of summer with its heat and sweat, the lack of bathing facilities became more pronounced. Beaches were closed for swimming being out of bounds as defence areas, and where there existed a bath in the house it was subject to different but similarly hard conditions. If one was lucky to have a bathroom, one had first to ensure the water was on, and if there were no disrupted mains there could be failure of pressure. Granted this there was the problem of soap which was hard to come by. Then having got round all this there would have to be faced the risk of being found in the bath when the alarm went. There was a common blitz story of the man who was found sitting on his toilet seat after the whole building around him had fallen down on being hit by bombs.

' What happened?' asked the ARP people who rescued him.

'I don't know,' said the dazed man. 'I just pulled the flushing chain, and the whole building went down.'

Apart from its humorous aspect the story drove home the risk of being caught in the bathroom during a raid. But even this was considered to be of little discomfort when one looked in a mirror to see a once strong frame now whittled down to a mass of skin and bones. Since rationing had been introduced, although a certain amount of food was ensured for everybody this was usually poor and basically inadequate with its lack of vitamins essential to maintain an overworked and now more worried population.

The same food situation applied to the services who shared the hardships, but this did not reduce efficiency. While the people carried on with their now monotonous way of living from hand to mouth the three services increased their offensive activities. More aircraft were sent to the island, and for the first time appeared the Beaufighter, which made its name as a night fighter and could take over from the adapted Hurricane. The army had more weapons and of course more ammunition which was added to that already held and being reserved for the big day. Even the newly organised Home Guard had its share, and as there weren't enough British weapons to go round some companies were issued with Italian rifles captured in North Africa. Grenades issued to the Home Guard were all Italian.

The Navy was represented by her submarines which now made Lazaretto their home. Of the eight submarines already mentioned that composed the first small flotilla some two months back, *Usk* and *Undaunted* were sunk. But in their place came *Umbra, Una, Uproar, Ultimatum* and *Upright*. Between them these knights of the deep harassed the enemy in every conceivable way. They were a direct threat to all enemy shipping crossing from Italy to North Africa, but more than this, they very often landed sabotage parties in Italy which wrecked essential transport services like trains, many of which were engaged in the daily transport of some 10,000 tons of munitions to Sicily, including bombs for Malta. Because of security such activities did not receive any publicity in those days of war and it is only fair to mention them now, not only to give praise where it is due but also for historical record.

Notwithstanding the superiority of British submarines in the Mediterranean, it had consistently become more difficult for surface maritime services to run convoys to Malta, and this was having a direct effect on the supplies situation. It was because of this that 'Magic Carpet' runs began to be made by submarines carrying stores, aviation spirit and even men from Gibraltar and Alexandria to Malta. There were various submarines which did these runs, including *Thrasher, Clyde, Cachalot* and *Rorqual*. These gallant submarines were fully armed when making such runs to Malta and after laying off their cargo they proceeded to harass the enemy by laying mines or torpedoing ships, thus killing two birds with one stone, and sometimes killing many more.

This was the harrowing but remarkable picture of Malta in the beginning of July 1941. Somehow the population had contained the never-ceasing air attacks, the destruction, and other discomforts brought about by the situation. Now they were facing the first pointers to the other and more personal threat of hunger which was knocking at their door. Even with all the courage and goodwill in the world there must have been those who welcomed a quick invasion. It would at least decide the future quickly and remove the agony once and for all. But invasion did not come, and the air raids had become again long and colourless ones like those in the first months of the war, also carried out by Italian aircraft. Savoia Marchetti bombers, Cants and sometimes even fighters crossed the coast at great height only to disappear again as soon as the defences tried to engage them. It seemed the enemy wanted to be more of a nuisance than an attacker, but this did not explain the occasions when radar plotted approaching bomber formations which never flew over the island. Local official reports began saying that some Italian pilots preferred to approach Malta, drop their bombs in the sea and fly back to base reporting accomplishment of their mission rather than facing the Malta defences.

This could have been only propaganda, and could not be expected to be officially confirmed. Anything in the way of confirmation could only come from the pilots concerned. That is where I found what I wanted. It was confirmed to me by an Italian pilot himself that many a time he and others dropped their bombs in the sea and turned back to base without flying over Malta and risking their life in the barrage.

With the air raid situation easing up during those first days of July there was relief. People could work and have more time for distraction, there was less inconvenience in having to run for cover. There was also time for airing the damp bedding in the public shelters. The boys in the Valletta/Floriana old railway tunnel had more time for their scouting activities, since there had by now been formed a boy scout troop for the young generation in that tunnel. Even British soldiers reappeared with their welcome intrusions with children during daytime and in the evenings with the men in the bars or girls in the streets of the nearest locality to their barracks or encampment. The Cheshires went to Vittoriosa and Cospicua, the Dorsets to Zabbar, and the Devons to Zejtun. Gudja had the Hampshires, and Qormi hosted the Royal West Kents.

Now that the evenings were warm those living in shelters all longed for an hour or two of fresh air under a mellow moon after the day was done. English and Maltese voices were raised again in sing-songs, which went on until curfew time.

Two weeks of this in July began to have telling effects. It began to be realised that since the soldiers were coming again there must have been relaxation in their stand-by duties, and this could only mean that there was no threat of imminent invasion. The absence of heavy attacks and German aircraft seemed also to confirm this, and the characteristically wary Maltese minds began to relax albeit with reservations. When there was a further third week everyone stopped talking about invasion, and tongues began wagging about lack of food and hunger. But even on this point fate seemed to be smiling when a convoy came in on Friday, 25th July. It attracted the usual attacks, first light with single reconnaissance aircraft trying to take a quick look at the ships in harbour already unloading, then with a heavy attack which was meant to be the highlight and sink the convoy ships. Instead, after a dose of barrage fire the Italian formations were dispersed, and the guns made way for the Hurricanes which dived on the Italians, shooting five of them down.

It must have been the first time since the invasion of Crete that the Maltese crowds left their shelters during the raid and assembled outside watching and cheering as the RAF went into action. When the enemy left, there were smiles and back-patting once again, as if everyone had regained the high spirits that for a time had been drowned by that other fear. It seemed as if everything was still moving in the way that had now become routine. Convoy comes in — the enemy attacks and is beaten back — his planes are shot down — and the ships are untouched. The gunners were happy with their contribution and so were the fighter pilots. The crowds were happy too, as with dusk falling they made their way home, whether this was a tunnel, shelter or a house. They knew that the stevedores they had seen working like ants simultaneously on the ships would continue throughout the night until the last case of corned beef or anti-aircraft shells was unloaded and removed safely away. When the ships were emptied by the morning there would be enough foodstuffs to keep them going till the day when there would be another convoy, just as the shells would keep the guns going and the aviation spirit would keep the fighters in the air. Life had become like that — living from hand to mouth — but it was better than that which they had for a while dreaded. And everybody was happy.

That evening even Giulio, Italian pilot of a Savoia Marchetti in the attacking formation, was to have something to rejoice over. He had nothing to be happy about as he tried to make his way back to base after his plane was riddled by shrapnel from the Malta guns. Many a time he had dropped his bombs in the sea and returned to base without flying over Malta reporting his mission to have been accomplished. But today his orders had been specific — to sink the convoy ships in port. But all he got was a shrapnel riddled plane with two of his crew dead while he himself was in agony similarly riddled by shrapnel which had entered his body in several places. His one thought was to make base before he lost consciousness which was fast approaching. If he managed to make it then he would certainly find himself in hospital. That, he thought with satisfaction, meant he would not have to face the Malta barrage again. When he reached his base in darkness he lost consciousness, but before losing himself into oblivion there had been the happy thought that he had made it.

The Maltese crowds had also retired by then, and lost themselves in the oblivion of sleep. Their last thought before losing consciousness had been one of satisfaction — that all was good, and that the enemy would probably not wake them up again after the beating he had taken. They would sleep peacefully through the night.

They were wrong however. The sirens began wailing again after midnight and those at home began cursing the Italians as they made their way to the shelters. It was only a nuisance raid, but it kept them awake until the sirens sounded the 'raiders passed'.

It was just past 4 a.m. on 26th July when they plodded their way back home. It was still dark, although the sun could be seen paling through the hazy mist as it always did one hour before dawn. Everyone hurried home trying to make the best out of the remaining hour for the start of another day. Half an hour later however there was an explosion which shook Grand Harbour and the cities on that side of the island. Immediately after, there was the sudden roar of gunfire which became a crescendo of noise as if a hundred mad gunners were let loose. The first thought that occurred to those at home not yet in their beds was that the enemy planes had turned back without warning, but it was soon noticed that the sound of those firing guns was different from what they had been hearing for the last thirteen months.

As if at a silent signal the people in Valletta, the Three Cities,

Sliema and Floriana rushed out in the streets and ran, not to shelters, but to bastions, and similar vantage points, curious, maybe, but more than curious for they were moved by a fearful thought that had suddenly occurred to them. And with them were running whose who left their shelters, similarly afraid of what they would see. Then all eyes converged on the sea outside the Grand Harbour's breakwater.

Searchlights from Forts St Elmo and Ricasoli were illuminating a wide expanse of the open sea and caught in that web of light was a tiny object moving fast trying to avoid the red tracer shells that were darting at it from the belching guns in the forts. The boat exploded, and the searchlights and guns found another one with the same result. As more boats were trapped into the illuminated sea the multiple six-pounders from both forts kept their rapid alternating fire with more explosions throwing fire and water in the white silvery beams as the gunners found their targets. There appeared to be no end to the number of naval units that were somehow attacking the coast line so close to Grand Harbour, but this did not seem to be worrying the gunners at the forts who were firing like madmen as they had never fired before — continuously, and, from what could be seen, with deadly accuracy.

On the eastern side of Ricasoli Corporal Ferris of the Cheshire Regiment who had spent that night with his men in a machine-gun post was watching all this as well, still not knowing what was really happening when out of the swirling and wreathing mist in the sea some fifty yards away from the shore there appeared the form of a boat crossing his sights silently towards Grand Harbour. He did not hesitate and gave a sharp order.

Similarly every machine-gun on that side of the coast was now shooting at every moving object that could be seen in the lifting morning mist adding more noise and action to that July morning spectacle.

The spectacle continued with the sheets of flame and red hot steel spurting from the shore batteries and the terrific din that was heard all over Malta waking up everybody in the far away villages to listen and wonder what was happening. With the first light of dawn Hurricane fighters appeared on the scene and joined in the fray.

For those first moments those who were spectators to all this gazed in awe at what was going on, enthralled with all they saw. But then they realised that the coastal defences were in action for the first time. It immediately registered with them that there was a seaborne attack from the enemy which could mean a landing, or what they had for some time feared — an invasion.

CHAPTER SEVEN

First Pangs of Hunger

The Italian human torpedo owed its beginning to as far back as 1935, when it was developed during the Abyssinian war, and it is interesting to note that with its successful development one of the first sure targets which the Italians earmarked for this weapon even then was none other than Malta. In the course of the weapon's development it was realised that if this weapon were to be used with effect against distant targets, means had to be provided to transport it and let it loose a short distance from its objective. So a particular motor vessel was devised as a motor torpedo launcher which would carry the torpedoes and their crews until the time when they were launched. For deeper incursions into bays and ports, the *Barchina* was developed, which was a small boat carrying an explosive charge through most of its length leaving space only for its motor at the back, and seating accommodation for its pilot in an ejector seat which he could dislodge to shoot himself away to possible safety before the moment of contact and explosion.

These *Barchini*, or E-boats as they came to be called, were carried most of the way in a big fast tender made for the purpose, which launched them some miles away from their target. To collect any of the pilots who manage to remain alive by using the ejector seat, there were MAS boats included in the team which would accompany the E-boats to the battle area and succour them with not only their presence but also with their armaments. This complete ensemble was organised under the name of La Decima Flottiglia MAS, and in 1941 its *commandante* was Valerio J. Borghese.

It is to be said that irrespective of the safety arrangements that were provided, it was a well-known and accepted fact that possibilities of saving oneself to fight another day were very remote, and the odds were heavily on the side of missions undertaken by this organisation being suicidal. Yet there were men to do it, which leaves no one in doubt about their courage and dedication.

It was the Decima Flottiglia Mas which delivered the attack on Malta's Grand Harbour on 26th July 1941.

According to their *commandante* there were several occasions when single elements of the *flottiglia* had come over to Malta for reconnaissance purposes. They came in singly close to the coast to observe the defences. There may be an element of truth in this since it was known, as I have in fact already mentioned in this book, that there were several occasions when the coastal batteries had engaged unseen targets, firing only on information from radar. Such incursions were attributed to mine-laying boats. Indeed they could very well have been the boats of Flottiglia Mas to which Valerio Borghese alludes. He even went so far as to claim that a member of his *flottiglia* had gone into Marsaxlokk Bay and landed at Marsaxlokk. The reason for such incursions was purely reconnaissance and the intention was to see what type of coastal defence could be expected if and when there were an invasion of Malta, for which it was already being assumed the Italians would have to provide both troops and ships.

Yet the most important point which emerges from all this, and which should be recorded for history, is that given by Commander Moccagatta who was in charge of the Malta operation when he said that the Italians had to rely on this type of reconnaissance because they could not find and they did not have a single spy in Malta.

Although the idea of an attack by the *flottiglia* on Malta had always been in Italian minds, they had never had the necessary determination to carry it out. They were well aware of the strength and determination of anti-aircraft and fighter defences and they could expect that coastal defences would be of the same calibre. But following the success of the *flottiglia* in penetrating the three nets of the boom defence at Suda Bay in Crete, on the night between 25th and 26th March 1941, when it sank the British cruiser *York* and three merchant ships at anchor there, a similar operation against Malta began to appear feasible. The first plan was started by Admiral De Courten exactly a month later, and he entrusted Commander Moccagatta with the operation. But when this was referred to the Italian equivalent of the Under Secretary of State it was rejected as being impossible. After insisting, Moccagatta was told that if he were to manage to reach Malta undetected on two occasions, then his request would be reconsidered. He did come to within half a mile of Malta with two E-boats on two occasions, and his request was then acceded to.

The attack was therefore laid down for 28th June, but the *flottiglia* had to turn back because of rough seas. Another attempt on the 30th failed as well, and Moccagatta was ready to give up the idea as impossible. It was a more determined member of the *flottiglia* who pressed him not to give it up — Maggiore del Genio Teseo Tesei, a fanatic about this operation and a man of stout heart. Prompted by Teseo Tesei's zeal and determination Moccagatta took up the operation again, and took the *flottiglia* on two training runs beforehand. On the second run on 23rd July the *flottiglia* met the powerful convoy that was sailing towards Malta amongst which there were the battleship *Renown* and the aircraft carrier *Ark Royal*, and the *flottiglia* very sensibly discreetly withdrew. But the anticipated presence of a convoy in Malta provided a worthwhile target, and the decision was taken.

The attack was delivered on 26th July. The force consisted of the overall fast tender *Diana* which carried eleven E-boats, the two MAS boats *MAS 451* and *452*, together with one SLC (Human Torpedo Launcher) carrying the human torpedoes and their crews, who were under the command of Maggiore de Genio Teseo Tesei. The overall command of the operation was under Moccagatta who himself was to lead the E-boats. The force was escorted by a squadron of Macchi 200 fighters which was to afford protection from British fighters.

The force left Augusta just after midnight. The general plan was for Major Teseo Tesei and Chief Diver Pedretti to approach the viaduct of the breakwater in the shadow of St Elmo on a human torpedo and blow it there to open the boom defence. The explosion would be the signal for the E-boats to begin their run and enter the harbour through the opening, thus avoiding the dangers of the other entrance between the ends of the breakwater which was closed by double nets. Another human torpedo ridden by Lieutenant Francesco Costa and Sergeant Luigi Barla had to make its way into Marsamxett Harbour in order to attack the submarines at Lazaretto. The whole operation was timed to take place during an air raid, in the hope no doubt, that the coast defences would be under cover, but the *flottiglia* was one hour late in arriving, and the sirens had already sounded the 'raiders passed' for the air raid. Not that it would have made any difference had they arrived in time, because unknown to them they were detected by the Malta radar soon after midnight, and the gunners of the coast defence were alerted.

Until the *flottiglia* was twenty miles away from Malta, it was tracked by radar. But then something strange happened. The track stopped, and seemed to remain stationary for fifteen minutes. Then it began moving away in the opposite direction, receding towards Sicily and gradually disappearing, indicating to the defences that whatever had been approaching the island had now turned back. Nothing of the sort had happened, however. What the radar was producing could have been caused through a phenomenon in that radar beams could be bent through temperature conversion, which according to experts was very common in the Mediterranean then.

There might have been another explanation for this, since during the fifteen minutes when the radar track had remained stationary, the Italian tender *Diana* launched the E-boats, and torpedo launcher and left them to proceed with their attack. Had the tender made its way back then, it could have been this that caused the track to withdraw and disappear from radar. After all we know that the radar had only been detecting the *Diana*, and not the E-boats which were until this time being carried in it.

Whatever was the cause, the 'withdrawal' of the unidentified force was passed to the guns in the coast defences to make them stand down. At that time, however, the E-boats were being escorted to within a couple of miles of Grand Harbour by *MAS 451* and *452*, while the torpedo launcher took the human torpedoes to about a mile off, and Major Teseo Tesei with Pedretti proceeded with their 'pig' (as human torpedoes were called) to the breakwater's viaduct.

It is interesting to note here that according to an entry logged in the records of the Malta Auxiliary Corps (a Passive Defence Unit) two members of the corps who on that night were on patrol in Gozo had heard the sound of voices talking in Italian as if coming from some boat in the darkness. Then suddenly there was a light put on which probed the shore as if for guidance to its proximity. It is possible that on their way to Grand Harbour in Malta, the MAS boats with the *barchini* they were escorting passed off Gozo and confirmed their position; only those boats could have had a light to put on.

It was expected that Major (later Colonel) Ferro who commanded the guns at St Elmo would send his gunners back to their beds on being informed that the detected force had withdrawn. But the behaviour of the approaching target must have seemed strange to him, and even though there was nothing visible he ordered his gunners to lie down and rest, but without leaving the gun emplacements. So, while they went to sleep on their blankets, doubtlessly disappointed at the turn of events, the Italian *flottiglia* was approaching silently, then stopping, unseen and unheard in the darkness to wait expectantly for the explosion which was to be the signal for the mass attack onto and through the opened boom defence. Not a sound came from the darkness beyond the coastline, but there were moments of tension for those who were looking over the dark expanse as if expecting something which they knew nothing of. This affected Lieutenant B. Portelli the officer in charge of searchlights, who without any positive reason ordered the fighting lights (as the two searchlights from the extreme ends of the line of defences were called) to be switched on. But when their silvery tentacles probed the sea, nothing was seen. The Italians were of course much closer to the shore than the points reached by the lights.

Then suddenly there was the explosion as Teseo Tesei blew up his torpedo. Lieutenant Portelli gave the order for all searchlights to be switched on and the sea outside Grand Harbour became an illuminated arena. The centre of attraction was the pack of eleven *barchini* now launched on their deadly attack. The gunners at St Elmo and Ricasoli were taken by surprise, but nonetheless rose up as one to their guns, and went into action with their multiple six-pounders, and with deadly precision, caught the enemy force in a crossfire. The first enemy boat was blown up within ten seconds, and others began falling to the guns at similar intervals.

According to Italian sources one of the *barchini* struck the viaduct, so it cannot be said whether it was Tesei's explosion which brought down the span of the viaduct or this boat. However the span which was brought down produced a further impenetrable barrier in that spot, and this, the Italians claimed, was what kept some of their E-boats from entering the harbour. This is contradicted in their statement when they say that it only took the defences two minutes to wipe out their share of the E-boats which makes it obvious that there was no time for them to go into the harbour, had Tesei opened the way as he had set out to do.

It was soon dawn, and the Hurricanes arrived on the scene to intercept the escort of Macchi fighters that had come to cover the operation. They found four E-boats running away from the harbour obviously trying to escape their doom, and sank them with machine gun fire. In the ensuing fight with the Italian fighters, three of them were shot down with the loss of one Hurricane. A significant point is raised here by the shot-down Hurricane pilot who baled out in the sea and swam towards a stationary Italian E-boat which he found abandoned by its crew. This indicates that in at least one case the Italians chose to abandon their boat and save themselves rather than press the attack. The boat involved was captured intact.

While this was going on, Lieutenant Costa and Sergeant Barla encountered difficulties with their human torpedo which they were attempting to take to Marsamxett Harbour. They had to abandon it and were captured later as they were found swimming into St George's Bay. It is not understood why these two men trying to save themselves should swim to a bay miles away from their abandoned torpedo, unless they had in the first place taken their torpedo to the wrong bay.

The final result was also confirmed from Italian sources that the tender *Diana* which had kept away from the scene of the attack returned to its base. But all the rest failed to return. Sixteen boats (including the human torpedoes) were destroyed, and one was captured. There were 15 Italians killed, and 18 taken prisoner in Malta. Amongst the killed there was their Commandant Moccagatta, and of course Major Teseo Tesei, whose water mask, it is believed, was picked up beneath the viaduct with parts of his brain and hair stuck to it. On that same day his relatives received the letter he had posted before going on the attack saying that by the time that letter reached them he would have died on Malta's breakwater to set an example for others on how to give their life for their country. Surely no one begrudges the *Medaglia d'Oro* which was posthumously awarded to him, and to Pedretti.

*

Notwithstanding the glorifying reports of the Western press of the successful repulse of the seaborne attack, all going a long way to dispel doubts about any invasion from that direction, behind the bright faces of lifted morale, there was a feeling of doom. It was true that land forces had by then with the intake of levies been increased to thirty thousand men; and the offensive action by air and naval units from the island was harassing the enemy and yielding splendid results; there was the unspoken fear about shortage of supplies — spoken of as a prelude to starvation, a determining factor in any siege. It was common knowledge that the island was always notoriously short of water, but it was not known if and how many of the reservoirs that collected rain water in winter for use during the months of draught were still standing and functioning. It was now the zenith of summer with the heat and sweat making more demands on drinking water. There were at least two months before the first autumn rains came, if they did come. Until then the rigs of the Water Works Department would keep on boring into unexplored depths of the globigerina limestone in their blind attempts for precious water.

The severe reduction of the stable foodstuffs by rationing had been expected and was a foregone conclusion, and there had been no complaints. Indeed it had been another limitation which was hitting every country involved in the terrible war, and even those who were not. It was in a way another form of making new characters of those who had never bothered to realise where the food and water that had made their lives easy were coming from and what they meant in others' work and sacrifice.

The dominating factor in this situation was the bread which was, as it still is, the mainstay of Maltese diet. Half a loaf of white crunchy bread sodden with olive oil, and a splash of tomato or tomato paste, seasoned with salt and pepper would make the most delicious of all meals. But even this was bound to become impossible under the privations of the moment. The harvest, even with most of it still green, had been brought in, and what grain had been produced and stored in old granaries of the Knights in Floriana and Valletta was already being used faster than it could be replenished, and the situation for future harvests was now bleak for the fertile ground had been made grey and sterile with the mixture of burnt TNT from bomb explosions, or, though to a limited extent, had been taken over for defence purposes. There was also a lack of young farmers, many of whom had gone into uniform although those of them who wanted it were given exemption. Apart from that of grain and staple vegetables there was also a shortage of clover, and whatever livestock was still available was bound to suffer as well.

It was the administration who had the major headache over the situation. What foodstuffs, petrol and ammunition the convoy of 25th July had brought in was expected to keep the people and defences going for three months, but this did not take into consideration the extra demands necessarily being made for petrol by the increasing aerial offensive action, and on ammunition by the constant air attacks which could any moment be intensified and leave the island open and bereft of its barrage which had until then kept it going. Besides, they knew that no amount of tinned stuffs could make up for the staple diet of bread and olive oil with which the Maltese had been blessed but which was now looking as if it could be their damnation, as the two items were becoming short. It was more than a headache to them on which a firm and wise decision had to be taken.

On 1st August the decision was taken to knead potatoes with the dough for bread. For the first time in their life the Maltese saw their beautiful loaves changing their colour and losing their crunchy and wholesome consistency. But what worried them was a more sinister thought, and as if in confirmation of their fears there was announced a few days later the rationing of kerosene and the precious olive oil.

Fredu Schembri was after all given his Home Guard denim uniform which was made for his measure. Now he made it his daily wear, not that this was required of him, but it was the final touch in giving him the air of importance he was always after. As if to emphasize this fact to those who sniggered at him, he made it a point to go out immediately on a self-imposed patrol after every raiders passed signal to look for any enemy flier that might have dropped by parachute in Vittoriosa.

Anglu Fenech did not carry on with his plan to apply for exemption from conscription. He reasoned that with Concetta to look after his sister during the day he could try to go into a unit which would require his services only by day so that he could be with his sister at night. After all there might also be that something from his rations which he would be able to share with his sister. Things did not work exactly as he had intended. He joined the Royal Engineers thinking of working at some trade during the day and be free during nights. But he was posted to a searchlight unit where, after he would have learned his job, all his duty periods would have to be during the night. His only consolation was that he could after all keep some of his rations to take to his sister. But he soon found out that after a few hours of the summer heat the bread which he kept for his sister was getting stale, as it was mixed with potatoes.

Carmelo Vella ate all his rations without any complaint. His life had always been based on doing what was dished out to him. Even the strange tasks that he was being given on operating a searchlight, running the generator, manning the sound detector or firing the Lewis gun were becoming routine to him. They had now given him a new feeling of interest in life which had never been there before.

Mary too had a new interest in life. Her days without John were now being occupied by the attentions of Bob. Resisting them at first, but after going out with him several times, each time deciding not to repeat it, she began to sense the difference in his caresses from those of John. When in the shelter during some long nuisance raid she began to feel the first pangs of remorse for her young Maltese consort, there was always Bob who would go to the same shelter to keep her company and dispel her remorseful thoughts. Then she would remember how John had lately become more occupied with his guns and the lance-corporal stripe on his arm.

Incredibly all could see and feel the change that was coming. It wasn't a change in raids or tactics, but something which was intrinsic, and characteristic in Maltese life itself. In the same way that the men in the services had now become accustomed to start the day with breakfast and to read vulgar humour from periodicals meant for men only, so the girls became at home with the romance British youth had brought to them. There was the feeling that an old flag had been hauled down, and never again would it be raised. That had faded. Instead, the young heads saw the beckoning image of a new life which was a straight road where the crooked path had been. Even the priests learned of new morals in confession, and they just had to keep with it.

Those times had introduced more than customs and philosophies into what had always been pure Maltese life. The barracks and the gun positions became a meeting place of jargon and routine. In the streets and shelters the civilian population adopted the wording which came easier on the tongue. So it spoke of *bomber* rather than *ajruplan tal-bumbardament*, and said *fighter* instead of *ajruplan tal-glied*. *Shelter* was used rather than *kenn*, as were *machine guns, air raids, dive-bomber, searchlight* and other words without a concise meaning in Maltese. Many of these have found a place in the Maltese language, and stayed there.

It was so on those hot days of a summer that seemed to have no end, that the sun continued to shine on the jagged edges of buildings, formerly the beautiful heritage from past civilisations, and stalwart hearts continued to resist. And as they toiled amid the now familiar debris of shattered glass, corpses, broken masonry and choking clouds of dust they tried to persevere in retaining their merry humour which would be needed in the days and months still to come, when they would be free to rebuild the country. In the meantime, life had to be carried on. The dead were buried, the young couples met and courted, and married bliss continued uninterruptedly with the act of procreation keeping Censu's rock-hewn maternity ward busy. For sustinence, food was somehow concocted, pilfered or through the way of least risk taken on the ration card, while the guns clawed at those who from the sky tried to disrupt all this. When the sky darkened for the night the black Wellingtons and dark grey Blenheims would be heard flying out, now identifiable by their familiar noises, to hammer the hornets' nests a hundred miles away in attempts to bring more peaceful days.

The submarine offensive from Malta had gathered momentum and between June and September had sunk eleven enemy supply ships totalling about 75,000 tons, besides others which they damaged. If one were to add another 16 ships with a total of 41,000 tons sunk by submarines based at Gibraltar and Alexandria, then the grand total could be taken as 27 ships and 116,000 tons. According to the German staff in North Africa these sinkings represented 50% of what was being sent to Rommel, which as one would have expected made the Germans see red.

It is not within the scope of this book to relate the stories of heroism and sacrifice which can be found in these submarine operations —and there were many, but I should not omit to mention that during this time of sterling action from Malta, one of the captains here — Lieutenant Commander M.D. Wanklyn DSO — the captain of *Upholder*, was awarded the highest British decoration, the Victoria Cross. This submarine which had suffered with the Maltese, bombings at Lazaretto creek, and whose officers and men often mixed with the locals and drank whatever providence provided at the Gzira and Sliema bars, had sunk thirteen enemy ships. It was no wonder then that there were many who shared in the joy at this coveted award.

When I mentioned in a previous paragraph that these successes made the Germans see red I was not exaggerating, because at this time of 1941 Hitler was complaining bitterly to Mussolini about the inadequate protection of reinforcements sent to the Afrika Korps, while Admiral Raeder himself, the Commander in Chief of the German Navy, concurred with this view and added that if the Germans were to lose North Africa they would lose the war in the Mediterranean with disastrous consequences for the whole war. This might have been another reason for deploying U-boats in the Mediterranean which provided another danger to convoys coming to Malta.

All the success and achievements throughout August and the beginning of September did not have the same effect everywhere. While the people and the naval and air authorities rejoiced, there were those at the top who were keeping their fingers crossed. The increased activities had demanded more fuel and ammunition which, coupled with the already heavy drain on supplies made earlier replenishment than expected necessary. An early convoy had to be attempted and it became imperative that it would have to get through.

If it did not, then the future of Malta would be in jeopardy.

CHAPTER EIGHT

Sacrifice and Sentence of Death

Convoy GM2 was formed in England and left for Malta, passing Gibraltar during the night of 24th/25th September. It was composed of nine ships : *Clan Macdonald, Dunedin Star, Imperial Star, Breconshire, Rowallan Castle, City of Lincoln, Clan Ferguson, City of Calcutta* and *Ajax*. It was an impressive collection of ships, but what was more impressive was the escort composed of Force H under Admiral Somerville comprising the battleships *Prince of Wales, Nelson,* and *Rodney*, the aircraft carrier *Ark Royal* and four destroyers, together with Force X under Admiral Burrough comprising the cruisers *Kenya, Euryalus, Edinburgh, Sheffield, Hermione* and eight destroyers. It was obvious that the importance of this convoy was realised and the British Navy had come out in force to get it through. This operation was code-named 'Halberd'.

With the absence of German aircraft from Sicily the British force was expecting attacks from German U-boats, which as has already been mentioned were now operating in the Mediterranean, and of course the Italian Air Force. However what the British admirals wanted most was an encounter with the Italian fleet. This can be evidenced by the presence of three capital ships in the escorting force.

The convoy was located by two Italian Cant Z 1007 aircraft at 1530 on 26th September, and the alarm was given. Both the Italian navy and the air force went into action. Admiral Iachino left port with a very impressive force which comprised the battleships *Vittorio Veneto* and the *Littorio*, the cruisers *Trento, Trieste, Gorizia* and *Duca degli Abruzzi*, the destroyers *Granatiere, Fuciliere, Bersagliere, Gioberti, Da Recco, Passegero, Folgore, Corazziere, Carabiniere, Ascari, Lanciere, Maestrale, Grecale* and *Scirocco*. Also despatched to the intended area of battle were 16 submarines. Had this been known at the time, a dramatic engagement could have been expected. Instead, the moment the British fleet tried to engage the enemy, Admiral Iachino withdrew without firing a shot and ran to Naples. Official records attribute this to the fact that the Italian admiral was under orders not to engage the enemy if it was found out that he was numerically

superior, and superiority was attributed to the three British battleships to the Italians' two. But one cannot help remarking that the
reconnaissance aircraft which located the British must have
reported the presence of the battleships. So why did the Italian
fleet go out only to refuse engagement?

What the fleet did not do was, however, attempted by the air
force, and squadrons of torpedo bombers escorted by fighters
launched a heavy attack on the convoy and escorts. A fierce
running battle ensued during which the ship *Imperial Star* was hit
and seriously damaged by a torpedo, and, rather than delaying
passage to Malta by towing it, the convoy commander sank the
ship. The only other casualty was the battleship *Nelson* which was
hit by a torpedo in the stern which reduced her speed. In the
battle area thirteen Italian aircraft were shot down but there were
other casualties on the Italian side not directly attributable to
enemy action, such as the loss of ten Macchi fighters out of a
squadron of fifteen, which failed to locate the British fleet and
used their petrol in looking for it.

Eight ships of the convoy reached Malta, and the wild reception
given to it by the population was noted for its impressive show,
even in Italian records.

That day spelled a respite from what was expected to be in
store for the future. In its sixteen-month life, war in Malta had
already grown old. There had been destruction, death and misery.
A repulsed seaborne attack, and notwithstanding the last few
months of respite from bombing, there had been the constant air
raids by Italian aircraft which although ignored as spelling no
danger still constituted a nuisance which called for patience and
sacrifices. But who wasn't making sacrifices in those days? The
pitiful conditions under which the population was living ranked on
the verge of impossibility. Work, sleep, and normal life were
tainted by daily expectation of death, schooling disrupted by the
ever-sounding sirens; food and drink were only available in
restricted quantities for the day not knowing what the morrow
might bring; new clothing became something of the past as there
was never space for it in convoy ships. When these hardships were
somehow lived with, there were the natural worries with women
of their menfolk on the guns or in naval ships at far away theatres
of operations. It had become a common occurrence for the
women to go hungry to leave some more for the children, or the
husband fasting himself for the sake of his wife. It had become a
life of continuous sacrifice, nobly exemplified by a village father

who covered his young sons with his body under enemy machine-gun fire and died so that his sons could live. It was, however, a sacrifice borne and shared by everyone who had been caught by fate or duty in the siege. It was this bond in purpose that raised hope in each and every one who forgot his troubles on seeing those of others. It was no doubt this same bond which had made the seamen in British warships and merchantmen face the ferocious assaults on the high seas whilst on convoys, and to die grinning, knowing it was a chance for others to go through where they were failing.

It was this kind of spirit which made Malta fighter pilot Flight Lieutenant MacLaughlan who at the age of 22 had an arm shot off by a Messerschmitt cannon shell, make his way back to fly and fight with a Hurricane with an artificial arm. It was also the same kind of spirit which made Mrs M. Barnwell bear the death of her son David, 19-year-old Malta fighter pilot who died after shooting down five enemy planes in a month. His father Captain Frank Barnwell, the designer of the Blenheim and Beaufort aircraft, had also been killed in an aircraft crash. Killed also were his two brothers Richard Anthony and John Sandes, both pilots.

'I am all alone now,' said Mrs Barnwell on hearing the news that her third son had been killed. 'David had last cabled me from Malta after he was awarded the Distinguished Flying Cross. But I am not down, and I have never felt prouder. All my four men have given their lives for this country. If they had to go they went the best way. There must be other mothers and wives who had such losses. Others may have it to come. They must carry on as I am going to do.'

The Maltese and British gunners remained shoulder to shoulder and continued to blaze away at the enemy as he appeared in the blue Malta skies. Wives and children, along with the rest of the population in Malta kept hoping that the cruel siege would be lifted, and the war would be won. But they did not shrink away from giving their contribution. Even if this was only to endure the hardships they were facing, silently and willingly.

There was of course another force which made the Maltese bear up with determination under the holocaust. It could be seen on their faces as they lifted their eyes to the sky, or heard from their mouths as they recited their prayers. It could be more easily understood as they were seen kneeling in silence in front of the altars in their churches; the big architectural beauties where they still stood, or the little derelict country ones which had to replace those that had been demolished. Whether they had to pray in the cool stark serenity of a spacious marbled aisle or in some small chapel where the rough wood of chairs and benches is often caught in the slanting sunlight, they did it fervently and with conviction. There was even a personal pride or maybe individualism, stemming from their identification of their God, Holy Mother or saint, and many a time this brought forth quickly made-up prayers. One such prayer for example was heard in a shelter in Senglea whose inhabitants always were and still are staunch devotees of the Nativity of the Blessed Virgin whose feast is celebrated on 8th September, the day commemorating the Maltese victory over the Turks in the Great Siege of 1565.

> *O Bambina tal-Vittorja*
> *Sultana tas-Sema u l-Art*
> *Ilqa' l-bombi fil-mant tieghek*
> *U ehlisna minn dan l-attakk.*

This can be translated as follows:

> Oh Maiden Lady of Victory
> Oh Queen of Heaven and Earth
> Gather the bombs in your mantle
> And deliver us from this attack.

Meanwhile the battle had to go on, and the hardships being endured were not only increasing individual determination of the people to resist but also that of their leaders who escalated the offensive being launched from the small island. The land battle in North Africa was still raging with a see-saw movement in the fortunes of fighting, and at this time the British and Common-wealth forces had the upper hand and were chasing Rommel back. The German General was frantic with rage at seeing his much needed reinforcements being sunk as ships kept trying to run the gauntlet from Italy and were prevented from doing it by the air and naval assaults from Malta. The improvement in the supplies' position brought about by the September convoy raised more confidence and no doubt, encouraged by the new long respite from heavy raids, the assault forces were increased. In October the two British light cruisers *Penelope* and *Aurora* were based in Malta with the destroyers *Lance* and *Lively*, and together with other destroyers, they became known as Force K under Captain W.G.

Agnew. This force achieved brilliant successes and destroyed whole convoys. It is interesting to record here that the Italians were fully aware of these ships at Malta and I found in their records, how at this time they were directing their air attacks on these ships in the harbour with their pilots never failing to report hits and sinkings of parts of this force. However they mentioned as well how even with such glorious reports, Force K kept turning up every time a convoy was found to attack. One such incident found in Italian records refers to 9th November. A few days before the Italian command was assured by its pilots that both *Penelope* and *Aurora* were so much damaged by their attacks, that they would not be able to move from their anchorage for a long time. On 9th November 1941 (I am here quoting their records) a convoy consisting of seven ships, *Duisberg, San Marco, Rina Corrado, Conte di Misurata, Sagitta, Minaulland* and *Maria*, was proceeding to North Africa. It was escorted by two cruisers and ten destroyers. Suddenly Force K from Malta appeared on the scene and in less than seven minutes had sunk all the seven ships and one destroyer, and damaging another which later sank. On 20th November another Italian convoy of four ships escorted by two cruisers and eight destroyers was attacked. As soon as the two cruisers were hit by torpedoes the rest of the convoy turned back into Taranto. Part of Force K however turned towards the Piraeus from where another two ships were coming to join this convoy, and this time these had no chance to turn back. They were both sunk by the *Penelope* and *Lively*. Italian sources record their shipping situation to have been catastrophic until then, and during the month of November they had lost 12 ships totalling 54,900 tons.

The flag of Malta and its command was flying high and proud now. Not without sacrifices, for during this month the battleship *Barham* was torpedoed and sunk by the German U-boat *U-331*. But what touched every Maltese heart more nearly that month was that the aircraft carrier *Ark Royal* was returning to Gibraltar after having delivered more Hurricanes to Malta, and was sunk by another German submarine — *U-81*.

*

Fredu Schembri soon found out that the Home Guard was not the easy pastime he had imagined it to be. He was required to attend drill sessions and weapon training twice a week, and after a month these were accompanied by firing practice on the ranges.

Fortunately for him, preserved meat and tinned fish were placed on the ration card and this removed the need to open his shop other than on ration days every fortnight. On other days there was nothing else to sell. So he could devote more time to his Home Guard duties which did not require any of the abilities in which he was lacking. He soon learned all the drill commands, however clipped was his tongue when he gave them, and he had become used to handling a rifle, so much so that he was soon promoted to sergeant.

After a short spell at a searchlight post in the countryside and far away from Valletta Anglu Fenech was transferred to a new post in Cospicua. It was a lovely place on a bastion overlooking what had once been modern roads and buildings, but were now all demolished. But there were still people living in shelters, who were often about, particularly now that there had been a respite from German raids. True, the post was in the target area, but the crew had orders to take cover in a nearby public shelter during daylight raids, as the searchlight's services were only required at night time. However, there was a distinct advantage which made up for all discomforts in the proximity of Cospicua to Valletta, and with the harbour ferries still running he could reach home in half an hour by ferry. So whenever he was not the duty telephonist he could always be away for an hour or two to be with his sister Sarah and Concetta, to whom he began to feel attracted. At night it was a different story as he had to be at his post.

Carmelo Vella was now also wearing his service shoes well. What's more, he began to like the life which seemed day after day to be bringing forth feelings which he had never felt before. He forgot all his inclinations for carpentry, and would have also put aside his love for the saxophone had some friends not often suggested that he should have gone into the Royal Malta Artillery where they had a good band and would have taken him as a bandsman. That was something, however, which did not appeal to him. Not that he did not like the artillery, because he admired it and particularly what it was doing in the defence of Malta. But if he had to go in that regiment, he was convinced it would not be as a bandsman. As a gunner, yes. There had been a time when he would have shirked from such a thought. Now he warmed to it, and became flushed, not in the way he used to do at the mention of women, even that was now over, but on realising that he wanted to get to grips with the change that had come over Maltese life and character. His, included.

John too was feeling he was a new man. Not because he was a lance corporal and ordering a couple of men about even though they were older than him, but because of other feelings. The drill, and physical training had built his muscles, and service discipline had instilled in him certain values of life that were not there before. When he played his part in shooting down two enemy aircraft there was no limit to his joy and satisfaction. When he talked about it he noticed the different attitude in his listeners, as they realised they were being talked to by a man and not a boy. One noticed a different outlook in everybody then, his parents, his brothers, sisters, and his friends. There was also a difference in Mary.

She had succumbed to Bob and went out with him. Repenting of her weakness she had gone to confession and told her fifty-year-old priest confessor all about it. He had told her that she had done wrong in giving herself to a man in her unmarried state, which was aggravated by the fact that she was promised to another man. He warned her as well that the English soldier was only a passing bird, and what's more, he was not a Catholic. Her way was sure to lead her to fire and brimstone. He then gave her absolution. She listened and repented, but two days later she felt so weak before Bob's approaches that she succumbed again. There was another rigmarole by the priest when she went again to confession, and he ordered her to desist from seeing the Englishman under penalty of refusal of absolution. She listened in awe with tears in her eyes and promised the priest, herself and God that she would not fall again. But Bob's charms were stronger than her determination, and when they met again she went with him and made love. On the following Saturday she did not go to confession, dreading having to face the priest. Three weeks passed during which she refused to submit to the shame and dishonour that the priest might bring down on her. She would have stayed unconfessed and unabsolved longer had there not been a new priest who came to her church to supplement the local confessor on the eve of the village feast. Many saw him for the first time. He was young. Not more than twenty-eight years old, she guessed, and on the spur of the moment she knelt and began to confess. She told him everything, and he listened in silence. When she finished he began to ask her questions. About John and Bob, and how she met them, and her feelings towards them. After questions came his words of advice which she felt helpful as a lantern in a dark stormy night. He spoke of love and infatuation, and guided her to know which of the two underlined her actions. God would help her, he said, but she had to make the decision. And she did, and marvelled at the easiness of it. Life had surely changed. And so had priests.

Manwela too never failed her Saturday confession when she spent the good part of half an hour relating to the priest her preoccupation which had nothing to do with the Ten Commandments. She told him of her worries about her husband who was away with his ship, and her eldest son who was on a cruiser in the Atlantic and who could not swim. Another one who had been with a destroyer at Narvik was now somewhere else and she hadn't heard from him for a month. The priest spoke words of comfort and explained that God would protect them. There were another two sons who had now joined up, one the Navy and the other the Royal Air Force, but both of them were in Malta. She cried when the priest told her that he would remember them in his prayers and that she was not to worry. Then she gave him a pound to say masses for their safe keeping. He took it and thanked her. After all priests must live. Even so, Manwela felt that a pound was cheap for the comfort it brought to her knowing that there was another One who was more powerful to look after her husband and sons.

Faith, hope and perseverance are good virtues, as fortitude, trust and determination are strong points in a human character; but they can never beat bread. An unvirtuous coward can live on food, but a virtuous one can't live without bread. This is a fact which had always been evident, as it was evident in that November of 1941. Fears of starvation began again as early as six weeks after the previous eight-ship convoy had sustained Malta. There were many who expected some relieving measures in the situation, and no doubt there were some in the way of replenishment of ammunition, petrol, spares and foodstuffs, but any effects that there must have been in this respect were certainly not visible. Commodities continued to be short and bread was still being served heavy and stale-looking with the addition of a 20% to 30% potato element, — that is when it could be found at all. For now it was in short supply. This had come even when there were still some potatoes to mix with the wheat. So what was going to happen when they ran out? It was one thing being brave and throwing defiance at the enemy, and another trying to do it on an empty stomach. Unless of course the respite from bombardment was to extend for ever, saving on ammunition and tiresome vigils on guns and defences, and passage from Gibraltar would remain as easy as it had been for the September convoy and make it possible to bring some more. It was a future based on hopes.

On the other side of the Mediterranean, the Germans in North Africa were convinced that something had to be done quickly to restrain the wolf that was eating 80% of what was being sent to them from Italy in the way of supplies, particularly now at a crucial moment in their campaign on which hinged not only the fate of an army and its general, but that of the whole war. It was not a difficult decision to arrive at, that Malta, the wolf, had to be immobilized. This intention had always been there. Now with the harassing and interception reaching their peak there was no more room for argument. There had to be action — and immediately. There was to be a man to do it, who had to be hard, decisive, and well-tried. There was indeed a man who had a year back been next to Göring himself in the direction of the Battle of Britain, and who was now in Russia. He had been sounded out about this possibility as long as two months ago. What had then been exploration of a possibility was now the implementation of a decision. Field Marshal Kesselring was detailed as Commander-in-Chief South. At the same time on 24th November, when Blenheim medium bombers from Malta were playing havoc with Rommel's petrol stocks and convoys to North Africa, and Wellingtons were pounding Benghazi, Kesselring was being briefed by Hitler in the presence of Göring, and told that he was to forget any plans to invade Malta but to remedy the situation by neutralising the island once and for all. And with this order the German squadrons in Russia were swung back to Sicily for their decisive onslaught on Malta. Kesselring arrived in Rome on 28th November. Two days later he was in Sicily. On that day Malta had its one thousandth air raid, which was the end of the respite, and the beginning of a holocaust, the kind of which had never before been seen.

An unexploded bomb being carried away
by Bomb Disposal Squad
(The Times *of Malta*)

An unexploded
magnetic mine
which, like
many others,
was dropped
on land
*(National
War Museum
Association,
Malta)*

Air Vice Marshal Sir Keith Park
(National War Museum Association, Malta)

Field Marshal Lord Gort VC
(National War Museum Association, Malta)

The Law Courts and other buildings in Valletta
destroyed by bombing
(National War Museum Association, Malta)

Barely afloat, the *Ohio* enters Grand Harbour
(Imperial War Museum, London)

CHAPTER NINE

Holocaust

It wasn't an easy situation that faced Kesselring. The German front in North Africa was crumbling and Rommel had begun his retreat from Tobruk which indicated that what was to be done had to be done quickly. But the German commander had no wild illusions. He was already aware of Malta's defences. Hadn't the Germans themselves only a month back described Malta's anti-aircraft barrage as the heaviest in the world? So he laid down a three-pronged plan. First he ordered reinforcement to the fighters protecting the most indispensable convoys. Secondly, intruder raids on Malta would have to commence which would be intensified until they could implement the third stage which would be a decisive air assault on the island to neutralise it once and for all.

These were the three points laid down by Field Marshal Kesselring, but there was a fourth point which was unspoken and nevertheless noted for implementation. An invasion of Malta. Hitler had rejected such a suggestion, giving as a reason that there were not enough forces to undertake it. But Kesselring was convinced that with the building up of the necessary forces, his proposal would not be rejected again.

So German aircraft reappeared in the Mediterranean, and began again to pound Malta on 4th December.

The re-entry of the Germans seemed to coincide with a drastic reversal for British naval forces. U-boat *U-557* torpedoed and sank the cruiser *Galatea* while the cruisers *Penelope, Aurora,* and *Neptune* ran into a newly-laid minefield. *Neptune* sank, while the other two were seriously damaged. The destroyer *Kandahar* also struck a mine and had to be sunk by her consorts. This brought Malta's K Force to an untimely end. As if this was not enough, the Decima Flottiglia Mas which had in July lost face in its attack on Malta, now delivered a similar attack on Alexandria and severely damaged the battleships *Queen Elizabeth* and *Valiant*. This run of misfortune was echoed in the Far East with the sinking of two other battleships, the *Prince of Wales* and *Repulse*.

To the ordinary man in the street who takes life as it comes such catastrophe might have brought a moment's pity to be shrugged off as yet another misfortune of war. But to the perceptive mind all this spelt a loud and clear message for Malta. These losses had weakened the British Mediterranean fleet to such an extent that with the German presence in this theatre of operations it had become impossible to attempt another convoy with any reasonable chance of success.

The battle was resumed in earnest with the Luftwaffe hammering Malta and the offensive operations against enemy convoys now mostly the responsibility of submarines, which of course in many cases had to depend on aerial reconnaissance. But more than a battle of aircraft and submarines, it now became also one of wits. From his end, knowing of the good defences at Malta, Kesselring ordered the attacks to be made by small formations, because, he reasoned, besides keeping his losses lower, this would exhaust more of the island's ammunition and petrol on less aircraft, thus weakening resistance for the invasion which, as has been indicated, he was still determined to carry out. On the part of Malta the authorities were alive to the food and supplies situation and immediately resumed a shuttle service by three submarines for the delivery of provisions and essential supplies. These were the *Clyde, Olympus,* and *Porpoise* which ran their supplies to Marsaxlokk. Theirs was a brave effort, but considering the fact that each submarine could carry only 200 tons of stores, mostly taken up by cans of aircraft fuel, it can be seen that this was only a drop in the ocean. Air Vice Marshal Lloyd also thought of the approaching day when the airfields would be subjected to continuous and murderous air attacks with obvious disastrous results for fighters. So a start was made to dig a parking place for fighters in the rock hill face at Ta' Qali Airfield. Another two measures which showed the sense of foresight in anticipating long continuous and heavy attacks were to encourage the population to dig private compartments in public shelters where families could remain for long periods and throughout the nights, and the introduction of the Compulsory Labour Service for everyone between the ages of 16 and 60 who was not in the services or in any essential job.

January 1942 brought with it merited honours for the three forces commanders. A KCB for Vice Admiral Wilbraham T.R. Ford, a Knighthood for Major General S.J. Scobell, and a CB for Air Vice Marshal Lloyd. There were also an OBE for Dr A.V. Laferla the Director of Education, an MBE to the Commissioner of Police Joseph E. Axisa, and Mr Emanuel Camilleri the Postmaster General. But any encouragement that such recognition of the island's efforts might have brought to Maltese hearts was shortlived, as it was overshadowed by a more sinister thought which was reflected in the New Year broadcast by Mr Nunn, Assistant to the Lieutenant Governor, clearly telling the population, this time without any innuendos, what was to be done in an invasion. There was the old fear again, and now with clear cut details for everyone to stay in his town or village, and keep off the streets. Protection Officers were to be given a stock of foodstuffs to see them through any emergency in their district. The warning of invasion would be by the ringing of church bells which from now on would no longer ring the All Clear. Until then it had been a prospect, imagined and unspoken, without the edge of a possible threat. Now it was officially given, and the exhausted public minds lost no time in turning it into an imminent one. And they could not be blamed.

The battle was continued in earnest with the Luftwaffe hammering every conceivable target in Malta. Stukas and Junkers 88 by day, accompanied by Messerschmitt 109 and 110s for low flying attacks and combat; Dorniers then took the night vigil. The guns and searchlights were fully extended; and so were the Hurricanes. But for these there had now developed a new threat with the German aircraft pressing their low flying attacks on airfields and destroying the precious fighters on the ground. It had become a common feeling for British pilots that it was safer to be in the air than in the now vulnerable parking pens. The Stukas had their vulnerable moments too. When they went into their renowned dive and flattened to come out of it they had a few moments when they lost control and formation. British pilots noticed this and that was when they attacked them with considerable effect. Kesselring learned of this after having paid dearly with many precious aircraft and he mentioned in his memoirs how he counter-acted by sending more of his fighters to dive with the Stukas so as to be at hand when the Hurricanes attacked. Not to be outdone the Hurricanes adopted another tactic by diving after the Stukas from altitudes as much as 30,000 and 40,000 feet through other German formations, even if they had to go after their prey straight through the anti-aircraft barrage, and there were cases of Hurricanes being hit by anti-aircraft fire. It could not be helped. It was a battle in which no quarter was being allowed. Kesselring himself did not fail to show his admiration and praise for these British pilots.

Like never before, it had suddenly become a straightforward fight for death between the Luftwaffe and the defences. With its small bomber formations, heavily escorted by fighters the enemy would pound a target until it got results, ignoring the losses it incurred in the process, and one after the other, every type of target was being attended to — harbours, dockyard, forts, airfields, gun positions; everything. Bombs were dropped by the hundred, hitting buildings and civilian areas together with the military, and making rubble out of cities which were once the pride of the island.

The gunners also had their ruses to adopt. St Peter Battery, one of the most prominent and hard-hitting, was from the very start manned by young recruits who were imbued with drill and tactics which had now become a part of their life. Being very often bombed the battery had adopted its own particular drill which 2nd Lieutenant Gerald Amato-Gauci, the GPO, had introduced. Two NCO's were always placed on the look-out with binoculars and they would follow the approaching bombers. As soon as they saw bombs being dropped they would blow a warning on a whistle which would be the signal for all exposed gunners to drop flat on the ground. As soon as the planes went past, the gunners would rise and go back into action. This drill was of course not adopted in dive-bombing attacks, when guns were kept firing in face of the diving planes. But in such cases 'Shrapnel Shells' were used, which when fired on Fuse 4 produced a 'Porcupine Barrage' and in more cases than not shot down or damaged the attacking aircraft. None of them would go unscathed, anyway, and very soon German pilots began to have a certain respect for this battery.

On 11th January the Germans pressed an attack on St Peter's and managed to place a few bombs in between the four guns. One of the bombs exploded only five yards away from the gun position in which 2nd Lieutenant Amato-Gauci was standing, directing his fire, and he was hit by splinters in the chin and in the neck. Although hurt and in great pain the Lieutenant carried on with the control of his guns, shouting orders and directing the fire, refusing to receive first aid until the attack was over. Afterwards he was admitted to hospital. This outstanding behaviour got him the Military Cross.

No one had noticed that on 1st January there had been 26 killed and 14 injured (which was a substantial number for people in rock bomb-proof shelters). There was neither any notice of the attacks on the airfields from 2nd to 3rd January, which kept going for 36 continuous hours; nor was there any satisfaction felt from the fact that notwithstanding all this the Wellingtons from Luqa bombed the enemy to smithereens at Castel Vetrano in Sicily, destroying 44 aircraft on the ground, 30 of which were troop transports ready to ferry troops to North Africa. It had, as has been said, become a fight of two blind giants pulping each other for dear life, with the civilian population, giving its share by sheer exhausted and furious resistance.

The long vigils in shelters during day and night were having their telling effect. Those who still had a house and belongings to go to, were spending hours listening to the battle raging outside, with hearts beating with every thud of an explosion or the rumbling of falling masonry, laying odds as to whether they would find their house again when they went out, or just a rubble of stone. This tension would not disappear after the raid was over for demolition and clearance squads were engaged in different and dangerous tasks, clearing roads and traffic arteries, demolishing dangerous buildings, carrying furniture and belongings to safety, and attending to a hundred and one tasks. They had to do ten jobs with one pair of hands. Police and ARP personnel had their hands full with different tasks as extricating dead and injured from beneath debris, reporting and guarding unexploded bombs. The rest of the population had a job to go on living — they had to queue for their foodstuffs and their kerosene, also for water when mains were broken, their children had to be sent to school, husbands had to be cared for, and houses or shelters had to be cleaned. For many of them there had to be the daily mass at the church or wherever services were held which not all the Luftwaffe's might could disturb. All this had to be done during intervals between raids, which were precious few, and thus putting more pressure and urgency on what had to be done. Time for life had become shorter, and it must have been this which brought about an amendment to legislation making it permissible for buses to keep running during air raids. But drivers could use their own discretion whether to stop or not. Even soldiers who were not engaged on anti-aircraft defence now had to take turns at the airfields clearing runways and filling craters after each attack, in order to keep the planes flying. More men were called up by conscription that month, and there were two changes in the military and naval commanders. Major General Scobell was replaced by Major General D.M.V. Beak, VC, DSO, MC as GOC, while Vice

Admiral Ford was replaced by Vice Admiral Sir Ralph Leatham, KBE.

Nothing was so important, however, that it could alienate one's attentions as long as the air attacks continued without respite. A heavy raid by Wellingtons on Catania on the 19th again went unnoticed, and even the reduction in kerosene entitlement failed to raise the expected comments, although it must have amplified the acute situation of supplies which everyone knew was fast approaching a climax.

There were no looks of preoccupation during the investiture held at the Governor's Palace in Valletta on 28th January, when Sir Edward Jackson the Lieutenant Governor was invested with the KBE, Professor A.V. Bernard the Chief Government Medical Officer was made a CBE, and the OBE was given to Dr P. Boffa, MD, and Lieutenant Colonel Edgar Salomone of the Royal Malta Artillery, while Mr Joseph Storace a Superintendent in the ARP Corps was awarded the BEM. These gentlemen had all been fully engaged in what Malta had been going through, and to some extent responsible for the good impression made by the various sectors they represented. But when they left the Palace to the sound of wailing sirens they knew that their fight was not over, and the awards they had received a short time before were in recognition for only a part of the battle. Because the fight would have to go on to the finish. What's more, they knew, as everybody else in Malta had noticed, that the air onslaught during January had escalated.

In fact against the 175 raids during December 1941, there had been 263 raids during January 1942, with casualties rising to 83 killed, and 135 injured.

One thing was certain which no one in Malta knew. This was only the prelude. Kesserling had still to launch the heavy assault.

*

There was no demarcation line between January and February, and everyone seemed to have lost count of time. Life had become like a continuous air attack and the only difference noted was the intensity which was constantly increasing with the obvious determination with which the enemy pilots seemed to be imbued in pressing their attacks home, notwithstanding the punishment they were receiving.

The local newspapers *Times of Malta* and *Il-Berqa* continued to keep the people abreast of the situation even when they had to come out with their pages charred by fire, and now they began to break down the tally of planes shot down attributing them to their avengers; anti-aircraft guns, Hurricanes and night fighters. It should be stated here that when their reports were verified thirty-seven years later they were found to have been more conservative than liberal, and the losses were indeed found to have been many more than was then given out. They did not report local losses and damage ; there was no need, as they were there for everybody to see. In a small island like Malta everyone could see the beacons from burning aircraft at the airfields, and the pulverized dockyard. The once beautiful harbour had become a fouled lake of wrecks and more than ever a dangerous gauntlet to run. Every tug boat and other vessel which could at some time be caught unaware during a raid, now had its Bren gun and the crew to man it. Not that this made any difference to the outcome but it made crews happier to know that if they had to die on their jobs they would die fighting. Docks, wharves and store houses were now rubble of cordite grey stone, the once white stone bastions were scarred, looking like multi-eyed monsters with eyeless sockets where bombs had struck. On 10th February, the feast day of St Paul, the patron saint of Malta, there was an additional wreck added in the harbour when the destroyer *Maori* was sunk during one of the ten raids on that day. At Lazaretto, in the port of Marsamxett, there was another daily story being related with the submarines which had their base there. Caught at their moorings as they were berthed at buoys only a few yards from the shore from which they could be reached by pontoons or floating cat-walks they very often became a sure target. After all they were still carrying out their offensive against German and Italian shipping to North Africa and between October 1941, and February 1942 they had sunk 54,000 tons of supply shipping, a destroyer, two submarines and two 7,000 ton ships near Taranto. Now the Germans seemed intent on vengeance, but when there was time the submarines submerged and lay on the seabed during a raid, sometimes going down and never coming up.

It was a situation which could not go on much longer. Every one knew it, but no one could say it better than the men juggling with the dwindling supplies. They had watched and hoped, and their faith in the Maltese had proved them right. The people had disciplined themselves and endured shortage. They had played up

and were even bearing hunger in silence. They had eaten carobs for
bread or drank murky concoctions for tea, smoked collected
cigarette bits wrapped in paper and in many other ways saved on
consumption of essential foodstuffs. But this could not go on
for ever. Even before the day when there would be nothing to
save, there was the question of ammunition and aviation spirit for
the fighters. There were no replacements for those. There had to
be another attempt made to bring in a convoy, however slim the
chances were. This attempt was made on 12th February.

Three fast merchant ships, the *Clan Campbell, Clan Chattan* and
Rowallan Castle, left Alexandria escorted by the anti-aircraft
cruiser *Carlisle* and seven 'Hunt' class destroyers. It was followed
further back by Force B under Admiral Vian comprising the
cruisers *Euryalus, Dido* and *Naiad* together with eight destroyers.
At the same time, and to be exact on the 13th, the empty
merchantmen *Breconshire, City of Calcutta, Clan Ferguson* and
Ajax which had been patiently waiting to leave Malta since the last
convoy in September 1941 left the island escorted by the cruiser
Penelope (now repaired) and six destroyers. The plan was for both
convoys to meet with the full ships going to Malta and the empty
ones to Alexandria changing escorts. With this convoy went also a
party of Maltese who had been interned since the outbreak of war
because of their sympathy for the Italian cause. They were to be
taken to Alexandria, on their way to Uganda, where they were
kept until the end of hostilities.

The convoy going to Malta was continuously attacked by
German aircraft from North Africa. *Clan Chattan* was hit by a
bomb from a Junkers 88, and as it was carrying ammunition it had
to be sunk by her escorts to avoid its exploding. The other two
ships were also lost, and not a single one reached Malta.

The impossibility of bringing in another convoy was a fact that
had to be faced. To make matters worse it began to be noticed
that rather than decreasing their efforts the Germans were still
escalating them not only with the number of incursions and size of
formations, but also with the use of faster and more battle-worthy
Messerschmitts. It must be said that the Hurricane had already
proved itself to be inferior to the faster type of Messerschmitt, and
if it had held its own so well it was only because of the excellent
pilots that flew it. But now, this difference was being felt in the
battle for Malta. There might have been other factors contributing
to this, such as the number of sorties that pilots had to fly every
day, the many times aircraft had to be repaired and be airborne

immediately after, and the numerical superiority they had to face in every air battle. The fact remains that Air Vice Marshal Lloyd knew he had to do something if the Royal Air Force was to remain in the Malta skies. The only solution was to get Spitfire fighters which were superior to the Messerschmitt.

So while those at the top put their heads together keeping their fingers crossed for time, the population continued with its fast, dug in debris to retrieve things from demolished buildings, cried over its dead and injured, and hoped for something to happen. It could not do anything else but hope. It had become clear that Malta had become a death trap and there was no possible escape. Nothing could go out and nothing could come in. Even the small fishing boats which crossed from Gozo were discouraged from coming after the many machine-gun attacks delivered against them.

It was unbelievable then how one could exist at all. The efforts that were being made by old and young alike were strenuous and required more and better food for achievement. Yet while the food situation was going from bad to worse there was not a moment's relaxation in the superhuman efforts that were surprising even the people who made them. The guns kept firing and shooting down the enemy with the same precision, the fighters kept flying and fighting against bigger odds, troops, policemen and civilians, Maltese and British worked round the clock on airfields filling craters and clearing debris to keep them serviceable. Farmers toiled in their blackened fields, trying to do the impossible.

All this was done on empty stomachs, filled only with defiance and hope. But hope for what? They just didn't know. Their only hope was in God and the Blessed Virgin, and faith never relaxed. It was this steadfast belief that kept them. They said it then; they still say it now.

While it was there, life went on, babies were born while their fathers fought the enemy or strived at their work, men and women died and their children grimly carried on; children somehow or somewhere attended school, and the priests were everywhere and with everyone with their holy administrations. The young in heart went to dances and the cinema. They were not even discouraged when the Regent cinema in Valletta was hit while the film *North West Mounted Police* was being run. The many killed and injured removed from the debris had become a part of history that was being made.

If this resistance was unbelievable in Malta it was equally astonishing all over the world. It surprised Kesselring himself. He knew his men and aircraft, and had no doubts about the havoc that the hundreds of heavy bombs, and incendiaries, must have wrought in Malta. If he wanted proof, this was given to him in the way Italian and German shipping losses were by February reduced from their previous 70%/80% to 20%/30%. But he could not understand how Malta still lived and fought. He thought he did, and attributed it to the rock shelters which in his opinion housed not only the people but even stores and aircraft. But he was wrong; very wrong in fact. The hundreds of guns that every day fired at his planes were not under rock. Neither were the men who manned them, nor the searchlight crews. The machine-gunners in the airfields, on searchlight positions, on the small boats in the harbours who fired at the attacking planes in defiance; these were not under rock. Nor were the Maltese and British infantrymen who took potshots with their rifles at low flying aircraft or the stevedores who stood by their cargoes until planes had passed over and unloaded in haste to take away stores by the time the enemy came for another try. Even Kesselring praised these stevedores. And were the fighter pilots that shot down his men under rock? The big losses that he admitted himself give him the reply. The hundreds of soldiers, policemen and civilians who were on the airfields waiting in slit trenches to rush out with spades and wheel-barrows of earth and fill the craters German bombs made on the runaways were not in rock. All this was brought forth from the brave and stout hearts of the responsible people — Maltese and British, which he could not bring himself to acknowledge. Under-estimation of Malta and her people was one of his errors.

As for the fighter planes, Kesselring was under the impression that there were rock hangars at Ta' Qali. It will be remembered that a start had been made on digging such a hangar but for some reason work was discontinued. However, when reconnaissance photographs revealed the ramp that had been made, and the mounds of rock and earth dumped close to it from the excavations that had been made, Kesselring concluded that the hangars existed and planned to attack them with special bombs which as we shall see later he did. His was only a waste of efforts, bombs, aircraft and men.

But even with these shortcomings he felt, as he himself wrote, that his second task in his three-pronged plan was accomplished. So he began preparations for his third task which was to be the big air assault. He explained this at a conference he held for his airmen at II Fliegerkorps Headquarters in Sicily. The basic idea, he said, was to surprise and neutralise the British fighters, or at least to cripple them so much that they would not be of any considerable danger to the ensuing bombing assault. He made his pilots aware at that conference of the powerful anti-aircraft defences on the island supported by naval anti-aircraft guns (so they were still there, even after he claimed he had accomplished his previous task?) which created a barrage to be penetrated only by stout hearts and at the loss of many aircraft. Another object in the assault would be that of heavy bomber raids on harbour installations during the day, with fighters for protection, while during the night there would again be nuisance raids by single aircraft to hinder the clearing up of wreckage and repairs. There was even to be the sinking of all supply ships making for the harbour and the blocking of this harbour by mines. Civilian buildings were to be spared.

This was the plan for his big air assault, which he entrusted to the direct command of Air Marshal Deichmann.

Being convinced that everything would go according to plan Kesselring was now ready to submit his proposal for the invasion of Malta again. He had already found support for his idea in the Italian Supreme Command (although support was promised subject to the destroying of Maltese coastal defences before the Italians would approach with their fleet) and with Rommel. Now that he had achieved his first success in restricting the sinkings of supply ships for North Africa he raised the matter again with Hitler in the presence of Göring. The Führer was adamant at first (as he had always been where paratroops were concerned after the invasion of Crete) but when tempers ran high Hitler grasped Kesselring by the arm and told him. 'Field Marshal Kesselring, I am going to do it,'

And the invasion of Malta was approved.

The draft plan for the invasion must have been burning in Kesselring's head since he had first thought of it. But only now he could speak confidently about it. This was his plan as reproduced, from his memoirs[1] :—

1. Attack by airborne troops to seize the Southern heights as a jumping off base for an assault to capture the airfields south of town and the harbour of Valletta, shortly preceded by a

---

[1] The Memoirs of Field Marshal Kesselring, William Kimber 1954.

      bombing raid on the airfields themselves and anti-aircraft
positions.

2. Main attack by naval forces and landing parties against the
   strong points south of Valletta and, in conjunction with
   parachute troops on the harbour itself, synchronized with
   bombing raids on coastal batteries.

3. Diversionary attack from the sea against the bay of
   Marsaxlokk.

With his plan approved he put it aside until he could accumulate
the forces that would be required to implement it. In the meantime the attacks continued on Malta in preparation for the big air
assault which he intended to launch in March.

Reverting to Malta, reeling under heavy attacks, in those last
days of February, let us have a quick recapitulation of the
situation. The island was virtually bombed out, and the harbours
in the process of being mined. Hurricanes had dwindled to a small
number which were being looked after like gold. Pens were built
for them in the dispersal areas round Ta' Qali airfield, with stone,
where it was available, then when this ran out, aviation spirit cans
filled with earth, were used. These pens gave protection from
splinters and bomb blast, but not from direct hits. But there were
so few planes that there was little time to be spent in their pens
during the day since they had to scramble five, six and even more
times a day; and each time they fought against bigger odds
inflicting damage but sometimes losing one or two themselves.
They knew that they were approaching the day when there would
be none of them to go up, or that there would be no more aviation
spirit or ammunition for those which remained.

It wasn't a healthy situation with a heavy air assault about to be
delivered. There were the anti-aircraft batteries which could after
all take the brunt of the attack on them. In this case any
destroyed guns could be replaced and there was no lack of
gunners. It would not be amiss to mention here all the anti-aircraft
forces that were available then, awaiting an assault of which they
did not know. There was first of all the 10th Heavy Anti Aircraft
Brigade which comprised two Maltese regiments from the RMA,
the 2nd and the 11th HAA, and two British regiments from the
Royal Artillery. Each regiment had 24 guns set up in 3 batteries
of two troops each with 4 guns. Between them these regiments
manned the following heavy anti-aircraft batteries, Tigne, Manoel
Island, Ta' Cejlu, Spinola, Ta' Giorni, Tal-Qroqq, Fleur de Lys,
San Giacomo, Hompesch, Zonqor, Marnisi, St Peter, Xrobb

il-Ghagin, Delimara, Ta' Karax, Gwarena, San Blas, Bizbizija, Gharghur, Salina and Wardija.

The 7 Light Anti-Aircraft Brigade provided the Bofors defence for low flying or diving aircraft. It was composed of the 3rd LAA Regiment of the Royal Malta Artillery comprising 10th, 15th, 22nd and 30th batteries. There were then the 32nd LAA, 65th LAA and 74th LAA of the regiment of Royal Artillery. Each Bofors regiment had 3 batteries with three troops of 6 guns each.

The 4th Searchlight Regiment comprised both Maltese and English soldiers.

It was an impressive array, without a doubt, that would be recorded in history for posterity. But would there be a history to be written? Those guns had already made it, resisting the Italian and German hordes and keeping the Malta skies free of the enemy. But for how long would they be able to do it? These questions were in the mouths of the gunners, as they no doubt looked at the dwindling number of shells in their magazines, dreading that hour when the word would come that there were no more. These were some of the feelings the whole island had about food, fighters and everything that was required to resist.

No one could do anything, but pray and hope.

CHAPTER TEN

O Lord, give us this day . . .

In the quiet of his study at the Palace in Valletta, Sir William Dobbie had sat hunched in his favourite chair, telephone cupped to his ear. He had been receiving a report about damage and casualties from the latest raids. Now he placed the telephone back and rose up from his chair. Dragging his feet he shuffled himself towards a big window and looked at the blue sky of that March morning. Although he was tall, now as he inclined his body forward his figure seemed that of a smaller man. The eyes beneath his bushy eyebrows that many had called 'magnetic' were feverish and red, as if he had not slept for days. His face was puffy, and its colour looked faded grey.

That last telephone call had told him of destruction in a town and two villages killing and injuring many and making four times as many families homeless. This would mean another journey to those places, as he had always done, to talk to the people who were hit and try to take some comfort to them. Not that this meant anything more than a few words that he knew by heart, but he would show that the stricken and the homeless were always in his thoughts — as if he had at any time been unaware of the people's plight throughout his term of governorship, twenty-two months of it under bombardment.

Indeed, the fate of Malta's population of nearly a quarter of a million was daily in his thoughts and his prayers. There was a time in the beginning when he was haunted by the possible reaction to severe bombing, but the Maltese had risen higher than his expectations and stuck to it admirably. There had also been the fear of invasion and the first shortages in food which had also been somehow surmounted. He had nothing but admiration for them. Their simple gestures whenever he talked to them after some raid, like kissing and wetting his hands with their tears or even patting him on the back left him moved beyond description. He even understood the sniggering of the gunners in anti-aircraft batteries when he left hastily at the sound of the alarm during any of his visits. But now there was a bigger fear coming to them of which they did not yet know. This time there would be no escape. Unless he got what he had been requesting.

He glanced at the sky again as if expecting what was uppermost in his mind to come from that direction, but there was only the open blue expanse which only an hour before had been full with the white cottony puffs of bursting anti-aircraft shells. Now it was clear again, but he knew it would not be for long. The sirens were bound to be wailing again any moment and the sky would then be full of death for the raiders as they themselves would rain death, as they had done one thousand five hundred times before. It would be resisted as the other raids were, but there was a limit to everything, and the feeling which had been weighing with him lately was heavy again telling him that the end was near. The gunners were tired, and so were the fighter pilots. Like them the people had suffered and borne everything with the stubborn faith they always had in Divine Providence. Now it had become a case of shells, aviation spirit and food, Providence could provide them, yes. No one believed that more than him. But they had not arrived yet, even if he had asked for them weeks before. He wanted them by 1st March. Now it was already the 7th.

There was a knock on the door and his ADC came in.

'The car is ready, your Excellency,' he said.

'I'll be down soon,' replied Sir William.

Alone again with his thoughts he felt the thrill of excitement he had been feeling lately when he thought of the hard decision he might have to make. That morning's run through the stricken localities would make him forget, but facing the misery that he knew was bound to be there would certainly not make his feelings any better, and the same problem would come to him again at the end of the day and haunt him throughout the night. What had he to say to the people he was going to visit? The same rigmarole as before . . . that the misery was bound to end? And when? In three months' . . . a year's time? But how could he bring himself to say something like that as he knew of the severe shortage of ammunition for the guns, and the inadequacy of the few remaining fighters, now, just when the enemy intended to launch a deadly final assault? Only he and another handful knew this, and he was appalled to learn of its imminence. All he knew about it was that it would come in early March. The news had sent him into a frenzy and he had pestered England for immediate reinforcements. He had then waited from day to day hoping that they would arrive before the Germans. Otherwise all would be lost. He needed planes, pilots, aviation spirit, ammunition, spares and food supplies as a first stage to resist the coming onslaught. If there were to be an invasion he would need more artillery pieces, tanks, petrol, ammunition and even more rifles for the new men that had been conscripted. He suddenly realised the impossibility of what he was asking, and the decision that had been eating his heart loomed stronger and unavoidable. He trembled; but it could wait.

There was a crowd waiting for him at Luqa, the village close to the airfield. The parish priest, police officers, ARP officials and the Protection Officer greeted him, then they walked together to the area where the last bombs had struck. Sir William stopped to look at what must have once been a busy village street. Now it was a sea of rubble lined on both sides by crazily tilted buildings which threatened to collapse at any moment. ARP men were still working on site, helped by policemen and some soldiers. A RAF ambulance was standing by.

'What's the score?' asked Sir William.

'Fortunately not many,' said a superintendent of police. 'Because all the people were in the shelters. There were only nine, all belonging to the same family.'

'Weren't they in a shelter then?'

'Oh yes they were. It was a private one beneath their house. But the shelter gave away into a cistern and the nine occupants were obviously drowned more than anything else.'

When he went to have a look at those who were rendered homeless it was a different picture. They were temporarily housed in one room in a school, and as he walked in, it appeared as if more people were filing in behind him into the already crowded place. For a moment Sir William stood silent, listening impassively to the din of conversation. He could not understand a word of it, but he could see from the looks and gestures that accompanied the talk that it was all about the ordeal that they had just been through, and on what awaited them. They stopped talking as soon as they saw him and realised who he was, then one after the other the women began crying and some of them began to speak in a loud voice trying to tell him in English what had happened to them. He had the disquieting feeling that those weeping women had somehow convinced themselves that he could work some miracle and give them back what they had lost. Then he felt like crying himself as he momentarily retreated into his black dream and felt impotent even to avert the worse that might come to them later. Sir William went round, shaking hands and saying a kind word. He assured them that they would be taken care of and be given money from the Relief Fund, but they needed their houses and belongings back, had it been possible.

'You will have them, don't you fear, when this is all over,' he told them.

'But when will it be over, sir?' said one of them.

'When we all are killed,' said another, pressing her baby to her chest and covering his face with kisses.

'Don't you worry, friends, we'll beat the Hun.' It was an old man in his late seventies who said this, and walking to him Sir William felt he had saved him from giving an answer.

'Has your house been destroyed as well?' he asked him.

'Yes, Excellency,' he said, and the everlasting smile on his face gave the lie to what must have been his inner feelings.

'I see you still retain your spirit?' remarked Sir William.

'Oh yes, sir, I am always like this, sir. I was at Gallipoli, you know?'

'Were you?' asked Sir William. 'I don't think it was as hot as this over there.'

'Maybe. But there we were shot at by our own ships. Here at least we're giving the Germans hell, and it won't be long when they will have no more planes to send over Malta.'

'It's good to see you in such spirits. What's your name?'

'Indri.'

'I suppose that is for Andrew. Well, Indri, keep hoping and smiling as you are and we'll win.'

'Hoping, Sir?' said the old man as if he was surprised that the governor should say such a thing. 'I *know* this from my sons.'

'Where are your sons?'

'They are both in the artillery, sir, and every time they come home they tell me how many planes they shoot down. We shall be better off when the Speedfires come.'

There was a sudden movement in Sir William's stomach when he heard the old man obviously referring to Spitfire fighters. He too was hoping for Spitfires, but all he had seen of them was the word spelt on teleprinter. Even so, he had ensured the news did not go beyond the four or five who knew of it.

'What do you know about Spitfires, Indri?' he asked the old man.

'All I know is that they are killers . . . and they will save Malta.'

'But who told you they were coming?'

'The airmen at the airfield told me, sir. I spend most of my days there, tending to their garden and growing vegetables for the cook house. They told me everything about Speedfires and they will come . . . soon.' He stopped to regain his breath, then he continued, 'I know they will, because I pray to God and ask him this. Every morning.'

It was a heartened Sir William who went to Floriana to see the next group of homeless. Instead of the normal fifteen minutes the drive took him twice as long. Again and again clogged streets forced his driver to make complicated detours. Then he had to make the last couple of hundred yards on foot since the main street was impassable. To his surprise he found only the official people awaiting him. No homeless, no curious crowd. What happened?

'Everybody is in the tunnel, your Excellency,' someone told him.

'The tunnel? But surely these people do not remain in the tunnel on such a sunny day? The more so after the long hours that they have been spending in that damp place.'

They were walking whilst he talked, and he looked at the desolation that was around him. The area resembled a battlefield, with huge craters in gaping streets, piles of masonry, smashed statuary and uprooted trees. The Church of St Publius was still standing notwithstanding the fact that its walls and facade were full of splinter marks but close to it there was an area with severe damage. Once magnificent gardens had been there. Now they were gone.

It must have been the pained look in his eyes as he looked at this that kept the others from answering Sir William's question when they entered the tunnel. The old railway tunnel was literally packed with people in a stifling and unreal atmosphere. There were men, women and children of all ages, pressed body to body in the centre space between tiers of sleeping bunks. Young boys not yet eighteen were with their beautiful consorts, and a couple of middle aged women gaudily coiffeured for the old profession which since time immemorial had its centre of activity at Balzunetta in Floriana and Strait Street in Valletta. They were now two sheep in a flock, with their sensuous lips moving concurrently with their fingers on the rosary beads. Nobody seemed to have noticed the entrance of Sir William at their back, and eyes never wavered from the small altar at the far end full of wild yet beautiful flowers and lit candles, where a priest was saying mass.

Sir William stood at the back, silent and apparently moved, as if listening impassively to the din of the prayers being recited. For the most part it consisted of the rosary which was now coming to the end. He would have remained silent had not the parish priest who was in the tunnel seen him and made his way through the crowd in his direction.

'I am sorry I wasn't there to meet you, your Excellency,' he told him in a subdued voice.

'It doesn't matter,' replied Sir William in a lowered voice. Then, looking at the Superintendent of Police, he said: 'So this is where the people are?'

'Yes,' said the parish priest, 'being the first Saturday of the month the people are holding the usual devotions to our Lady. It was the same yesterday having been the First Friday of the Sacred Heart devotions.'

Sir William knew of those two days in the Maltese Catholic's life and looking at the sea of faces intent on the altar and the officiating priest he guessed what the congregation in that tunnel was praying for. There were words being uttered that he could understand, and there was a moment when he could have sworn he heard the word Speedfire, even as Indri had pronounced it. Then he concluded it must have only been his imagination. Without another word he left, with his entourage following him.

The blue waters of Calcara, like a series of moving mirrors, reflected the multi-coloured boats as they pulled at their moorings It seemed that every one of the two hundred odd persons that still lived beneath rock in that picturesque fishing village had a boat. It wasn't exactly so, but many of the shelter families in Coronation Garden in Vittoriosa which was quite close to the bay had obtained a boat even if it was never taken out of the bay. Until a month before there had been more boats, but many of them fell victim to bombs and mines that were dropped there.

Today the word went round that the Governor would be paying a visit to the village to see the damage that had been caused during the morning raid, and the people had gone to the bay to see Sir William. Maybe it was only an excuse on their part to enjoy the warm sun of that beautiful March day. There were many flower beds in that area, most of them with wild white, red and yellow flowers which were all out, and although it was only 7th March even the air was redolent of spring. The characteristic peacefulness of the village was broken by the voices of those who had flocked there as if in a festive mood. Never had Calcara seen so many

people since some months back when an Italian hospital ship
crossing from North Africa to Italy had been taken there by
British warships in order to be inspected. I was there on that
occasion, when an Italian General, frightened of flying the
Mediterranean, had taken passage in that hospital ship as a
stretcher-case, and was removed and taken ashore.

When the Governor's car arrived, the crowd broke into clapping.
Two men broke the police cordon and rushed to open the door for
him and when he came out he was shaken by the hand and patted
on the back. For them he was their hero. His imposing figure did
not belie the image. He had the usual words of welcome and
encouragement, then followed by the crowd he walked to where
thirty people rendered homeless lined up to meet him. There were
the usual pitiful sobs, but on the whole it was not too bad. There
had been only two killed and five injured who were already
comfortable in hospital. The homeless had lost their houses but
they had already been living in shelters. What belongings they
could save were already being removed to a boathouse.

The easiness of this, his last task for the day, made him linger
and talk to the people who seemed to be so excited to have the
Governor amongst them. The parish priest and the superintendent
of police were busy telling him about war life in the village and
were continuously interrupted by those who wanted to give their
own version of the incidents being related. After half an hour he
decided he had had enough. He remembered he had to see Sir
Edward Jackson his Lieutenant Governor, about a meeting he had
to attend on that day about the introduction of a communal
feeding scheme. That brought back the thoughts that had tortured
him during his previous two visits to Luqa and Floriana; but he
found consolation in the fact that at Calcara there had been no
mention of Spitfires. However, if this thought had been absent in
the village minds, it now became stronger in his. He looked at his
watch and saw that it was half past one. Time was running fast
towards the end of another day bringing closer what had by now
settled heavily on his heart.

Then it happened. It began with the noise of aircraft engines,
far away, but steady. Some of the crowd began walking away at a
fast pace, knowing immediately what the noise was. Others were
looking at Sir William's face now uplifted to the sky intent to see
what was approaching. Then the noise became stronger and nearer.
There was now no doubt it was that of fast low flying aircraft,
coming below radar coverage as the Germans sometimes did, to

drop bombs before any alarm was given.

'It's the Germans,' someone shouted, 'they came in without warning.'

The crowd took up the shout and began dispersing quickly. A couple of women screamed, others took up children in their arms and ran. Someone told Sir William to take cover; but he didn't budge. This was it, he must have thought, as his gaze did not move from the blue sky above. Then they came, silvery streaks skimming the bastions of Grand Harbour climbing steeply to avoid steeples and cupolas as if they had not expected them and vanishing in the distance to make place for others. Sir William stood there watching, and counting . . . one . . . two . . . three . . . Then a small boy who had stood alone gave a shout.

'Hurrah . . . Spitfires.'

His shout stopped everyone in his tracks. Those who were running away turned round and ran back, all began to clap, some were suddenly shouting hysterically but not forgetting to exclaim words of thanksgiving to God, Santa Maria and a host of saints. And their shouting was joined by that from a thousand throats from the bastions on the other side of Grand Harbour.

Only Sir William remained silent, as if unmoved. But there were tears in his eyes, and something in his throat was choking him from saying anything. When finally he found his voice after the fifteenth Spitfire had disappeared he was heard saying faintly : 'So they have done it after all.'

Indeed they had. Those first fifteen Spitfires had flown straight from the aircraft carrier *Eagle* lying south of the island of Majorca.

*

There was an enthusiastic air everywhere on Sunday 8th March 1942. The same people who had daily been showing their preoccupation and fear about the obvious situation were all suddenly talking about the arrival of the Spitfires. The young were explaining to the old how these planes were superior to the German fighters and how they would turn the tables in Malta as they had done in Britain. Those who did not understand just nodded ; those who were not impressed fought down their fears by listening to what was being said without commenting. When the first raids of the day came there were many new faces outside by the shelter entrances, bubbling with expectation to see the Spitfires beating hell out of the Germans. It would now be possible for convoys to reach Malta unmolested. Their faith was almost childlike, however — vague and unclear. But there were no engagements for anyone to see.

Then when the darkness of night fell and the sirens began wailing again for a series of attacks the radiance that had been shared with everybody soon dimmed. The thuds of exploding bombs were heard in the shelters of Rabat and Mosta, and it wasn't difficult those inside them to know that the airfield of Ta' Qali was being bombed.

'Santa Maria', exclaimed one woman hysterically, 'they must be attacking the Speedfires.' Her words gave birth to a new prayer that night for the safety of the planes. The attacks continued right through the night and most of the following day, and when the news ran that four planes were shot down there was the same question on everybody's face. But no Spitfires were mentioned.

The new darlings went into action on 10th March. The sirens wailed, and a formation of three Junkers 88s, heavily escorted by Messerschmitt 109s flew in. The Spitfires had flown high where they were hardly visible to the naked eye; the guns opened up on the bombers; then in the Fighter Operations Control Room, the Duty Controller got the clarion call — 'Spitfires engaging'. The blue sky outside became like a circus arena with the British fighters swinging out of formation one after the other and diving onto the Messerschmitts. The guns had shot down one Junkers, then suddenly they stopped as if the gunners too wanted to watch the show which was entertaining the crowds that had come out of their shelters. There were noises of cheering at the aerobatics in the dogfights that ensued, and suddenly crowds broke into mad clapping as one Messerschmitt went spiralling down to earth. Two others were seen flying away with smoke coming out of their engines, and children were dancing and calling out in loud voices *'Achtung Spitfeur'* which they had learned from days of the Battle of Britain.

The final score for that day was one Junkers to the guns, with two definite and four probable Messerschmitts to the Spitfires. The Hurricanes, because they were also in the scuffle, had two probables. It was the needed tonic to close the day on an enthusiastic note.

But Sir William could not share his people's enthusiasm and their triumph. Three more days had passed with a steady flow of foodstuffs, aviation spirit and ammunition, without any indication of possible bulk replacement. This line of thought had become methodical with him since the last month. He had always been a hopeful man, but now he was seeing his hopes for relief like running through an hour glass. In all his years as a professional soldier he had never imagined being faced with such a situation. Yet, he had to find answers for each problem — and quickly. The question of food supplies took priority. It was one thing imposing half rations and sleeping parades to avoid food consumption on the disciplined garrison, and another dealing with civilians. He had just agreed to reduce the issue of safety matches to a ridiculous two boxes every fortnight per family, but food was a different matter. Yet, it had to be done. A communal feeding scheme had been worked out whereby all remaining foodstuffs would be pooled to provide cooked meals for distribution in every town and village, and every head of the population would be sure to get one meal a day, and no more. This would bring some control and much saving on provisions, even at the expense of sacrifice and discontent. It would bring also another advantage in distributing what was left in equivalent portions until supplies ran out. If the people were to die of hunger then they would die together.

It had been a hard scheme to work out, and harder to decide upon, but now, with no news about the convoy that was to be attempted there was no alternative. As for aviation spirit and ammunition it was a harder problem. He couldn't very well stop the barrage and the fighters. There could be some sort of restriction . . . yes, that was what had been mentioned at the last meeting — restricting gunfire and flying sorties.

'Oh God', he exclaimed to himself, 'how could one think of having to watch the Germans pick on their targets and destroy them piecemeal, without lifting a finger? Because it would come to that whenever a day's allowance was exhausted. Maybe it would have to be done until the convoy came in. But when was it going to come? And if it never arrived? Or should the onslaught which was inevitable took place before it? In moments like this he thought that he would have preferred it to happen; he would at least have no choice and would use everything until the island went bust. There was a moment of indecision — maybe it could be called weakness, but he decided not to press for the restrictions.

He decided on the launching of the communal feeding scheme, and had no difficulty in agreeing to the Red Flag arrangement which the meeting had proposed in an endeavour to leave more time for work. The arrangement was to hoist a red flag after air raid warnings, to indicate the areas on which attacks were likely.

Those outside these areas would be free to stay out of shelter and continue with their work. The master flag was to be hoisted on the Palace Tower where the one controller would be, and other areas where work was to be done, like Sliema, and the airfields would have to receive their instructions from there.

This arrangement was put into operation on 17th March, with the addition of the flying of a red and white pennant when a raid was not expected to develop into bombing.

The people were quick to give the arrangement their own interpretation — red for bombers, red and white for fighters. The dockyard where most of the essential work was done introduced also the sounding of a fog horn when it was indicated that the attack was likely to be directed against the harbour, and it was this warning which sent the workers to their shelters. There was also the question of more men being required to help the airmen, soldiers and policemen standing by at the airfields to make them serviceable after each raid, and he had no difficulty in agreeing to the issue of a call for volunteers to go and do a spell of work at Ta' Qali airfield every day. Notwithstanding all the hardships there was a very good response to this call and truckfuls of men began flowing in from the very first day.

These were some of Sir William's problems which he tried to solve. Indeed everyone had problems. Churchill was urging early action in the Middle East theatre with the fighting almost at a standstill while Malta was being reduced to the extremity by the Germans' sustained air attacks. Whoever was responsible was in a bundle about mounting a convoy for the island if heads were not to roll. From the Western side too preparations were hurried to mount another force to deliver more Spitfires to Malta. Plans were completed to move out both convoys at the same time, and the date was fixed for 20th March.

Kesselring too had his problems. He had initially given his orders for the onslaught on Malta to begin at the beginning of March, and Marshal Deichmann, his chief of staff, had issued instructions to his units. However, a Security Officer happened to find the original stencil used for these instructions still intact in a dustbin where a Sicilian orderly had dropped it. Hell was raised by the suspicious officer, obviously presuming that unauthorized eyes might have seen those instructions, and the onslaught was postponed, conveniently allowing Malta to receive its first Spitfires. Any Maltese would have interpreted this as an answer to prayer had it been known. And nobody could say it wasn't.

Now Kesselring gave his second and final orders for the onslaught. Malta was to be heavily bombed without respite. The job was entrusted to the II Air Group Messina under the personal direction of Air Marshal Deichmann, and the objectives were three — the aircraft on airfields, the anti-aircraft batteries, and ships and warships in harbours. All these had to be destroyed, with the heaviest bombs available. The mining of harbours from the air was also to continue. German pilots had already reported the mounds of accumulated earth which they had noticed at Ta' Qali airfield which had come out from the tunnelling of a hangar in the rock face. Although this was discontinued, Kesselring was convinced that it had been completed, therefore he ordered attacks to be made against it by Jabo bombs. These were rocket-propelled bombs which would be fired horizontally at the cliff face to penetrate into the rock hangar, which in fact did not exist.

The onslaught, which would continue until Malta was completely neutralized, was ordered to start, as fate would have it, also on 20th March.

CHAPTER ELEVEN

The Assault

Even as the last bombers from the night raids which had lasted from 2230 hours of the previous day were turning away from Malta, the first rays of light were coming up in the east. The stillness of the morning was broken by the first people coming out of their shelters chattering as they hurried to their first tasks of the new day. Two pillars of smoke drew silent attention to the residue of a night-long enemy activity. Dockyard workers gulped quickly a cup of sugarless tea from their home or shelter, took up what Providence and a thoughtful wife might have kept for them from the previous day and hurried for their day's toil. Those who could get the early papers were scanning the headlines, most of which were on the machine-gunning of the two Gozo Boats *Royal Lady* and *Franco* on the previous day during their passage between the two islands. Fortunately there had only been three injured. But even these incidents had now become almost insignificant occurrences to be waved aside in the face of other problems. There were heavier pre-occupations to tax one's mind. The blackened remains of desolation where whole neighbourhoods had disappeared accompanied one throughout the way to house or work, and these were enough to anchor one's own feelings and living to the ever-existing danger the end of which no one could foresee; the empty larders, patched up trousers and coats which at any other time would have disgraced a scarecrow; empty stomachs which could not even be given what water was required, and much less the food. There was all this, and the stark expectation of what the new day would bring.

The first hours of 20th March went past as others before them with a mixture of relief from the respite and the sadness of conviction that this would not be for long. Housewives hurried with their first chores of the day after they had seen their husbands off to work or duty, and their children to school where this was still functioning. But hardly had they settled down for the coming day when across the tormented island the sirens began wailing an air raid warning. Those at home dropped everything and rushed out. It had now become their drill. In the harbour area those who remembered the new instructions looked at the Palace Tower, but they need not have troubled, the red flag was up, and the dockyard typhoon was blaring its macabre note. At Ta' Qali airfield Spitfires and Hurricanes were scrambled, and the anti-aircraft batteries were fed with the plot. Whatever warships were in harbour had their anti-aircraft guns manned to join in defence. Those were the new orders.

The enemy lost no time in arriving — six Junkers 88s, and a horde of Messerschmitt 109s. The guns went into action against the bombers while Spitfires and Hurricanes took the superior force of fighters aside. One Junkers 88 was blown to smithereens, but not before it had released its bombs, some of which fell on civilain buildings. The other five bombers flew lower and pressed their attack home on ships and warships in the harbour. As they came within range they were taken in hand by the Bofors, and one persisting Junkers pressed a sole attack on the submarine base at Lazaretto with a Bofors from Hastings Curtain on the Valletta Bastions pumping tracer shells into its fuselage. However, it persisted, dropped its bombs where it intended, and then flew out. It was the same story with the others. They all received heavy punishment, but they carried out their mission. No one could deny them that.

Those who were out watching the dogfights on that morning had their first experience of the Spitfire's versatility. In the midst of a mixed action one Messerschmitt climbed up towards the sun, and a Spitfire broke the ranks to go after it. It reached the German plane as it was flattening from its climb, obviously assuming it had the advantage of the sun blinding any pursuer. But there was the Spitfire on its tail, and as it flattened out the British fighter opened fire. The Me rolled over on its side and went down in a spiral spin, and the watchers on the ground expected to see the Spitfire breaking up the action. But it did not; it kept following the Me firing at it all the time and stopping only after it had dropped into the sea. Then the Spitfire broke off at 200 feet over the water, and climbed back to find another one.

There were two further attacks that morning, similarly by formations of 6 Junkers 88s and a swarm of Messerschmitt 109s, and they were also directed against shipping in the harbours. The toll for that morning was one Ju88 destroyed with two probables, and one Me109. One British fighter was also lost. There was a lull during the afternoon, which was broken only by one alarm because of a single reconnaissance aircraft which was engaged by anti-aircraft fire. It must have observed the results of the morning's raids. What it might not have noticed were the submarines *Pandora* and *P-36* which were now at the bottom of Lazaretto Creek, never to surface again. The Polish submarine *Sokol* which was close to them had been missed and was still at its mooring.

In themselves these raids did not give any indication of any escalation in attacks, and if there was anyone who was unduly worried it was Sir William who had by then received information about the two convoys which had left Gibraltar and Alexandria together and was keeping his fingers crossed that they would reach Malta without mishap. But the determined attacks on shipping did not augur well. Even so, he could at least hope that the convoys would reach Malta before the onslaught.

There, however, he had no chance.

Half an hour before dusk, on that same day, the onslaught proper was launched. Following the alarm, a plot of 200 plus was indicated. Gunners and pilots knew that this was something new. In fact it was, in many respects. The first formation of fifty Junkers 88 heavily escorted by fighters crossed the coast and was immediately engaged by the 3.7 guns of 'Sally', the anti-aircraft battery at Salina. When German raiders attacked after noon they always took this route in order to get the sun behind them, and 'Sally' was necessarily always the first battery to open up on the raiders, with the inland batteries following up as if they were players in an orchestra in which 'Sally' was the conductor. Either the psychological effect of this or the precision of the firing placed this battery at the top of the German list for annihilation. On 20th March it was no exception and the men of 9th Battery, of the 2nd Heavy Anti-Aircraft regiment who manned the guns blazed away with relish. The enemy formation however was soon out of touch as the bombers flew through the inner barrage until they reached Ta' Qali airfield where they commenced their dive. As they released their collection of heavy bombs, the whistling like that of a thousand lost souls intermingled with the hammering sound of Bofors and the rattling of ground machine guns, to make what one could only describe as an infernal pandemonium. The fighters overhead had in the meantime engaged the enemy force. The smoke from the explosions had not yet cleared when a second wave came in, and this time the bombs were being dropped line by line in the system of carpet-bombing. Wave after wave of attacking aircraft kept coming in at regular intervals for a steady half an hour, dropping a variety of bombs; the heaviest contact fuse bombs; delayed action; deep penetration; incendiaries and anti-personnel. One of the last waves was armed with Jabo rocket-propelled 2000kg bombs, which they fired horizontally at the cliff face where Kesselring thought there were rock hangars. Finally there were the Messerschmitt 110s flying low with small calibre bombs and sweeping machine-gun fire. The pressure was eased only when darkness had fallen and it was time for the searchlights to light up the skies. They made three illuminations, and what guns could fire played up with gusto.

After the planes had left it looked as if there had been the day of reckoning at Ta' Qali. Devastation reigned supreme both on the runways and the dispersal areas. Aircraft pens disappeared, buildings were demolished and the whole area was like a moon landscape pot-holed with craters. The soldiers, policemen and auxiliary workers that were there emerged with their spades and wheelbarrows to fill up the craters on the runways but there was the immediate problem of unexploded bombs which began to go off. There was no question of waiting for the bomb disposal squads to clear the ground because there were fighters with almost empty tanks wanting to land. So they set to work, throwing caution to the wind, and the fires from still burning aircraft provided what light was required.

This attack cost the enemy heavily. No British fighters were shot down in fighting, but some were destroyed on the ground. The people in the shelters who heard the continuously rambling sounds of battle knew that this was something out of the ordinary. Sir William was aware that Kesselring's onslaught on Malta had begun.

Whilst this drama was being enacted in Malta there was other activity going on both to the east and west of the island. The convoy from the east had left Alexandria. With code name MW10 it consisted of the merchantmen *Breconshire, Clan Campbell, Pampas* and *Talabot*. These were escorted by the anti-aircraft cruiser *Carlisle* and the destroyer *Zulu, Hasty, Havoc, Sikh, Hero* and *Lively*. But Admiral Vian followed further backwards with the light cruisers *Dido, Euryalus* and *Penelope*, together with some destroyers. As soon as the convoy was located it was reported to Admiral Iachino of the Italian Navy who hurried to it with his squadron composed of the battleship *Littorio* and the destroyers *Aviere, Grecale, Ascari, Oriani, Scirocco* and *Geniere*. At the same time he signalled to another squadron made up of the cruisers

Gorizia, Trento and *Giovanni delle Bande Nere,* accompanied by the destroyers *Fuciliere, Bersagliere, Lanciere* and *Alpino,* and asked them to meet him so as to make a combined force. The rendezvous was for Sunday 22nd March when he expected to meet the convoy in the Gulf of Sirte where he was convinced he would destroy it since his force was extremely superior in power and gunfire to that of the British.

On the same day Force N had left Gibraltar with the battleship *Malaya,* the cruiser *Hermione* and eight destroyers, together with the aircraft carriers *Eagle* and *Argus* which were carrying Spitfires for Malta. It was a heart-rending drama that was being enacted. With Malta in her last throes, needing fighters, foodstuffs, and ammunition if she were not to succumb, she was fighting it out trying to keep out the enemy until the fighters from the west, and the foodstuffs and ammunition from the east could reach her. But, in the circumstances, both convoys had to get through. One would not suffice.

Only Sir William and his crowd knew that was going on. What the garrison and the people knew was that they would never be let down, and since stocks were at rock bottom there must be something in the offing. Because of this they continued to fight and resist.

March 21st was similar to the day before. It began with a mass attack on Ta' Qali airfield by waves of bombers escorted by fighters. Then there was a second attack in the afternoon with 75 Junkers 88s coming in waves with Messerschmitt 109s and 110s. The story of the previous day repeated itself. But there was a bright spark to the black outlook that was left by the raids when sixteen new Spitfires flew in after having been launched from the *Eagle* and the *Argus* south of Majorca, One convoy had done it. In the three attacks on Ta' Qali the Germans lost twenty planes.

As soon as Admiral Vian knew of the approaching Italian squadron he moved forward with his small force to stand between the convoy and the Italians. When these were sighted on the morning of 22nd March, Vian knew immediately that he was not only heavily outnumbered but also outgunned since Iachino had the 15-inch guns of *Littorio,* and 8-inch guns of the cruisers against his 6-inch and 5¼-inch. So the British ships laid a smokescreen to prevent the Italians from taking proper range. They began to dash in and out of the smokescreen firing damaging salvoes at their superior opponents and then doubling up behind the smoke before the Italians could take range.

The engagement was broken off that morning, but the Italian squadron approached again in the afternoon. This time Admiral Vian closed the range to under 10,000 yards and emerging out of the smoke screen succeeded in hitting the *Littorio* with a salvo which started a fire on the battleship. Then the British destroyers attacked out of the smoke blanket and succeeded in hitting the *Littorio,* again with a torpedo and the *Giovanni delle Bande Nere.* The Italians withdrew, though there was more to it than this, because, as Italian reports say, two of their destroyers sank on their way to their base, while the stricken *Giovanni delle Bande Nere* on her way to La Spezia was torpedoed and sunk by Malta-based submarine *Urge.* This was recorded for history as the Second Battle of Sirte.

In the meantime the convoy was untouched by the Italians and carried on towards Malta when the Germans took over and attacked it from the air. It soon became a running battle with all the British warships closing up to take the brunt of the attack and firing madly at the German planes in an effort to save that convoy, which they knew must reach Malta.

On the other hand the Germans were determined to prevent it from reaching harbour. The drama had suddenly switched to the convoy on which so much depended. There were 26,000 tons of material being carried in those ships which was a prize for both sides, to be saved or destroyed. But when the ships were fifty miles away from Malta, the Germans hit *Clan Campbell* and sank her. Admiral Vian was desperate and continued to fight for the rest. On 23rd March the convoy moved within reach of fighter protection from Malta, and from daybreak Hurricanes and Spitfires flew out to protect the remaining ships. From 8 a.m. the first engagement took place, and relays of Hurricanes and Spitfires took it in turn to fight off the German planes which were now doing their utmost to sink the ships as they plodded their way towards Malta. By 5 o'clock in the afternoon the Germans had lost two Junkers 88s and a Heinkel 111, and a further eight Junkers 88s were so damaged that it was unlikely they reached base. There was not a single casualty in British aircraft. Malta as such was not touched on that day as the Germans were concentrating all their efforts on the convoy.

On the following day, 24th March, the ships were within sight of Malta, only eight miles away and Admiral Vian breathed a sigh of relief. Another hour or two and they would come within shelter of the Malta guns, but as luck would have it, in the next attack the *Breconshire* was hit. Fortunately she did not sink but was considerably slowed down in speed. Admiral Vian was faced with a dilemma as to whether to slow the whole convoy or to leave the *Breconshire* to make her own way. It was an obvious decision. He made the destroyer *Southwold* take it in tow. Then leaving the cruiser *Penelope* and the anti-aircraft cruiser *Carlisle* to defend her, he proceeded with the other two ships to Malta, now so near and yet so far.

Air Marshal Deichmann in Sicily was soon informed of the *Breconshire's* plight and quickly despatched 30 Stukas escorted by as many Messerschmitt 109s, with orders to destroy her. They arrived like hounds with the scent of the hare in their nostrils flying in pairs and line astern at a height of 5,000 feet, and following a zig-zag course so as to evade attack. But the Spitfires and Hurricanes were ready for them. They were determined that the *Breconshire* should enter port. While the Spitfires took care of the Messerschmitts the Hurricanes went onto the Stukas and broke up the formation before they could dive. An aerial battle ensued which ended with two M109s being destroyed and fifteen Stukas being so damaged that they would probably not reach their base. Heads became so hot and tempers frayed in the fighting, that one Hurricane pilot pumped not less than 1,200 cannon shells into the fuselage of a Stuka before letting go. The *Breconshire* was not hit, and made to continue her way for the last two miles to Malta, when suddenly there was an explosion as the destroyer *Southwold* which was towing her struck a mine and sank. There was no time to lose and reaction was quick and efficient. The two towing tugs from Malta *Robust* and *Ancient* came out to help and between them towed the *Breconshire* into Marsaxlokk harbour.

The *Pampas* and *Talabot* had in the meantime entered Grand Harbour. The Germans would however give no chance to unload and resumed their heavy attacks. These were delivered by strong formations of Junkers 88s and Stukas, always escorted by Messerschmitt 109s with no more than two hour intervals between one attack and another. Attacks were also maintained through the night. However on the night between the 24th and 25th the last of five raids was over by midnight, and work however light could be started on the unloading from *Pampas* and *Talabot*. On that first day of the drama that ensued, with the *Pampas'* derrick gear put out of order, stevedores unloaded 310 tons of stores by hand. Another 330 tons were unloaded from *Talabot*. But there wasn't much that could be done because very early on the morning of the

25th the first reconnaissance aircraft were over the island, and soon after breakfast the first heavy attack of the day took place. This time waves of bombers, as always escorted by Messerschmitt 109s, flew along the eastern coast as if to deceive the defences about their intention. Then suddenly they swerved inland and attacked Hal Far airfield. No sooner were the first bombs being dropped on Hal Far than half the aircraft force turned round and proceeded into a straight attack on Grand Harbour.

In the afternoon there was a repetition by a heavy force of Stukas and Junkers 88s, but hardly had the first bombs dropped on the airfield than half the force turned back and proceeded into another unexpected attack on Grand Harbour. This raid also over, there was another one, this time by a formation of Messerschmitt 110s as if to clear the field for another attack which in fact came later after teatime by a heavy force of bombers. Their objective was again the Grand Harbour.

Another attack which began at dusk was prolonged until darkness fell and searchlights had to be used. It was a very exhausting day for the defences and the population who had to remain in the shelters throughout. Consolation came at the end of day when it was confirmed that 7 Stukas, 4 Junkers 88s, and 3 Messerschmitt 109s were shot down, while 13 others were so mauled as not to have reached their base. 27 planes in all, and, strange but true, with not a single British loss. But the biggest consolation came after the smoke and water spouts from the last bombs had settled and the *Pampas* and *Talabot*, against which most of the bombs were directed, were still intact. There were other raids during that night, but stevedores, dockyard workers and soldiers made all possible use of the intervals to unload. 310 tons were unloaded from *Pampas* and 497 tons from *Talabot*.

Consolation was however shortlived because in the raids on the 26th the Germans seemed to have lost their heads, and ignoring the heavy barrage that was cutting them to pieces they kept diving until some of them managed to hit their precious target. At 1230 they hit *Talabot*, setting her on fire and two hours later they hit *Pampas* which began to sink. By that time 145 and 289 tons had been discharged from the respective ships. The stevedores and soldiers showed their worth on the following day 27th March, when notwithstanding eight raids by day and one of two hours by night they managed to unload by hand 603 tons by day and 345 tons by night, from the still sinking *Pampas*.

It was, however, a different story with *Talabot*. She was still burning fiercely, and only 5 tons could be discharged. The rest of the time was taken by fire fighters going all out to put out the fire, now knowing that the ship carried ammunition. There were four determined raids on 28th March and the *Pampas* was shaken by a number of near misses. Following the failure of electric current from the dockyard, HMS *Avondale* was moved alongside to provide current and a further 243 tons of stores were unloaded. Stevedores and soldiers were now diving into the flooded holds and retrieving stores. The situation became desperate requiring hazardous measures. It became similarly desperate in *Talabot* where the fire had reached the kerosene and aviation spirit stores. Two fire floats manned by seamen from *Penelope*, and the Maltese-manned harbour tug *Ancient* were now pumping water into the burning ship, and did not move away when German bombers dived in a further bid to finish the fiercely burning sihip.

The Bren gunners on the *Ancient* faced the hungry Germans with steady firing, which stopped only when the gunners and the firemen were blown overboard by the explosion of a stick of bombs which slightly missed the *Talabot*.

The drama continued for three more days and nights with the men on *Pampas* working like dogs, with electric current going off, being repaired, and going off again, under constant attacks, to unload 905 further tons before the ship sank. From the *Talabot* only 30 tons of floating stores could be saved. As the hull became red hot and the ammunition began exploding, the ship had to be scuttled, as otherwise she would explode and destroy what was left of Grand Harbour. With the ship expected to explode any minute Lieutenant D.A. Copperwheat of *Penelope* swam out to the blazing ship and attached charges to the sea cocks, then swam back to shore and exploded them to flood the ammunition holds. For his feat he was awarded the George Cross. A dockyard worker who by an oversight was left on the burning ship jumped into the sea and found himself in difficulty. Two police constables, M. Fenech and C. Cassar, dived in the water and rescued him. Both of them got a BEM.

The two ships finished up at the bottom, and the gallant stevedores, soldiers and seamen had lost only a part of the battle, because they had managed to unload no less than 4,952 tons of stores from them, which were worth their weight in gold.

The Grand Harbour and the Dockyard were a shambles and presented a bitter picture. Nothing had escaped the Germans' wrath. Every ship which happened to be in harbour during those days of March was now a wreck or almost one. Even the cruiser *Penelope* which had contributed so much to the battle of Malta with her convoy work and actions, and during those three days of attacks with her anti-aircraft guns, nearly met her Waterloo on the 26th. When the *Talabot* was hit, *Penelope* sent some of her crew to fight the fire on the ammunition ship. Then a bomber dropped a bomb down aft of the bridge between her and the jetty, and she was holed all over by splinters. A stick of bombs aimed at her then hit the jetty and one of her close range guns was blown away. It had become obvious that she could not stay in harbour any longer. But on the other hand she was damaged all over with splinters, so much so that she earned the nickname of 'pepperpot', besides other damage to her deck which made repairs imperative before leaving. No other ship would have consented to enter dock in the Malta dockyard in those days; but *Penelope* did.

Captain A.D. Nicholl DSO, her commanding officer, however had no illusions. He knew he could not hope for the normal dockyard work which was being interrupted continuously by raids, so he had to improvise, since he wanted to leave Malta as early as possible. He mobilised his shipwrights and artificers into a team to help the dockyard workers and work on the ship day and night.

Some said this was madness, but who wasn't mad in those days? The Germans looked certain death in the face in hitting targets or making it possible for others to do it; the gunners were lost in wrath from their first shot and did not stop firing until the enemy was shot down or got them; the fighter pilots pressed their attacks on the enemy irrespective of the deadly anti-aircraft barrage. Even those civilians who were called for dangerous tasks seemed not to care any longer and did what was beyond their normal capacity.

My father was a very timid person. When the destroyer *Jervis* was attacked five miles away from Malta and became a sitting duck for German bombers with her engines stopped, she called for someone to go and effect emergency repairs to her engines so that she could move away or enter harbour. My father volunteered for the job, and was taken to her by boat. Under the continuous threat of air attacks on the paralyzed ship he effected emergency repairs, and left the ship when she could use one engine and make port. She managed this, but was hit again and sunk as she entered Grand Harbour. Ironically enough the British foreman who had contributed grandly to this action by calling for the volunteer was decorated for his action. My father received overtime pay.

This was in fact a very sore point with dockyard workers who were always volunteering for such tasks with others getting the decorations. Joseph Zerafa, another fitter, quickly volunteered to clear a torpedo which had jammed the firing tube in a submarine. The dock and the area around it were cleared of all people when he worked on it, because of the imminent possibility of an explosion. But he cleared the tube, and made the submarine operational again. He got a thank you, and was happy.

A great event during the March raids was that of the Polish submarine *Sokol* which we have already seen being missed by bombs at Lazaretto when the *Pandora* and *P-36* were sunk. Submarines were ordered to dive by day whilst in harbour to avoid detection, but as *Sokol* could not do this until her damage was repaired she was camouflaged and removed to Rinella Creek in Grand Harbour alongside the hulk of the sunken *Talabot*. The Germans however detected the move and bombed her in her new position. She was therefore surrounded by barges and camouflaged again, but to no avail, and the Germans bombed her. Fortunately they sank the barges but failed to damage the *Sokol* any further.

With the help of other submarines much of her damage was repaired until she could dive by day and continue with repair work at night. Back at Lazaretto she had almost completed her repairs and getting ready to sail away when one of her periscopes was damaged, and proceeding to the dockyard in Grand Harbour for a replacement she fouled the boom and smashed the starboard propeller on a rock. She would not have made her scheduled sailing date had it not been for an expert fitter who volunteered to work on her throughout a night of raids. It was again my father, who made the first aid repairs which would make it possible to sail.

Impressed with the job done, Lieutenant Commander Boris Karnicki DSO, the *Sokol's* commanding officer, thanked my father and asked him how he could ever repay him for making it possible for the submarine to leave. My father shrugged the commander's thanks away but asked for a packet of cigarettes. The Lieutenant Commander sent a pillow case round amongst the crew who quickly filled it with red packets of Craven A. He completed the service by sending a seaman to carry it out past the dockyard gates for him. On the following day the *Sokol* sailed for Gibraltar with half her batteries and only one propeller.

With an average of four daylight raids by formations varying from 70 to 100 bombers the situation became very grim. When it wasn't the harbour and dockyard under attack, it was an airfield, or an anti-aircraft battery. St Peter Battery had four guns blown away with all their crews. Ta' Cejlu got it too. 'Sally' at Salina Bay was no better and was being continuously blasted with bombs. One tactic used by the Germans for this and other batteries was to drop a number of time bombs in the battery quadrangle set to explode at one hour intervals which would obviously leave the gunners uneasy and wary thus reducing their alertness and efficiency. But Salina Battery never went out of action completely, and its men always rose to the occasion.

It was in fact an officer at this battery who received a merited Military Cross. During a late afternoon raid a heavy bomb hit one gun position without exploding. At the same time a store where shells were kept was set on fire. Lieutenant Joe Agius, the troop commander, sent his men away from the fire and the unexploded bomb which still rested close to the burning store, and while the men filled up buckets of sand he took them up and went alone to douse the fire. Besides the risk of the bomb going off, there was the possibility of the fire reaching the shells in the store. But with calmness and disregard for his personal safety, Lieutenant Agius kept at his task and got the fire under control. Things got hectic when the fire was still burning at dusk, and there were frantic telephone calls from Headquarters to put it out before darkness fell, as otherwise it would pinpoint the battery and make a beacon for night raiders. But Lieutenant Agius calmly carried on until he put out the fire. It was a three-hour ordeal, for which he was awarded the Military Cross. Lieutenant Agius already had another meritorious action to his credit, for at Fort Ricasoli, in company with two other men, he had dived into the sea at night to save eleven people from thirteen who were drowning after their boat was capsized by the explosion of a bomb during a raid.

Attacks on anti-aircraft batteries were becoming so deadly and frequent that it had become a daily fight with death for the gunners. To men like Sergeant John Abela, an excellent No 1 on the guns at the Salina Bay Battery, the ordeal became a challenge. It was similarly looked at by the men who had to keep the guns going, like Sergeant Artificer Ross of the Royal Electrical and Mechanical Engineers, of the same battery. Both these men were awarded the Military Medal.

One also can understand the plight of the chaplains who were always on the spot in moments like this. No amount of danger would keep people like Father Henry Born, Father Raymond

Formosa and others from giving their men the comfort of their religion which gave them the courage they needed. The life of the chaplain had become a very hard one. Maybe it was harder than that of the individual soldier since he had to spread his time between several gun detachments using any type of transport he could lay his hands on. Whether it was pillion riding with a despatch rider, the rations carts or by walking he always reached his men when they most needed him. This service which was the mainstay of a heroic defence was rarely if ever recognised by citations or decorations, but chaplains got the rewards they expected through the appreciation of the men they served.

Fredu Schembri was now living for only two aims in life. One was to fight the enemy in the Home Guard (it was the only place where he could render service) and to meet a German pilot. The first one was, as indeed he hoped a little far fetched, but the second one became an obsession with him. He increased his self-imposed patrols in Vittoriosa which had become like a city of the dead, but his only find was an unexploded bomb. In the absence of a pilot this offered him an alternative for his bravado. So he picked up the bomb and lifted it on his shoulder and slowly walked with it to the police station, a mile away.

'What have you got there, Fredu?' asked the sergeant as he saw him entering his police station with the deadly cargo. 'That's a bloody bomb,' he continued this time shouting in a tremulous voice which he could not control. What constables there were, disappeared.

'I found it in Victory Square, Sergeant,' said Fredu, surprised at the reception he got.

'Are you crazy?' shouted the sergeant.

'Well.....' stammered Fredu, 'what should I do with it now, that I brought it?'.

'Do with it?' replied the sergeant in search of a brainwave.

'Go and put it back where you found it,' he said.

And Fredu obeyed.

It was the wave of madness that had overtaken desperate minds which sometimes bordered not only on the humorous but also on the dramatic.

Anglu Fenech now thanked his lucky stars for his posting at the searchlight position at Cospicua from where he could easily skip to Valletta to be with his sister, particularly now that already shattered Valletta was being continually hit again, losing bit by bit what little semblance of a place fit for habitation had remained. There was now also Concetta, who had become for him more than a mere companion for his sister. These two women had become his only reason for living. He only worried when he had to take cover during daytime and heard bombs exploding at Valletta. His thoughts would then go to the two women, and many a time he left the shelter to look across the harbour and see in which direction bombs were being dropped. He could even pinpoint the place where his sister's house and shelter were. During night raids he never worried as he was occupied with the searchlight. Anyway, when there was an illumination on the single raiders, which was very often, he felt he had control of the situation since he knew where the danger was. But one day after an attack on the harbour he was sent for by his NCO and told that he could go home on two days' leave. It was generosity coming at a strange time, and Anglu knew what it might mean.

He was away like a flash to find only a rubble of stone where his house had stood. He realised what this meant for him, but then he tried to face the situation. After all the war was not for ever, and with Concetta at his side he would rebuild or buy another house for themselves and his sister. There would be a good bonus paid at the end of hostilities he was told, and that would help. Suddenly he went to look for them in the shelter where he knew they would be. He would smile at them and do everything to mitigate their loss. But the Dominican monk who held him by the arm told him not to go. Looking at his face, Anglu saw it was full of pity and he knew the worst.

'Yes, my son,' the monk told him. 'They were both extricated from beneath that masonry.'

'Dead?' was all Anglu could say.

The monk nodded, then tried to say something meant to console. But Anglu was not hearing. He broke out crying, as he remembered later, he had never cried before. He felt the anguish of separation from his sister whom he adored, and Concetta, the first and only woman he had loved. They had died together, and he had lost both of them. He cried for two days and nights as he roamed all over the place that was once the proud city of the knights, now turned into mounds of stone that were the monuments of a barbaric enemy as his house had become a tombstone of an unfair God. But tears could not bring them back, not the blasphemous thoughts, either. But what could release him from

the anguish and preoccupation that he was feeling in his chest
growing like a balloon? He found some murky wine, and he drank
it. But it still did not clear his chest and his head. Then he became
strangely quiet, and spoke no more to any one, not even to his
friends when he returned to his post. And his friends did not speak
to him as they understood.

The first day he was excused duty, and while they manned the
searchlight that night he was allowed to stay in his bed, awake and
uncertain of what was going to happen next. The following
morning there was a heavy raid and when he showed no incli-
nation to move from his bed his friends stayed with him, giving
companionship with their presence, even if they were uselessly
risking their life. There was the noise of exploding bombs, and the
endless clapping of guns, then the sounds of fast flying aircraft
which indicated an air battle. But nothing was bad enough to
make Anglu leave his bed. Then one of his friends called the others
and shouted.

'There is a Messerschmitt shot down. Look,' and the others
went outside leaving Anglu alone. Then he heard one of them
saying that the pilot had baled out.

'There he is, look.... and he is dropping quite near.'

Anglu jumped out of his bed and rushed out of his quarters like
a bull on seeing red. As he looked at the sky his eyes bore the
glassy look of madness. Then he saw the parachute, and the pilot
dangling from it dropping slowly. With a blasphemous word he ran
to the Lewis gun that was mounted in a sandbag emplacement. It
was the only weapon of defence on the post, to be used against
aircraft attacking the position. But for him it had become a
weapon of vengeance. His friends ran after him, realising what he
was doing. But he reached the gun before them and turned it on
them.

'If you come closer I'll shoot the whole bloody lot of you,' he
shouted.

The look in his eyes showed that he had lost his senses. But
nobody doubted that he meant every word he said, and they did
not dare go closer. For a miniute or two they all stood there as if
in a tableau.

His corporal said only one sentence. 'Don't be a fool, Anglu.
Leave that gun alone.'

But he did not. Instead, he turned the gun round and before
they could stop him aimed at the German pilot and pressed the
trigger. By the time his friends were on him Anglu had emptied

the whole drum, and with the bullets he fired went all his tension and preoccupation. When they took him away he was crying like a baby, and the calmness of before returned to him.

*

Even the most staunch optimists had to admit that all seemed to have finished for Malta, and what resistance was to be made during April would only delay but not prevent the end. One had only to look around and see the Lazaretto base in Marsamxett, now silent and closed after all the submarines had left, intending never to come back again. There was the haunting sight of Grand Harbour, full of wrecks, with the remains of the destroyers *Gallant* and *Kingston* broken up in their docks where they had been blown up. The dockyard was like a cemetery for decapitated and smashed installations. The only living object was the cruiser *Penelope* still in dock where she had defended her tenancy with all the might of her guns and paid her rent in blood. It was however evident that her efforts were being made until such time as she could finish the necessary repairs so that she could leave as well.

The same situation prevailed at the airfields with destroyed pens, demolished buildings, and burnt-out aircraft. There was life only in the ant-like army of exhausted men working round the clock on the craters that still covered runways and dispersal fields, and of course the few still standing planes and their fliers, struggling along against the enemy hordes which kept coming daily in bigger formations and without respite.

Even those who could not see all this, were soon made to taste their fate in the bread, after the sodden grain that was salvaged from the *Pampas* was used, giving it a taste of remains from the morgue, but none the less eaten and fought for. There was now the daily reminder of Victory Kitchens which had been extended to all towns and villages, dishing out a daily portion to all those who registered for it, which meant everybody. There was of course a menu for each day varying from *minestra* (vegetable soup), beans, tinned sardines, herrings, *balbuljata* (beaten egg powder with tomatoes and what left-overs the cook happened to have) and of course goat's meat. Of course only one item was served every day. Even the Maltese goat herd had to submit to the supreme sacrifice to make up for the lack of meat and livestock. With this obviously went out pasteurized milk on which children and the old thrived. The Victory Kitchens introduced a daily drill for everybody, without any distinction — everyone had to queue to collect his points-worth of meagre rations. But what was going to happen when stocks ran out? Run out they must, for the situation had no chance of any foreseeable relief.

In the meantime the assault continued with an ever increasing intensity. The Germans kept coming between four and ten times a day, every time with formations of 100-plus raining a variety of deadly merchandise, tailored for the target, big high explosive and incendiary bombs for the airfields, deep penetration bombs for the dockyard, parachute mines supposedly for the harbours which found their way on land. There were delayed action bombs, dropped together with other impact bombs on forts and gun positions, as well as anti-personnel bombs which were meant for troop concentration areas, but were dropped in the streets and the fields. Indeed, there was allowance made for the civilian population areas, because they had all the bomb varieties, including the diabolical strings of bombs chained together for more concentrated explosions and damage. By the first week of April, the damage to civilian property rose to 15,500 buildings destroyed, including 70 churches, 18 monasteries or convents, 22 schools, 8 hospitals, 10 theatres, 8 hotels, 8 clubs, 5 banks and 48 other public buildings including 6 Knights' *Auberges* in Valletta. Most of this was despite Kesselring's order, which had stated that civilian buildings were to be preserved. The casualties for the same period ran up to 1,104 killed, 1,318 seriously injured, and 1,299 slightly injured, which represented 1 in every 70 of the population becoming a casualty. Had there been no rock shelters there would have been a wholesale massacre.

Hungry downcast looks could not be helped, and no amount of reading, working, doing chores or anything else would make up for them. There were bound to be moments during a day or an hour when thoughts roamed to wonder at and doubt the words of praise and congratulations that were continually flowing in to Malta from all over the world. Was it possible that no one of those who spoke or wrote such words of gold could supply a nugget's worth of material help? Even the Germans had praised Malta for her astounding resistance. They had called her the unsinkable aircraft carrier, and they were now throwing everything they had against her in a bid to destroy her once and for all. The Maltese could not do more . They had resisted in silent defiance and their gunners had a good share of the 177 enemy planes destroyed or hopelessly damaged during March. April looked like bringing a bigger harvest, and they would go for it. But before such determination could be put into effect they had to have food, planes and ammunition. They had never mentioned the word surrender; and they would not; they would rather die. But they did not want to die.

Food, planes and ammunition. Those were the three phantoms that had been haunting Sir William's mind. He had been asking for them for so long, but they had come in short supply, and the enemy had destroyed most of it. He could not blame anyone, and it was certainly not his fault. But there was one thing which he felt was his responsibility, and he had to do something about it.

As if to keep in line with the rising state of desperation, the attacks continued to escalate during the first days of April, both in frequency and intensity. Good Friday on the 3rd, had 8 attacks, and Easter Sunday on the 5th had another 8. There were 12 attacks on the 6th, and another ten on the 7th, during which was notched the 2000th raid on Malta, and the only standing remnants of a civilized heritage in Valletta — three *Auberges* and the Royal Opera House — were destroyed. In the midst of this time of destruction, King George VI, obviously moved by what was going on in Malta, assumed the Colonelcy-in-Chief of the Royal Malta Artillery.

'I have been watching with admiration the stout hearted resistance of all in Malta — service personnel and civilian alike — to the fierce and constant air attacks,' read his message, 'in the active defence of the Island the RAF have been ably supported by the Royal Malta Artillery, and it therefore gives me special pleasure, to assume the Colonelcy-in-Chief of the Regiment.' This infused more determination in Malta's gunners to be worthy of the honour bestowed on them.

In the midst of it all there was the cruiser *Penelope* now caught with her panties down in dock as she was about to put the finishing touches to her emergency repairs. That day the Germans attacked her she was peppered again with holes. She began to flood, while all the electric wires in the dock were destroyed and had to be replaced. She was firing every available gun at the attackers, and two of them nearly crashed on her as she shot them down in flames. The order to the gunners that day and been: 'Don't fire until the enemy planes are on the tip of the barrel.' Shells had to be continuously brought to her by lighter and all hands helped in unloading.

Penelope had become an obsession with the raiders, who were throwing in everything in their attacks on her. This brought about a new type of cameraderie between her and Maltese gun crews in the vicinity who went into action in direct defence of the ship. As a gesture of appreciation, maybe at the suggestion of Captain Nicholl, an issue of rum was made to these Maltese crews. But for some unknown reason a naval store officer stopped it.

In another raid *Penelope* was attacked again, and her deck became like a rock garden with the chunks of masonry that crashed down on her from near misses. Some of the stone weighed as much as half a hundred weight. But 8th April was the blackest day. There were 14 raids, one of them by as many as 300 bombers. It was realised that if *Penelope* did not get to sea that day she would be lost. So, plugged with wooden pegs from stern to stern she was taken out of dock and put alongside the quay to oil. That was when the Germans attacked her. She opened her terrible fire and as always Maltese gun batteries opened up in her defence, even though the rum issue had been stopped. However the officer who had stopped it had his apartment at the dockyard shattered during those attacks, not by enemy bombs, but by shells from a Bofors gun whose crew might have unduly depressed the barrel in the heat of action, as if in defiance of the officer's uncalled step.

When *Penelope* was down to her last fifteen rounds the Germans left her, hit and battered, but just able to make it. Seven of her crew were killed and more than 30 injured, amongst them Captain Nicholl. But he came back from hospital that same night, walking with the aid of a stick and hardly able to move. At 9 p.m. he took the ship to sea, steering her only by the engine to Gibraltar.

With the departure of *Penelope,* the only vessel capable of movement in the Malta harbour besides the tugs, it was as if the last breath which could rescusitate a dying island had expired. There was nothing more to do for anybody. The gunners began counting the shells they were allowed to fire for the day as per the last order for rationing ammunition, and the fighters had to limit their sorties, all with the hope of extending as much as possible the tentative target date that had been arrived at. They couldn't do the same with food, for rations were already at their lowest. Even so, everyone except the people knew that Malta must fall.

The people sensed this, but could not believe it, since they still had their faith in God. Nothing would shake that faith, which was keeping them strong in resisting and surviving the monstrous attacks ... every day .... and in every raid.... like on the following day, 9th April, when a 2000 kg bomb pierced the Rotunda at Mosta — the third largest dome in Europe, falling among the congregation praying in the church, without exploding or hurting anyone. That bomb still lies in that church today, as a silent witness of Maltese faith. And more than ever before their prayers rose in unison.

CHAPTER TWELVE

The George Cross

Because it seemed certain that Malta must fall, the British Cabinet was in a dilemma. Britain had come to realise the importance of the Mediterranean, where its only remaining foothold was in North Africa. The British star had risen in that theatre of operations until Malta could interfere with Rommel's supplies and sink them on their way to him. Now, since its power to do this had decreased considerably, the German forces in North Africa had received all the supplies they required, and it was known that in February a convoy carrying a large number of tanks had reached Tripoli, giving Rommel the required strength to resist the attack which General Auchinleck was preparing for. It was this desire to prevent the fall of Malta that made the British Cabinet strike on a new idea of securing the airfields of West Cyrenaica so as to be able to give support to Malta and to the relieving convoys. And there was pressure to have this carried out soon. How soon? 'Now,' was Churchill's view.

There was however a point raised that should an offensive be staged right away to secure those airfields it might cause the piece-meal destruction of the new armoured forces that Auchinleck had been building up for the big offensive against Rommel. What this meant was that in an attempt to save Malta, Britain might lose Egypt and the whole of the Middle East. What was it to be? Malta or Egypt?

At the same time that the fate of Malta was running in this vicious circle on the British side, a similar argument was going on between the Germans and Italians, where the capture of Tobruk was concerned, which would open the way to Egypt and what would follow. After a lot of discussion and confrontations the Commander-in-Chief South and the Africa Panzer Army were agreed that the next operational objectives must be Malta and Tobruk. Tobruk without Malta was not enough, while the sea route from Greece to Tobruk was within range of British bases in Egypt. There was however only one bone of contention between Kesselring and Rommel — the order in which the two operations were to be carried out. At this time Rommel's star was very high with Hitler, who was as always supported by his yes-man Göring. It was therefore not difficult to expect that Hitler would establish priorities as first the occupation of Tobruk, and then Malta. Kesselring took his defeat very well, since at this time he had not yet built up the forces he wanted for Malta's invasion. Until Rommel would take Tobruk however, he would have plenty of time to do it, and then there would be nothing standing in his way for the invasion of Malta.

While Malta took second place with the Germans, it took precedence with the British Cabinet which decided that to save Malta the risk of losing Egypt must be accepted.

General Auchinleck was ordered to prepare for the offensive to occupy the airfields of West Cyrenaica, and it was to take place not later than the middle of June 1942. In the meantime steps were to be taken to reinforce the island, first of all by more fighter aircraft since their force had dwindled. While these decisions were being taken, Malta's resistance was not only justifying what had been decided upon but was pricking human consciences in acknowledging what the Maltese effort was worth in saving the Mediterranean for Britain, and indeed for the Western world. There was no appropriate way of payment, but some sort of recognition had to be made, even to justify the admiration and appreciation which every peace-loving nation had found for the small island. Indeed someone wrote to the British press suggesting a Victoria Cross for Malta. But nations were never decorated. That would make it better still because it would be something unique in the annals of history, and have more weight and effect. King George VI then decided to award Malta the George Cross.

It was against this background that Churchill received the reports by Sir William Dobbie which implied exactly what the Prime Minister and his Cabinet did not want to happen.

Steps for the replenishment of Malta's fighters were taken immediately. On 14th April 1942, the American aircraft carrier *Wasp* left Glasgow with 47 Spitfires bound for Malta. It was escorted by the battleship *Renown*, the anti-aircraft cruisers *Cairo* and *Charybdis* and a number of destroyers. When this convoy had already been a day out at sea, on 15th April, King George VI made his award to Malta.

> To honour her brave people I award the George Cross to the island fortress of Malta, to bear witness to a heroism and devotion that will long be famous in history.

This was the message he sent to Malta, and which spread throughout the world. Sir William Dobbie replied to that message as follows:

The peoples and garrison of Malta are deeply touched by your Majesty's kind thought for them in conferring on the fortress this signal honour. It has greatly encouraged everyone, and all are determined that, by God's help Malta will not weaken, but will endure until victory is won. All in Malta desire to express once again, their loyal devotion to your Majesty and their resolve to prove worthy of the high honour conferred.

A George Cross was to be embedded at once in the Maltese Arms, and this unique award which was the one and only of its kind awarded to a Commonwealth country was very well received. There was no clamour or noisy rejoicing; the Maltese were past that now, but the most important message behind the award, the Malta was not alone, was understood, and one could detect this in everyone's talk and behaviour.

The assault had in the meantime not eased up and the daily raids by big formations of bombers continued. The gunners had by now learned well the intricacies of the box barrage and once an aircraft was caught into it, and most of them were, it became difficult to escape unscathed.

The Germans too had learned their tricks of war, and the Maltese came to know this very soon. The convoy with the *Wasp* had on 19th April passed Gibraltar. Possibly it did not enter port so as to avoid being reported upon since it was known that there were many German agents in Spain who made it their business to report ship and convoy movements. Notwithstanding this the Germans learned of the convoy and knew that it was carrying aircraft for Malta, which they wanted to destroy at all costs. They tracked the convoy by radio interception after it left Gibraltar and until it reached a point south of the Balearic Islands. They even knew exactly when the *Wasp* launched the Spitfires, losing one in the process, and from that moment the aircraft were timed to the hour they would reach Malta.

Forty-six Spitfires make a lot of noise, and as they flew low over Malta people were again rushing outside to laugh and point at them, and to clap. There were even those who cried, associating no doubt their arrival with the thought that had been generated by the award of the George Cross — that Malta was not alone. The

Spitfires separated with half of them going to Ta' Qali, and the rest to Hal Far. Twenty minutes after they had landed, their pilots were still getting acquainted with others when the sirens started wailing. A strong formation of Junkers 88s and Messerschmitt 109s came in, separated in two and attacked the Spitfires. Twenty of them were destroyed while another twelve were damaged.

This disaster of April 1942 came as a staggering blow. But nothing shook the British more than the realisation that Kesselring seemed to be running a step ahead of them, and that the Germans believed like them in the importance of Malta to the present struggle. It was now time to be realistic and this drove the fact home that the Germans were not likely to give Malta the time to live until the scheduled offensive by General Auchinleck to occupy the airfields in West Cyrenaica could get on its way. It was the time to do away with arguments and silence the exasperated participants with a one way decision in taking the bull by the horns. If the immediate priority was to give Spitfires protection to Malta then it should be done now, and if the airfields in Western Cyrenaica were still not available then the planes were to be sent to Malta, even at the risk of having them destroyed and replaced again. There was the other immediate problem of foodstuffs to be tackled, and here there was a possibility of consultation over the target dates given; one would know what time there was to play with, however short it was. It was not so with ammunition, which had to depend on enemy action which was an unknown factor. What was known was that the AA batteries were already keeping only half of their guns in action to save precious shells and this established the priority. What was required was a crash plan, and what's more, to have the right man on the spot to run it.

Even while this crash-planning was going on, the last efforts by a totally exhausted garrison and people continued, not caring and impervious to fear, giving every iota of strength and determination to battling with the enemy of that day, and at the specific moment, letting fate and God take care of the morrow. Such was the desperate situation which prevailed at that time. The battle had become one for Malta rather than of Malta. But more than this it became for each individual more like a personal feud.

Carmelo Vella, the timid searchlight man who had been posted to the harbour searchlight position at Cospicua, where we have already seen the desperate outburst of Anglu Fenech, was now at a complete loss. The war had already transformed him into a new

man, but the German attack had offered a challenge to his newly
discovered qualities which he was not in a position to take up. He
welcomed his turns on the searchlight during nights, or on the
Lewis gun whenever his position was attacked, but he still felt that
he had never came to real grips with the enemy. This was having
its effect on his state of mind. All his preoccupation had funnelled
into one ardent desire to face the enemy at closer quarters. With
the coming of the assault his desire had become an obsession of
which he wanted to be rid, without knowing how.

It was in April that he broke down. Because searchlight crews
were ordered to take cover during the day, and also because of the
rationing of ammunition, his position was left attended by only
one man during day raids, while the rest took cover. But one
afternoon Carmelo remained at his post watching an attack by
Junkers 88s on Grand Harbour, with his heart aching for action.
Suddenly he saw a Junkers 88 flying in the direction of his post
after flattening from his dive. The plane was so low that he could
see the front gunner's face behind the perspex. His heart filled
with anguish, and without knowing how and why he rushed to the
Lewis gun, and as the plane flew overhead Carmelo let go, seeing
his tracers drawing a line from nose to tail of the aircraft. His
companions were there and told him to desist, not to waste
ammunition, and I was with them. But he persisted.

We saw that plane turn round and fly back straight at the
position, and we all shouted to Carmelo to leave the gun alone and
run with us for cover because that German had taken a personal
interest in the matter, as in fact all of them were doing. But
Carmelo would not listen; instead, he armed the gun with a fresh
drum and shouting at us to leave him alone he took a position to
meet the Junker's challenge. We saw the plane approaching, and
Carmelo calmly moving the gun to keep it in his sights. Then we
ran for the shelter which was close.

It was at that time that Carmelo opened fire, and as I took a
last look at him over my shoulder I saw the tracers flying straight
into the aircraft as it flew overhead. Then there was the shrieking
of three bombs.... and all of us who were some distance away
dropped ourselves flat on the ground where we were shaken by
the explosions, but unharmed. When we ran back, we found a
mound of masonry where the machine gun post had stood. We
began clearing the masonry and it wasn't long before we got to
Carmelo buried underneath, but still alive.

When he opened his eyes and saw us looking over him, he said, –

'Did I get him?'

Both Mary's parents were killed in an air-raid, and this was enough to throw her into a state of desperation which the war itself had not done. When after her last confession the young priest had shown her that her true love was for John, and that her attraction to Bob was only a matter of passion, which was to be expected in the prevailing circumstances, she had repented, and promised God and herself to reform. But now during John's long absences when he was on the guns it was only Bob who would come to her. She had lost the comforting companionship of her parents. The priest had told her how she could stop seeing Bob without offending him, but when she had to, she found it so difficult to do. He had noticed her hesitation and restricted himself in his caresses, thinking it was all due to her loss. But when she had broken down and cried on his shoulder trying to bring herself to tell him of her difficulty, his hand went to her chin which he lifted so that he could look into her eyes. She wanted so much to tell him then and was stopped by his lips closing down on hers. When once she allowed it, it became so more difficult to deny it again, and before she knew it, they were back to where it had all started.

John had somehow come to know and faced her with it. She told him everything, but he was adamant in refusing to accept her explanation, and left her. She could see how distressed he was, and began to feel for him what she had never felt before. None waited in more anguish during the following night than Mary. Her thoughts were all of John, and how she might have destroyed him by treating him the way she did, knowing how he had to face daily death at his battery. which, as he had told her several times, was one of the most bombed of them all. She could not get out of her mind the details he had so often related to her of what he was having to face at his battery. Dive-bombing, machine gunning, blown up positions, slow going time-bombs. Indeed, his battery at Salina, which everybody called 'Sally', had been hit by 115 bombs, and it took a steady hand and a stable mind to have to go through such an ordeal and stay alive. If he did not, then it would be because of her. She suddenly felt the urgent need to go to John, and ask for his forgiveness once and for all. She wanted to hug him, and kiss him, and to be kissed in return. And as she had him in the picture in her mind she could feel her body waking up for him, and to give him anything he might want. This was love, as her young confessor had hinted to her.

The following day she waited, her mind made up, for Bob to call for her with a landrover, as they had arranged. But when he did, she told him that she could not go out with him as agreed. Instead, there was an errand she had to run, and he could take her. She got into the vehicle and asked him to take her to Salina. It was such a strange request, and Bob wondered and wanted to ask her what was she going there for, but the look of determination he saw on her face kept him back. On the way he tried to take her hand, but for the first time she pulled it away. When they reached Salina, and the battery came in view she asked him to stop the vehicle, and as he did she got out and began running. Bob called after her to ask whether she wanted him to wait, but she didn't hear him, and kept running.

Half way to the battery she saw men running about, camouflage nets were being removed from gun positions, and men with steel helmets on their heads were rushing to take positions. In the distance she could hear an air raid siren wailing. She kept running, and was about to stop as she reached the gate. But seeing no one there, the guard having been attending to something in the guard room, she ran into the battery and stopped to look for John. No one seemed to have noticed her. All dutiful eyes were intent on instruments and the sky. Those who were not on duty were under cover. She looked at the gun positions, then she saw him. Just his sun-burned face under the steel helmet.

She called out his name, but her voice was lost in the sound of orders being shouted and the noise of approaching planes. Then hell was let loose as the guns opened up. She put her fingers in her ears and lowered her face down as if to keep out the din which looked like bursting her ear drums. Then there was the whining of diving planes, and looking up she stood transfixed looking at the black metal eagles that seemed to be diving at her. She ran to a slit trench, and had just dropped into it when she heard the shrieking of bombs.

After the raid was over and Salina Battery was for the umpteenth time taking the toll of damage from another direct attack, no one could explain the naked body of a female, shrunken and disfigured from blast effect, which was found amongst the other male dead bodies. As John looked at it he could not help remembering Mary. For a moment he had thought he heard her voice calling his name, before the raid had began. But it had all been his fancy, because of the love he still bore her.

Notwithstanding the British Cabinet's bold decision the intended convoy for May had to be cancelled, and any hopes Sir William had of being able to put forward the target date for his supplies disappeared. What was to be done? Nothing much. Rations had been so diminished that the next step down was nil; there was nowhere to go. Whatever reductions and belt tightening were made had been in theory at least, balanced by the fact that bread, the main staple element, was left in just reasonable proportions. But now even this had to be cut. What's more, there was no more white flour which the Maltese had always known. As from 26th April there was to be only dirty brown bread, and this to be reduced to 3/8 rotolo per person as from 5th May. It was just enough for any city man for his breakfast. Those in the villages were used to having twice that. For lunch and supper there would be no bread, unless of course one went without it in the morning. In a few weeks' time, two or three may be, there wouldn't even be that. Lack of wholesome and insufficient food soon had everyone infested with scabies. The one only good prospect was for what food was left to run out before ammunition. At least Malta would die fighting.

Strangely enough what effects the situation was having on living were not reflected in the fighting output. Spitfires and Hurricanes kept harassing the heavy enemy formations, and guns, although halved, kept engaging with more than usual efficiency, and planes were being shot down in bigger numbers. It could have been because the Germans were getting more desperate themselves, or maybe they knew this was the island's last breath. St Peter Battery, which held the record for the number of planes shot down drew its number in those days and was attacked. Only two of the 4.5 inch static naval guns were manned and in action, and one of them received a direct hit which destroyed the gun and caused many casualties. It might have been worse had it not been for the drill adopted with two NCO's being detailed on the lookout with binoculars, who, as soon as they saw bombs being dropped on the battery, would blow a whistle and the crews would drop flat on the ground for protection.

This drill was introduced at this battery by Lieutenant (later Major) Gerald Amato-Gauci, whom we have already seen being awarded the Military Cross in January for meritorious action at this same battery. This drill was later adopted by other batteries.

Doomsday kept approaching with the Germans becoming bolder and fiercer. Attacks were also more widespread. On

28th April, the electricity supply was disrupted, and people in shelters had now also to endure darkness to their other inconveniences. St Publius Church in Floriana, one of the most treasured edifices in the island was wantonly destroyed, and fun made of the occasion by a German broadcaster. A shelter in Senglea, the most bombed city, received direct hits from a stick of bombs and gave way during one of the six raids of the day, with many killed. During March and April the Germans had used 2,150 bombers in the assault, which dropped 1869 tons of bombs on Grand Harbour area. All this had forced 162 hours in alerts. During April, there were 177 German aircraft destroyed or damaged and not likely to reach their base. The total number of killed was 297. But thanks to rock bomb proof shelters, these cannot be taken as heavy casualties considering the fact that between 20th March and 28th April the Germans had flown 5,807 sorties by bombers against Malta, 5,667 by fighters and 345 by reconnaissance aircraft, and dropped on the island 6,557,231 kilograms of bombs, which was almost as much as had been dropped on the whole of Britain during the peak of battle in September 1940. But what was more serious belonged to the five fighter squadrons which were then operating, i.e. No 185 (Hurricanes) at Hal Far; Nos 126, 249 and 603 (Spitfires) at Ta' Qali, and No 601 (Spitfires) at Luqa. By 30th April they had only seven serviceable Spitfires between them.

Those who hoped for some respite in May were disappointed because the assault was continued even with more vigour, and the first day was taken up by 12 raids. The target date for the exhaustion of supplies was closer by one week. When electric current was resumed on 2nd May, after a week in darkness it was being remarked that at least one was spared to die in light. But there were those, who, dazed by the exploding bombs around them could not even muster force to speak. The end was near.

As the last handful of Spitfires and Hurricanes scrambled to intercept the enemy, the guns kept giving their support with whatever shells the gunners could lay their hands on. Sir William made his last reports on which Churchill had to act. In the meantime the Maltese waited — and prayed. The nearest feast would be that of Our Lady of Pompeii, on 7th May and this time there would not be any roses for the characteristic offering. Instead, the people had only hunger, sorrow and fear — a sacrifice which they were bearing, not more for repentance of their sins or in thanksgiving for their safe keeping in the raids, but for Malta, and its preservation. As they prayed, however, their voices were drowned by the noises of German planes now flying desperately closer, and the deafening explosions from the bombs that kept raining down. Eardrums could bear it no more, and the rock trembled. Even babies in their mother's womb were shaken up.

At that same time the aircraft carrier *Eagle* was proceeding at full speed to her usual rendezvous, dead set on the urgency of her mission and hastened by a frantic Churchill. The fast minelayer *Welshman* too, had entered the Mediterranean on a cloak and dagger mission trying to pull a fast one on the Germans in an attempt to break the blockade.

Another event which also had the look of a secret operation was the arrival of General Lord Gort VC who was that day appointed Governor and Commander-in-Chief of Malta to replace Sir William Dobbie. He arrived at Kalafrana at dusk during an air-raid, where he found waiting for him the Chiefs of the Three Fighting Services, the Lieutenant Governor, the Chief Justice, Members of the Executive Council, and a host of others. The whole party proceeded to a bomb damaged building nearby where Lord Gort was to take the Oath of Allegiance and the Oath of Office. Hardly had the party entered the building when bombs were heard exploding quite close and the Chief Justice, Doctor (later Sir) George Borg dived under a table. When the situation was restored, it was found out that the Clerk to the Council, had left the Bible behind, and for a moment it looked as it the swearing could not take place. It was Sir William who saved the day by producing from his pocket the Bible he always carried with him. When the Chief Justice signed the deed it was noticed that there was blood on his hand from a cut he had received following the explosions. After the party left, the new Governor devoted the next two hours to discussing the situation with Sir William Dobbie. That was all Sir William did in the way of a handing over. Then he left for England via Gibraltar, accompanied by Lady Dobbie and their daughter Sybil.

No speeches, no fanfare, nothing. Not that anyone wanted it. Much less the people. There was however room for celebration the following day, 8th May, when *Eagle* reached her rendezvous and lost no time in launching Spitfires V for Malta. There were 64 of them, of which she lost three. Most of the 61 Spitfires which reached Malta some hours later had had their machine-guns removed, and carried spare parts in their place. Immediately the planes reached Malta, machine-guns began to be fitted to make them serviceable and bring the fighter squadrons to their full strength. That day the *Welshman* still hugged the Algerian coast at her full 40 knots. It is found mentioned in books of fiction that the *Welshman* made her dash rigged up as a French light cruiser of *Le Tigre* class, to which it was similar in shape and superstructure. But this is not true, and the caper of disguising the ship as a French vessel was carried out by the *Welshman's* sister ship *Manxman,* when on 25th August 1941 she went into the Gulf of Genoa in such fancy dress and laid mines off Leghorn. She got away with it since the Germans had long been trying to bring pressure to bear on the Vichy Government to put the French fleet, keeping out of the war at Bizerta, at their disposal. It was therefore thought that it would not do to spoil such possibilities by attacking what could after all be a French warship.

Lord Gort was Churchill's new man for Malta, and with him he had brought the George Cross, and the scroll written in the King's own handwriting. Every Maltese saw the new Governor's picture in the papers the following day. There were those who saw in his steadfast eyes the look of the gallant and determined fighter who might take Malta out of its ordeal. But many did not comment. After all they remembered his heroic achievement in the evacuation from Dunkirk. He wasn't by any chance expected to have a repetition at Malta? Indeed when Churchill had spoken to him about his new appointment he had mentioned the possibility of his having to attend to the island's surrender. But the Maltese did not know that. What they knew was that unless food would be coming soon not even Gort would save them. The only good omen that registered with the people was that the new man had arrived on 7th May which was the feast of Our Lady of Pompeii. And that was something.

The merciless pounding continued on 9th May, but now there were the Spitfires to scramble, which took back some weight from the guns. Ten raids, some fierce air battles and thirty enemy planes destroyed. But the apex was reached on the morrow, which unknown to anyone was to be the last day of the assault.

There was first of all a flurry at the harbour since the early hours of the day. Stevedores and soldiers were called to stand by as when some convoys came in. But there weren't any ships expected. As the first rays of the morning sun from the east were clearing the last misty wisps over the water of Grand Harbour there was a strange apparition between the breakwaters. Then someone who knew called out: 'Here comes the *Welshman*.'

Yes, she had made it and entered port as nonchalant as a girl of the house. Soldiers had in the meantime been given green canisters to place on the jetties and even some bastions, and as soon as the *Welshman* reached her wharf there was a sudden bustle as the stevedores and soldiers went forward. Cargo hoists began working, and an officer was shouting orders to his men to form a human chain from the ship to the trucks that had arrived. Work started in earnest and the first canisters were ignited to lay the first palls of a smoke screen. When the German and Italian planes (this time they came together) came over for the first raid of the day they found a harbour lost under a blanket of smoke, which, according to what Cajus Bekker wrote in his *Luftwaffe Diaries*, was thought to be fog. They knew there must have been something going beneath that dense blanket, and they must have known of the *Welshman*. But they could not see where she was or what she was doing. They could perhaps cover the area with their bombs trusting in pot luck. But not today. They were not given the chance to pause and think — two squadrons of Spitfires hurtled down from above and the first air battles of the day ensued. Five Savoia Marchetti flying in beautiful formation, no doubt their pilots with minds at rest because of the screen of fighters around them, found three Spitfires on them. Before they knew what was happening three of the bombers were shot down in flames, bombs and all, and before the pilots of the other two could think about it the Spitfires were back on them as well, riddling them with cannon and machine gun fire. Those two bombers turned tail hoping to reach base even with the smoke that was coming out of them. There were 12 shot down during that attack. But there were seven more attacks during that day with as many air battles, which were the fiercest that Malta had ever witnessed. But for the first time ever, the Spitfires enjoyed numerical superiority over the enemy fighters and tore them to pieces. 63 enemy aircraft were destroyed or sent limping back home to fall on the way. Only six of the enemy fell to the guns that day; the rest belonged to the Spitfires. It was their well-deserved day of vengeance. That day brought the total of enemy planes destroyed during the last 72 hours of Kesselring's assault to 112, with the loss of only three Spitfires, two pilots of which baled out to safety.

When the word went round that a ship had broken the blockade the people wanted to rejoice again, but they couldn't very well do it because of the smoke. When after six hours it lifted completely everyone rushed to the bastions to get a glimpse of this sole hero which had risked so much for them. The *Welshman* was there for all to see — free and empty, with its cargo of provisions, ammunition and aircraft spares already taken away to safety. On enemy losses on those days it is recorded in the *Luftwaffe Diaries* that between 10th and 12th May, Italians and Germans lost more bombers than during the previous five weeks of the assault when the enemy had flown 11,500 sorties against Malta. As Ciano stated in his diaries, those days were the turning point of the battle. Even so, on the following day Kesselring signalled to Hitler that enemy naval and air bases at Malta had been eliminated.

It took only a short time to show him how wrong he was.

CHAPTER THIRTEEN

The End in Sight

Field Marshal Kesselring stopped his air onslaught on Malta and transferred the greater part of his remaining air forces to the Russian front. What was kept behind was to collaborate with the Italian air force in maintaining attacks on Malta with the purpose of curbing any possible attacks on German and Italian shipping to North Africa. His reports on this stage of operations are not only not based on facts but in some cases contradictory. His first sweeping statement was that he had accomplished his task of neutralising Malta, which was certainly not the case. Malta was truly broken up, with her towns and villages in shambles; and her people were hungry, because the *Welshman* had only provided a brief and temporary relief; but she wasn't finished.

Indeed, if Kesselring wanted any proof of this he got it soon, when a force of Wellingtons from Malta carried out a heavy bombardment of Messina, Palermo, Augusta and Catania, which according to Italian sources was very effective. Indeed, if he was so convinced that Malta had been neutralised why did he leave a part of his forces to continue attacking the island with the Italians, so as to curb attacks on shipping? Reading his reports one cannot but realise how misinformed Kesselring had been about Malta. Later, he admitted in his memoirs how even his forces had proved too weak to neutralise the island.

When attacks were resumed by mixed formations of German and Italian aircraft these didn't stand any comparison with the German-monopolized raids of the previous months. Particularly because most of the bombers were Italian, whose crews were now assailed of fear and trepidation when coming to Malta. From months back, flying over to Malta was being described by them as a mission to hell, and they did everything to escape such missions. After all, the anti-aircraft barrage which had earned respect throughout the world was still intact (notwithstanding that the destruction of anti-aircraft batteries was one of the objectives which Kesselring had stated he had accomplished), and Spitfires were still in Malta, and greater in number (these, he was also supposed to have eliminated). It is interesting to note that one of the most enlightening documents which still exists in Malta was a charge sheet recovered from a dead Italian pilot which shows that he was specifically sent on a mission to Malta as a punishment for his crimes, which in his case as in those of many others finished in death. It is therefore no wonder that many of the Italian crews resorted to the old stratagem of dropping their bombs on their way to Malta, and flying back to base reporting mission accomplished. The stories they had to make up were reflected in many of the Italian war bulletins which were also heard on radio in Malta, and made up humorous anecdotes.

No doubt worried by the frequent occasions when German aircraft came over from different directions, sometimes enough to baffle radar detection, an RAF Observer Corps was formed. There were about 45 Maltese airmen posted to it, and with a few British NCO's were stationed in five AMES's (Air Ministry Experimental Stations) each of which was manned by a few men and an NCO who were trained in aircraft identification and the use of a plotting machine through which they could pinpoint the position and flight of aircraft and report it accordingly. There must have been many occasions when the surveillance of these posts was essential in determining air-attacks and defining plots before such information was flashed out by the fully occupied radar. The service was later extended to Gozo with the establishment of a sixth post there. This was something which functioned very well and rendered good service for the rest of the battle of Malta and was only disbanded on 22nd March 1945.

Now that the Spitfire had established itself as the specific defensive weapon for the Malta front, Britain did not lag behind, and in mid-May seventeen more Spitfires were flown to Malta from the aircraft carriers *Eagle* and *Argus*. The *Eagle* had become an expert in this kind of shuttle service. It was hoped that there would be no further need of this when British forces in North Africa occupied the airfields in West Cyrenaica, the launching of the offensive had been fixed for about this time, the middle of May, but it was deferred till the end of the month. This plan was aborted however, as Rommel attacked first on 27th May. Instead of driving towards the airfields, the British forces had to fall back in front of German pressure. It thus became clear that Malta's future defence rested solely on the island's forces, and replenishments had still to run the Mediterranean gauntlet.

Lord Gort had from the very first days of his governorship become a people's governor. Rather than waiting for attacks and damage to make him go to the people he began to make the rounds for himself. Town after town, and the villages were all visited; he talked with the people and got to know everyone that counted. When he was out with his car on the roads and met pedestrians, he picked them up, for there was no public transport. But this was only for a short time, because to save on petrol he began to use a bicycle for many of his trips, thus giving an example to service chiefs who were now prohibited from using their cars unless on essential service. He soon became at home with the anti-aircraft batteries and other military establishments, and air-raids did not disrupt his visits. These were little things perhaps, but they brought him closer to the people than his predecessor had been. There was the bishop of Malta, Dom Maurus Caruana who was a very important person to know, and Monsignor Michael Gonzi, the Bishop of Gozo who had been dubbed as being anti-British, but Gort felt he would meet him some day and decide for himself.

There was now more recognition being given to acts of gallantry by Maltese members of the garrison and the passive defence. There had been a time when such acts remained unmentioned or were simply recorded, while much less meritorious acts by Britishers were getting all the medals. 'If a Britisher sneezes,' there was a common saying, 'he gets a medal for it.' Picking on an example at random one may mention the cases of two Maltese gunners, L.V. Bone of the 7th Heavy AA Regiment, and Carmel Briffa of the 2nd Heavy AA Regiment. Bone was hit between the shoulders by a shell splinter during action. In great pain and unable to move his neck he remained at his post without showing that he was hurt so as not to stop firing, and carried on until the attack was over. Briffa was thrown off his balance by the blast of a close bomb when his position was under attack, and got the tips of two fingers caught in the mechanism of the gun, between the breach ring and the mounting when the gun ran out after firing. With his fingers trapped and in excruciating pain he calmly waited for the gun to fire again so that the recoil would release his crushed fingers. He then carried on at his post until the raid was over, and only then reported for medical attention. After this was given he insisted on resuming his place and carrying on. Neither of these gunners was considered for a medal, and only received an entry in their records. But a British Warrant Officer got an MBE for saving pots and pans from the debris of a bombed kitchen so that he could make a meal for the men. A British Major also received the

Military Cross for swimming across the harbour to attend to the
batteries on the opposite side, his citation read. Those close to him
said that he could not even swim. After Lord Gort's arrival there
were many unglamorous jobs which brought their holders
recognition for meritorious service. Louis Demajo Albanese, and
Charles Jones, both Superintendents in the ARP services, received
an MBE for their sterling work. So did Anthony Attard, John
Attard, and Arthur Mortimer, three engineers in the Telephone,
Electricity and Water Departments for their tireless service in
keeping the service going under the danger and difficulties of the
moment. Superintendent V. De Gray of the Malta Police, and
Passive Defence reservists F. Calleja and C. Galea received BEM's.

But even with all the impact Lord Gort had made and the
relations he established, he was well aware of the two imminent
dangers that had to be faced — a possible invasion, which he knew
Kesselring had had approved by Hitler, and which Rommel's
successful offensive in North Africa could make easier and more
possible, and the other ever persistent shortage of provisions. This
latter was more like the wolf at the door. A crash plan entailed a
review and redeployment of the forces available to meet the first
contingency, and strong-handed action for the second one. While
his call which carried more weight went out for the second
requirement, which had now more than ever become urgent, Gort
proceeded with the first task. He appreciated the importance of
anti-aircraft defences in any eventual invasion by airborne
landings, but he was more in his element with the infantry, which
he was immediately convinced would have to play a major part in
repelling any invader. What were the forces at his disposal in this
quarter?

The main force he had to rely upon was the 231st Brigade
which was made up of the following British regiments. The Royal
Irish Fusiliers, The Buffs, Royal East/Essex Kents, The Queens'
Own Royal West Kents, Devonshire Regiment, Dorsetshire
Regiment, King's Own Royal Regiment, Lancashire Fusiliers,
Royal Hampshire Regiment, Durham Light Infantry, Inniskilling
Regiment, Manchester Regiment, and Cheshire Regiment. To
supplement the British Brigade there was the versatile and highly
trained local King's Own Malta Regiment which had three
battalions (1st, 2nd and 3rd) and No 10 Static battalion. For
artillery support there were the 12th and the 25th Field
Regiments of the Royal Artillery equipped with field guns and
howitzers of the moment. There was no armour to speak of in the

way of tanks, as the restricted local terrain did not offer much scope, but there was a good number of the versatile Bren gun carriers.

Although doubtful about the kind of contribution it made, one must mention the Home Guard which was composed of hundreds of men, by now trained and armed with rifles and hand grenades, and whose objective was to man defence posts in their particular town or village. Between Home Guard, Police, Air Raid Precautions personnel, and Demolition and Clearance Squads, and Auxiliary Corps, there were 4,000 men. It was now a set-up, which together with the Coast and Anti-Aircraft regiments of the Royal Malta Artillery could handle any situation. There was of course the Royal Air Force, and particularly the Spitfires which on the end of May were again strengthened by another 55 delivered again by *Eagle* in its shuttle service.

So the end of May brought in June, and crucial expectations on both sides. Kesselring, who had by now assembled most of the forces he had been building up for the invasion of Malta, was looking expectantly at Rommel's progress as he believed that as soon as Tobruk would be occupied he would be given the go-ahead for the attack on Malta. Gort, on the other hand, satisfied that he had the forces he wanted was endeavouring to bring the necessary provisions and ammunition not only because they were urgently needed, but also to have a reserve for any eventual attack. Notwithstanding the easing up of air-raids, May had also produced a tally of 116 enemy aircraft destroyed. With the pangs of shortages, now particularly that of kerosene, playing on everyone's nerves, news was received of an early attempt to relieve the situation. The plan was to move out two convoys from the west and the east timed to converge on Malta with a view of breaking down enemy attacks that were sure to be forthcoming. The first convoy which was given the code name of Operation Harpoon left Clyde on 5th June, under the command of Admiral Curtiss flying his flag on the cruiser *Kenya* which was accompanied by the cruiser *Liverpool*. There were also the destroyers *Onslow, Middleton, Kuyawiak* (Polish), *Escapade, Bedouin, Icarus, Matchless, Blankney, Marne* and *Badsworth*. This force was escorting five merchantmen, i.e. *Crari, Troilus, Burdwan, Tanishbar* (Dutch) and *Chant* (American). To join them at Gibraltar was Force T composed of the battleship *Malaya*, the aircraft-carriers *Eagle* and *Argus*, the anti-aircraft cruisers *Cairo* and *Charybdis*, and the destroyers *Partridge, Antelope, Westcott, Vedette, Ithuriel, Wishart* and *Wrestler* together with the minesweepers *Hebe, Rye, Speedy* and *Hythe*. With these, there were to join the convoy as well the *Welshman*, again fully stocked, and the tanker *Kentucky*. When this convoy reached Gibraltar on 11th June, the other one from the east left Alexandria. Code-named Vigorous it was under the command of Admiral Vian flying his colours in the cruiser *Cleopatra* which was accompanied by the cruisers *Dido, Euryalus, Hermione, Arethusa, Newcastle, Birmingham,* and the anti-aircraft cruiser *Coventry*. There were also 26 destroyers, 4 corvettes and 2 mine-sweepers. The merchantmen being escorted were the *City of Lincoln, City of Edinburgh, Ajax, City of Pretoria, Elizabeth Bakki* (Norwegian), *Potaro, Butan, City of Calcutta, Rembrandt, Aagtkirk* (Dutch) and the tanker *Bulkoil*.

It is not known how the people came to know, but rumours were rife that a convoy was on its way to Malta, and there were prayers being said for its safe arrival. To the Maltese, the endeavours and sacrifices of the men in those merchantmen and their escorts had become also their own. This feeling was predominant on 11th June, the second anniversary of the Battle of Malta, up to when the island had been attacked from the air 2,537 times. These raids had made havoc of their homes, and killed 1,215 of their people, but had not destroyed their spirit. The enemy had paid his price too, not only in ships and men which met their doom at sea from action by the Malta forces, but also by 590 planes which were shot down over the island.

The eastern convoy ran into immediate trouble when heavy formations of German aircraft from Crete attacked it just after it had left. *City of Calcutta* was hit and could not continue, so she turned back to Tobruk. The Dutch ship *Elizabeth Bakki* was also hit and had to return to Alexandria. When the first formations emptied their bombs other aircraft from Tripoli took over and the *Aagkirk* and *Butan* were sunk. The cruiser *Hermione* was also sunk without any survivors. The Italian fleet had gone out, but before it could intercept the convoy it was attacked by torpedo bombers from Malta and also from the United States Army Air Corps which had now been operating in the Mediterranean, hitting the battle-ships *Littorio* and *Cavour*, and sinking a heavy cruiser and damaging two destroyers. From the continued air attacks the three destroyers *Hasty, Grove,* and *Airedale* were lost, and what remained of the convoy had to turn back as there was no chance or scope to proceed to Malta.

The western convoy was having similar difficulties. After it left

Gibraltar it was attacked by U-Boats, and then by German and Italian aircraft from Sardinia. One by one the convoy ships began to be picked out and the escorts made the usual spirited defence. Two Italian cruisers and five destroyers tried to make an interception but they had to withdraw quickly in face of the heavy escort. What ships were not sunk by air attack, were destroyed when hitting mines, and this left only two ships intact. The destroyer *Bedouin* and the Polish *Kuyawiak* made the supreme sacrifice and were sunk, but there were no more casualties until what remained of the convoy approached Malta where it was given air cover by Spitfires from the island. Tension increased when on 15th June there were continuous sounds of gunfire at sea heard all over Malta. Everyone knew that a battle was in progress for what was left of the convoy.

The following day, two laden merchantmen reached Malta and of course there was also the *Welshman*. The Grand Harbour was soon covered by a smoke screen, and the preparations which Lord Gort had introduced for the quick unloading and carrying away of merchandise were put into operation, notwithstanding the 7 raids the enemy carried out in an attempt to destroy the ships. These included also a clearance of the routes beforehand so that vehicles carrying the stores would not be delayed on the road. On 17th June therewere six more attempts to sink the ships in harbour, but now there were ample Spitfires to protect them. This time not a single object was lost from the ships.

Had all the ships in the convoys reached Malta, Field Marshal Kesselring would still not have been disturbed. His next move against the island was now going to be the invasion. It had been agreed by everybody that it should take place after the occupation of Tobruk.

Rommel was now poised for the final assault. His plan included a dive bombing attack by Stukas, and he had asked Kesselring to supply these. Every available plane from Greece and Crete that could dive was sent to North Africa, and Kesselring himself flew there to be with the crews. But his bigger interest in an early occupation of Tobruk was fanned by the impending invasion of Malta. His preparations in that respect were now completed, and since February he had accumulated two parachute divisions under General Student (the victor of Crete) one of which was the German-trained Italian 2nd Parachute Division 'Folgore', troop transport aircraft, heavy freight carrying aircraft, and Giants for tank transport. In addition there were two to three Italian assault divisions, and elements of the navy to shell Malta's fortifications and escort the troop transports and assault craft. All this was to be capped by strong air formations. The operation was code-named Hercules, and the date tentatively given for its implementation was 10th July, provided of course Tobruk was taken by then.

More than ever before, worried because of their lack of knowledge about Malta and her defences, the Italians were in a frenzy about not having managed to find a single person in Malta who would do their bidding and give them information, now that the time had come when their fleet would have to face the deadly coastal guns. It was probably this that made them jump at the idea of a young Maltese turned Fascist in Italy stepping into the breach. Carmelo Borg Pisani, a 26 year old Fascist diehard had been studying in Rome before the war, and he relished such a job. He was given the necessary training, but his biggest asset lay in the fact that he knew Malta and spoke Maltese. He was carried over by submarine during the night, then a dinghy put him on the shore in a heavy swell which turned against the traitor and played havoc with him and his equipment. With the coming of dawn he was located by soldiers, who picked him up and took him to Mtarfa Military Hospital. The fact that he was sent to a military hospital indicates that he was either taken for a Maltese soldier, or an Italian to be taken prisoner. Probably it was the latter. Whichever it was, while in hospital he was recognised by a Maltese military surgeon, and the cat was soon let out of the bag. The crime of treason could have finished Borg Pisani in front of a firing squad, but in an expression of true faith in the Maltese Courts, he was remanded to a civilian trial, which found him guilty of treason five months later, and had him hanged.

Kesselring had no doubt that Tobruk would fall. In fact at 5.20 a.m. on 20th June the attack was launched with a hurricane bombardment by artillery and Stukas, which was followed by an infantry assault. Three hours later German tanks were pouring through the defences and Rommel was on the spot with them to speed the operation. By the afternoon of that same day Tobruk fell.

Two days later, Kesselring visited Rommel, now promoted to Field Marshal at his new Headquarters in Tobruk, with more than congratulations on his mind; he wanted to ask for the return of his air force units for the invasion of Malta, as had been earlier agreed. But Rommel was already briefing his officers for an attack on Sidi Barrani that very morning, indicating that he intended to press on with his advance to Egypt in preference to invading Malta. When the divergence in opinion of the two Field Marshals was referred to Hitler and Mussolini the decision did not take long to come, obviously because it had already been burning in the minds of the two dictators.

Hitler had been very dubious about the success of the invasion because he felt that the Italian Navy would fail to back the invasion force in the face of the British Navy. Besides the fact that the invasion plan included a sea-borne landing of Italian troops at Malta, the success of which he doubted, there was the question of supplies and reinforcements; in this, Hitler told General Student when discussing the plan with him in that month of June, that although his paratroops would probably be able to land in Malta, he felt convinced that the Italian navy would run away the moment it saw the British navy, and leave the German parachute troops stranded in Malta without the supplies and reinforcement they were bound to require.

Mussolini was indeed relieved by the possibility of an easier and more glorifying operation than the invasion of Malta which had been terrifying him. Moreover, Rommel's suggested alternative of pressing on to occupy Egypt weighed more in appeasing his vanity. He was the first to give his reply, and on 24th June sent Rommel this message: 'Duce approves Panzerarmee intention to pursue the enemy into Egypt.' A few days later, Mussolini flew over to Derna, with a white charger following in another aircraft, for his triumphant entry into Cairo.

Italian sources have it on record that Kesselring had agreed that pursuit into Egypt was preferable to an invasion of Malta. But this is not exact. What happened was that when Rommel met stiffer resistance by the British who stopped him at El Alamein, he needed reinforcements which Kesselring had to give him from the forces which had been earmarked for Malta, thus making any invasion impossible. So, Operation Hercules fizzled out.

*

After the menace of the much important invasion had loomed so large for several months, only to fizzle out so incongruously, it would not be amiss to pause here and see what might have been its chances of success, had it been carried out. Other than Kesselring, all those who had at some time expressed themselves so convincingly about Malta's invasion were now suddenly keen to try it. One must ignore Mussolini's assertion of taking Malta in four days; that was only one of his empty boasts. But Rommel had at one time said that he could occupy Malta by paratroops and smoke, while General Student, after having occupied Crete, said that Malta would be easier. There had never been a more irresponsible misrepresentation of facts. Any assessment of possibilities can only be based on the invasion of Crete. It has to be said that Hitler did not want to invade Crete, and he had reluctantly agreed to do it after pressure from General Student. After the island was occupied however, Hitler repented because he felt that the price he had to pay was excessive. This was why he rejected all further overtures that Student was enthusiastically putting forward for similar operations against Cyprus, the Suez Canal and Malta. This was when Student described Malta as being easier than Crete. In my opinion he was then being stupidly enthusiastic as Rommel had been capricious.

If we were to look at the factors that in the opinion of military tacticians contributed to the fall of Crete we will have our answer right away. The principal factor to that disaster was the lack of anti-aircraft defences in the island. They were then described as scanty; therefore troop carriers and gliders could fly at ease and drop their troops where they were wanted. Can anyone in his right senses believe this could be similarly done against Malta with her anti-aircraft barrage? Kesselring's mighty armada of slick Stukas and fast and manouverable Messerschmitts had experienced their worst moments in this barrage, and I have no doubt that any force of heavy troop carriers and gliders would have found its Waterloo in it.

Kesselring himself admitted in his memoirs that two months of intensive air assault by the cream of his airforce had failed to subdue the Maltese anti-aircraft defences (and this we know, as not a single anti-aircraft battery was put out of action indefinitely). How could he hope therefore to do in the few days before invasion what he had failed to do in two months of incessant bombardment? It must also be emphasized that during the time when the invasion was to take place, in July, the RAF had more than enough Spitfires at its disposal.

The second factor that contributed to Crete's fall was the geographical terrain of that island with a few towns and villages, and much more open land where gliders and paratroops could land and regroup away from the eyes of defenders. Malta was certainly different and there was hardly any area in the 95 mile square island where one could land and remain unnoticed. A third factor was that Crete being so close to the Greek islands, the Germans could transport their artillery and heavy equipment by caiques which they commandeered from those islands. To Malta, such equipment would have had to come from Sicily, running the gauntlet under the eyes of the British Fleet, aircraft from Malta, and of course the coastal defence batteries. The last factor was the element of surprise which was prevalent in Crete, and which would certainly not have been reflected in Malta. In fact it can be said, and I can vouch for this, that the proposed date in July for the invasion was known in Malta, where the code word 'asia' was already established signifying invasion. What the British did not know was that Hercules was cancelled, and when Kesselring's troop carriers left Sicily one evening, troops and Home Guard in Malta were alerted, and were not ordered to stand down until the following morning, after it had been ascertained that the troop carriers had gone to North Africa to reinforce Rommel. There was also the other factor of half of the invasion force being Italian, with instructions to effect a landing. Had this been attempted in 1940 they might have had a chance of making it, but in 1942 it was certainly a different matter. And the Italian command knew this, otherwise it would not have imposed the condition on Kesselring to have the coastal defences obliterated before any Italian would approach Malta.

My final comment on this point is that an invasion with the conditions mentioned would have probably failed. I add that Hitler knew all this, and that is why he resisted and finished by cancelling Operation Hercules, which was never raised again. Kesselring too, after the Battle of Sirte, lost all hope in the Italian navy and became openly critical of its inefficiency in battle. This made him realise what would have been the likely outcome, had it been involved in an invasion.

*

The convoy ships that had arrived on 16th June raised many hopes among the population. Sweeping assumptions of the breaking of the blockade, wild hopes of the raising of the siege, and an imagined step towards normalising the situation when every one would be able to get what he wants and as much as he wanted. It was however a totally different picture for Lord Gort. Truly, the convoy ships had brought in 15,000 tons of stores, but they had only been part of a convoy of six ships amongst which the package of essentials that were required with priority had to be balanced. It could therefore not be helped when it was found out that the most essential items happened to be those in small quantities on these vessels. Such shortages were of course balanced by bigger quantities of others with less priority where requirement was concerned. So while there was little wheat, there was more tinned fish; the little tinned milk was balanced with beans. It was an explainable situation, but none the less worrying. If there was no wheat, as most of it had gone down with another ship, no amount of tinned fish was going to substitute for bread. One couldn't very well issue beans instead of milk, now that the goats were all going to be slaughtered for Victory Kitchens. What was to be done? Nothing much. A balance had to be struck somehow.

That something like this could happen seemed to have been foreseen, and the services of Sir Jack Drummond from the Ministry of Food in London, and another, had been acquired, who were now in Malta. Lord Gort gave them this nasty problem to sort out. The rest he would do himself. What was to be the rest? The first thing he wanted to do was to tell the people the truth about the situation.

On 20th June Sir Edward Jackson told the people everything in a broadcast. He chose his words and balanced his arguments, but no amount of balancing could shift the weight from the side which was already hard pressed in the scales. There was not going to be any increase in the bread ration, and this was because bread was the main Maltese meal (obviously it would have been reduced if it wasn't for this). There will be no reduction in tinned meat, and there would be an increase in tinned fish. Luckily this was fish in oil, which could therefore make up for reductions in the ration of edible oil. Then there was a long list of items which would be reduced by half on the ration scale. Kerosene was one of them.

The talk was padded by information about the extension of Victory Kitchens to cover all Malta and with promises of attempts to improve menus, and the subtle mention of a target date up to which essential supplies must serve and be replenished. All attempts would be made to make it before then, but what would happen if they were not, was left to the imagination of the listeners.

One thing which was not mentioned but which became obvious was that no supplies of fuel had been received. This of course did not only mean lack of petrol for the buses, but also less aviation spirit for aircraft, no oil for generators which were used for searchlights and other defence machinery. If there was no petrol for buses there would similarly not be any for army transport, bren gun carriers, fire-engines, ambulances, cranes, bulldozers, and other equipment which had become tools to be used daily in a place like Malta, still under daily bombardment, and awaiting an invasion. This had of course come about because the only tanker in the convoy had been lost.

The surprise item in the goods brought by the convoy ships was a consignment of knitting wool and clothing, mostly underwear, and these were put out for fair distribution by coupons. Knitting would shorten time when waiting for one's doom, and new underwear can make a corpse look neater. It provided some badly needed humour when an old priest received as his share, a pair of bloomers. Gort was now too busy understanding what his predecessor had suffered, but with him it was a little different. Dobbie had waited in anguish for a convoy, but Gort wanted one and a tanker, as no merchantman could carry all the fuel he needed. And tankers were priority targets for enemy attacks.

Even with all the subtle technique he had brought with him, and the appeal and respect he had oozed out of the Maltese, and the George Cross he had brought them (he remembered he still had to have a presentation ceremony) he finished by being faced with the same thorny problem that faced Sir William Dobbie. It was now that he would have to act differently. To the public he promised that somehow he would get them through, and he took severe action against hoarders and black marketeers. To the British Cabinet he explained the situation — not in a negative attitude of having to ensure a convoy for Malta's sake, but in a positive way linking the island's revival of offensive activity. To himself he promised that he would get the supplies he wanted. He was well aware that there could be an invasion, which if it did come would be over in a matter of days, whether it was won or lost, making no difference in the eight weeks ahead which would bring Malta to its target date. If it was relieved by then.... he stopped thinking in this direction, because it must, and it would. Perhaps this was how Lord Gort differed from Sir William Dobbie. With Sir Alexander Hardinge he could afford to be a little more open. 'Everything depends on a convoy' he told him 'and especially an oiler.'

The fall of Tobruk made invasion more imminent, and even Gort had to put aside his worries about the supply position. Now that he had the date of 10th July for a possible invasion, and there was no hope of getting his convoy by then he was methodical enough to temporarily ignore the convoy and concentrate on invasion. After all if it did come he would resist it or bust, and if he failed, the question of supplies in eight weeks' time would be somebody's else's problem. The American aircraft-carrier *Wasp,* now forming part of an American Naval Squadron in the Mediterranean, delivered some more Spitfires to Malta. They arrived during an air raid, and as soon as they landed they hastily refuelled and went straight into action. At Luqa airfield the first Liberator aircraft landed, which would contribute to the offensive effort of the island, which was immediately geared up. On 21st June, two transports of 10,000 tons were located while they were proceeding to Tripoli, and torpedo bombers from Hal Far got them just outside Tripoli Harbour. They attacked them, sinking one and hitting the other which managed to make harbour in a damaged condition. Both of them were carrying troops and tanks for Rommel. On the 22nd a tanker was bombed on its way from Naples to Palermo. On the 23rd, two ships which had left Palermo were both hit, and had to be towed back to the harbour delaying supply of material to Rommel. Two others which had left Taranto on 30th June had to return there after being hit.

These delays must have irritated Rommel, and this could have been the reason why air attacks on Malta were intensified at the beginning of July, but as it was not yet known that the invasion had been cancelled it was thought that the heavy attacks were the expected prelude. During June, the defences had destroyed 140 enemy aircraft, 54 of which were shot down by Spitfires.

This time attacks began with a heavy night raid just after midnight on 2nd July in which several formations of bombers took part dropping high explosive and incendiary bombs. Guns and night fighters shot down 4. From the morrow attacks kept mounting up, and so did the toll of those being shot down. Attacks reached their heaviest on 7th July when mixed German and Italian formations attacked the airfields six times. Several dogfights took place, and 24 enemy planes were shot down while another 26 were so damaged that they were unlikely to reach their base. Five Spitfires were lost, but all their pilots baled out to safety. Each day was pointing to an imminent invasion, and no chances were taken. The people had already received indications about the possibility of invasion, and although they had no dates they could see the preparations as troops were deployed. However, if they did know what was going on, they did not say anything about it.

It is possible that the British already knew about the cancellation, and were taking precautions just in case, but I still remember clearly when as the officer in charge of the Home Guard platoon at the city of Vittoriosa I was called and given instructions to await a possible attack. We were mobilized, given ammunition and food so as to be self-contained, and during the evening I went round myself calling all my men from their homes, and after a pep talk by the area company commander saw my men to their various posts where they were to spend the night so as to be in position for any eventual attack at first dawn, when paratroops attacks generally take place. When I was asked to stand down my men, I was told that a force of troop carriers had indeed left Sicily, but flew past Malta, obviously to North Africa. By that day, which was only the tenth one of July the Spitfires had shot down 78 enemy aircraft.

With the threat of invasion virtually over, attention could be concentrated on other problems, but while a solution was readily found for operational commitments, what problems involved supplies could only be patched up. What milk remained was restricted to children, while potatoes were exhausted and disappeared from sight. Indirectly this brought more pressure on wheat since there wasn't any more puree to mix with it. Soap had become worth its weight in gold. With the list of available commodities getting shorter every day it soon became obvious that what the enemy had not succeeded to do by bombings and invasion would be obtained by the blockade. Operationally, things were looking brighter, and on 18th July Air Vice Marshal Lloyd, the Air Officer Commanding who had borne so magnificently the brunt of the blitz, and never slept away from his office in order to be at hand at all times during his 14 months of command, was substituted. In his place was appointed Air Vice Marshal Keith Rodney Park, one of the officers who had played a big part in the defeat of the Luftwaffe in the Battle of Britain. He was considered to be one of the biggest exponents in operational command of fighter aircraft.

As if to reflect the newly infused spirit in the RAF there was the incident of 29th July when an alert was given on the approach of one enemy aircraft. It was an Italian Cant Z 506B flying boat, approaching the island surprisingly low, and without any escort as if to challenge the defences which were bound to blow it to blazes. Onlookers said they could see something like a white piece of cloth stuck to the pilot's cockpit, while communications reported receiving a friendly call sign from the aircraft. The defences desisted from opening fire, and the flying boat came down at Kalafrana. From its bowels emerged Flight Lieutenant E.T. Strever and the rest of an RAF crew of a Beaufort aircraft, who had been picked up by the Italian crew of the flying boat to be taken into captivity. But on the way to Taranto, the British airmen had overpowered their captors and brought over the Italian aircraft to Malta. Lieutenant Mastrovieni and his captured crew looked none the worse for their ordeal as they left the flying boat under escort.

Because of the change in the situation it was also decided to re-establish the submarine base at Lazaretto and the submarine *Utmost* blazed the trail from the west, to be followed by *Unbroken* and within twenty four hours by *United*. Victory Kitchens were extended to every available place and the whole population was soon eating what it was handed, which began to get less every day. There was only one occasion when the people rose up in arms, this was when green stinking liver was served, and most of it was pelted back at those who served it. But what could they do? It was all they had for that day. It had become a situation which called for tears of desperation as an encore, and Lord Gort bore with it all, thinking no doubt of the obvious outcome if his pressing calls for a convoy were not acted upon. But if it was to meet the need of the moment it had to be a super convoy which would ensure provisions, ammunition and fuel. The three items had more or less the same target date on his list which would be reached in three weeks' time. If any one of them failed to be brought through, then the other two would be useless, and Malta would fall.

His thoughts were not spoken of again since the tailored but outspoken speech by his Lieutenant Governor, but the people knew. They knew as they noticed the firing getting weaker and shorter during attacks, and the Spitfires flying in smaller formations. They knew as they saw the sausages and beans being ladled out more sparingly as they queued for their daily portion, as if those items too were like the shells and gallons of aviation spirit all numbered. Indeed, as the last days of July rolled on to August, everyone was convinced that Malta's days, which meant their own, were numbered. Worse than this was only the lurking feeling that not even Lord Gort could save them. There had only to be a miracle.

Gort had appealed to them as being more determined and sure of himself and their fate than Dobbie had been, and unlike him he did not often have recourse to God in his steady and bold speech. They had trusted him, and still did, but it now seemed to them that there was no further place for boldness and determination. The target date for these virtues had been reached, and fizzled out, and they were only left with their last morsels to crunch and watch the last fighters and guns straggle with their last drops of aviation spirit and ammunition. Their only hope was not in Gort, but in God. It was to Him they had recourse. As always their hearts and prayers went to the Blessed Virgin, whose feast would fall in two weeks' time under the title of Santa Maria.

CHAPTER FOURTEEN

The Santa Maria Convoy

If Gort was preoccupied with the situation, the British Cabinet was no less worried. Every possibility had been tried to relieve Malta without success. Gort was well known, and if he was saying that Malta had only three more weeks to live, then it must be so, and the Cabinet was all behind him. The fact had to be faced that the zenith had been reached, and there was no other way but to attempt another convoy. This time, however, it would be bigger than any that had been ever attempted before, and it would have the most powerful escort so far. This gave birth to Operation Pedestal.

The convoy was to have two naval escorts: Force Z, which would accompany it as far as the approaches to the Sicilian Channel, and Force X, which would continue as far as Malta. Force Z was to be under the command of Vice Admiral E.N. Syfret, flying this flag on the battleship *Nelson*. It would have another battleship, *Rodney*, the aircraft-carriers *Victorious* (Rear-Admiral Lyster), *Eagle*, *Indomitable* and *Argus*. There would be the three cruisers *Sirius*, *Charybdis* and *Phoebe*, accompanied by the destroyers *Eskimo*, *Somali*, *Zetland*, *Antelope*, *Laforey*, *Lookout*, *Quentin*, *Wishart*, *Tartar*, *Lightning*, *Ithuriel* and *Vansittart*. Force X was to be composed of the cruisers *Nigeria* (Rear Admiral H. Burrough), *Manchester*, *Kenya* and *Cairo*. In support there would be the destroyers *Ledbury*, *Penn*, *Bicester*, *Ashanti*, *Icarus*, *Fury*, *Pathfinder*, *Wilton*, *Intrepid*, *Foresight*, *Derwent* and *Bramham*, together with the tow vessel *Jaunty*. There would also be the supply Force R to replenish the warships, consisting of the tankers *Brown Ranger* and *Dridgedale*, escorted by the corvettes *Spimea*, *Coltsfoot*, *Geranium* and *Jonquil*, with the tow vessel *Salvonia*.

As wards of this strong escort there were to be the merchantmen *Warrangi*, *Empire Hope*, *Brisbane Star*, *Santa Eliza* (American), *Port Chalmers*, *Rochester Castle*, *Dorset*, *Glenorchy*, *Melbourne Star*, *Warmarana*, *Almeria Lykes* (American), *Clan Ferguson* and *Deucalion*, together with the tanker *Ohio* (which was American but captained and manned by a British crew).

To follow further back there was the aircraft carrier *Furious*, which was to carry and launch Spitfires for Malta, together with its escort consisting of the destroyers *Vedette*, *Venomous*, *Amazon*, *Keppel*, *Malcolm*, *Wolverine*, *Wrestler* and *Westcott*. The three aircraft carriers responsible for the air defence of the convoy were to fly squadrons of fighter aircraft constantly which were to be Hurricanes, Fulmars, and Grumman Martletts. In coordination with the convoy when it reached the dangerous zone near Sardinia, bombers were to attack the Sardinian airfields so as to harass the torpedo bombers which normally attacked convoys from there. The Malta submarines, now numbering eight, were to be placed in a patrol line of six to the south of Pantellaria, which was considered to be the likely route of attacking Italian naval forces, with the other two to go to Cape St Vito and Cape Milazzo on the north coast of Sicily.

The first handicap to the convoy was that the Italians knew of it before it left Britain, and knowing of its importance to Malta's survival and the outcome of the war in the Mediterranean, they made, in conjunction with the Germans, all the preparations for its destruction. The naval forces alerted for intervention were the 3rd and 7th Divisions of their fleet, consisting of the heavy cruisers *Gorizia* (Admiral Parona), *Trieste* and *Bolzano*, with the destroyers *Camicia Nera*, *Aviere*, *Geniere*, *Legionario*, *Ascari*, *Grecale* and *Corsaro*, for one division, and for the other, there were the light cruisers *Eugenio di Savoia* (Admiral Da Zara), *Raimondo Montecuccoli*, and *Muzio Attendolo*, with destroyers *Maestrale*, *Oriani*, *Fuciliere* and *Gioberti*. There were also to be light surface forces comprising the No 15 and No 20 E-Boat Squadrons. For underwater attack there were the submarines *Ascianghi*, *Dessie*, *Dandolo*, *Wolframio*, *Granito*, *Grada*, *Bronzo*, *Dagabur*, *Cobalto*, *Atogi*, *Avorio*, *Emo*, *Axum*, *Brin*, *Veletta*, *Uarsciek*, *Asteria* and *Otaria*. The Germans also provided two U-Boats, *U-73* and *U-333*, together with four Motor Torpedo Boats.

With the two forces thus arraigned, the stage was set for what could prove to be one of the biggest convoy battles of the war.

The convoy left Britain without fuss, and in the early hours of 10th August went past Gibraltar, to be immediately reported upon by a Spanish passenger plane flying to North Africa. The remaining hours of the day were uneventful, but at 1000 hours of the following day there was the first attack by Junkers 88 which was met and contained by the Fulmars and Hurricanes from the carriers. At about that time British Beauforts and American Liberators attacked the three Sardinian airfields at Elmos, Decimomannu and Vellacidro, where, the Italians admit, 22 aircraft were put out of action.

As the convoy reached the usual position south of the Balearic Isles at 1229 the carrier *Furious* launched 38 Spitfire Vs for Malta of which only one could not make it. It was while they were engaged in this operation that U-Boat 73 (Lieutenant Rosenbraun) penetrated the destroyer screen and hit *Eagle* with four torpedoes, sinking her immediately. The Italian submarine *Dagabur* was trying a similar attack on *Furious* but was pounced upon by the destroyer *Wolverine* and sunk by depth charges before it could do any harm. A further attack was made on the convoy that day by 37 Junkers 88 all diving like devils on the ships, but they hit only the merchantman *Deucalion* which had to leave the convoy and proceed towards the Tunisian coast.

The worse attacks came on 12th August beginning with a formation made up of 14 S79 torpedo bombers, 28 Macchi 202, a squadron of Me109s and two formations of Stukas (piloted by both German and Italian pilots). Their attack was directed at the aircraft carriers, and they hit *Indomitable* setting her on fire. *Victorious* was also hit, but with less damage. The destroyer *Foresight* was also seriously damaged in this attack and had to be sunk by her companion *Tartar*.

During these attacks Italian aircraft used their new weapon, the Motobomba FF, which was a bomb/mine, dropped by parachute, with an automatic pressure device, which activated a motor on contact with water, and drove the bomb in a circle with a radius of some 15 kilometres chancing to hit some ship. But it was not effective. It had now become time for Force Z to return to Gibraltar and leave Force X to carry on with the convoy. One may question the wisdom behind such a decision in the circumstances. It is true that there were two damaged carriers to be taken back as they were of no further help to the convoy, but there were also two battleships and aircraft carriers, three cruisers and twelve destroyers being denied to the convoy when it was approaching the most difficult part of its journey, and only 36 hours away from its destination. Had half of this force been left behind it would have added weight in the holocaust that was destined to hit that convoy, which was now without fighter protection. So Force Z turned back as ordered.

It was at dusk that the enemy launched its next heavy attacks, no doubt now encouraged by the weaker escort and the absence of fighters from the damaged carriers. The first attack was by a pack of submarines, and the submarine *Axum* hit the cruisers *Cairo*, and *Nigeria*, as well as the tanker *Ohio* with one torpedo each, sinking the *Cairo*. Another submarine hit the cruiser *Kenya* with another torpedo. With three of the four cruisers hit, the convoy was put in confusion, and it was at that time that thirty Junkers 88 and seven Heinkel 111 torpedo bombers swooped on the ships hitting *Brisbane Star, Empire Hope* and *Glenorcky*. *Empire Hope*, however, seemed to be singled out. Before it was hit, she had no less than 18 near misses. When she received a direct hit, a 15 foot hole was opened on its side, and the bomb blast wounded her gunners and threw many men overboard. A fire was started and it soon reached the cargo of aviation spirit being carried on the bridge deck. It was merciful when the ship was torpedoed and sunk by the submarine *Bronzo*. The damaged *Glenorcky* was also finished by a torpedo from E Boat 31. The *Brisbane Star* was hit by a torpedo from a Heinkel and was stopped. It instantly became a sitting target, but rather than being discouraged her crew went all out to make the necessary repairs. When they did, and the ship could make headway at a slow speed, her captain decided to leave the convoy and head south in the hope of finding shelter closer to the Tunisian coast. *Clan Ferguson* was also first hit by a Heinkel torpedo. It was set on fire, and as it was carrying ammunition it became an immediate hazard. There was no hope of it being saved, so it was fortunate when it was finished with another torpedo from submarine *Alagi*. As darkness fell the enemy E Boats pressed home their attacks, and while two of them took up and sank the cruiser *Manchester*, the others sank the merchantmen *Wairangi*, *Santa Eliza* and *Almeria Lykes*.

No one can give the exact details of what went on throughout that night, and the position could only be properly reviewed the following morning when dawn showed only the *Melbourne Star*, *Waimarama* and *Rochester Castle* in their convoy position. The tanker *Ohio* was farther back with the destroyer *Ledbury* in attendance, while 10 miles behind could be seen *Port Chalmers* and *Dorset* escorted by the destroyers *Bramham* and *Pathfinder*. *Brisbane Star*, which had also been hit and tried to get close to the Tunisian coast, could not be seen. This was what remained of the mighty convoy on which so much depended. With only some ten hours away from Malta, but within range of enemy forces from Sicily and Pantellaria, and with all the cruiser force out of action, rather than being near, it seemed still so far from reaching its destination. If there was any reorganisation after the night's confusion it had to be carried out quickly. But the ships were not given time. At 0810, twelve Junkers 88 delivered a diving attack, sinking *Waimarama*. At 1050 a formation of Stukas and Junkers 88 divebombed the remnants of the convoy hitting *Dorset* and *Rochester Castle*. One of the two Stukas which were shot down in this attack, which was manned by Italian airmen Sergeant Raimondo Oscar and air gunner Aldo Tarabotti, crashed on to the *Ohio*. At 1125 there was a further attack by Italian torpedo bombers.

Most of the ships had then moved forward to come within cover of Spitfires from Malta, but the *Ohio* and *Dorset* could not move as fast and lagged behind. When 14 Stukas came to attack they found only them, and unleashed their wrath on the two ships. *Dorset* was sunk.

The convoy was now dispersed. A part of it had proceeded forward on its own leaving the stricken *Ohio* behind. It looked as if everyone was trying to make it on his own. If the convoy was in such a confusion, the Italians were not less confused, and this is indicated from their records of this action where it is found that a squadron of Junkers 77 (Pichiatelli) flown by Italians operating from Pantellaria, was the whole time under the impression that the *Ohio* was an aircraft carrier. It was this squadron escorted by 23 Macchi 202s which delivered the last attack on the tanker. The report made, which still appears in the record was that the aircraft carrier *Ohio* was hit, and probably sunk. The truth was that they had hit only the minesweeper *Rye* which was with the tanker, together with the destroyers *Penn* and *Ledbury*.

For the whole series of attacks the enemy had paid with 66 aircraft which were shot down. But these would not be of any value to Malta's needs. What were needed were ships, and the tanker.

The people had been talking about a convoy since 11th August, and the tension from uncertainty as to whether the ships would make it could be seen on every face. Prayers were more fervent in shelters and in churches, and the convoy was on everybody's lips, even though no one knew what and how many ships were attempting to reach the island. The only contact with them was kept through the distant sound of gunfire which could be heard throughout 12th August. When on the 13th gunfire was heard closer and Spitfires were seen flying out in formation it became evident that whatever ships there were, must have been very close, and the tension increased.

In the afternoon, the word went round that the convoy ships were seen only a mile or two away from Malta. The word spread like wild 'fire, and all the people in the Grand Harbour area left home and shelter and ran to get a position of vantage on the bastions. Men, women, and children; soldiers, sailors, airmen, priests and nuns; they were all there to be in the crowd to witness the ships' arrival which would decide whether Malta would survive or not. As time moved forward without any development, people from the villages began to arrive to join the crowds on the bastions. Lord Gort, was also there, sharing in the heart-rending tension that was on the sea of faces. He had a word and a smile for everyone, but he had done that even at Dunkirk. There were also other things in doubt; hadn't the *Talabot* and the *Pampas* reached harbour as well in the last convoy only to be destroyed in port? Gunners and Spitfires however were now on the alert ready to prevent that happening again.

Suddenly, the first ship appeared, and wild cheering went up from the thousands on the bastions. Everyone could see the black twisted metal of the ship's deck which did not even leave space for members of the crew to stand and acknowledge the cheering that was already reaching them. But crew or no crew, the ship made harbour like a lady. Even with the wrong type of make-up she became the toast of the crowds. Union Jacks, and Red and White flags went up in the hands of children, and their young voices began singing 'Rule Britannia'. It was a hero's welcome for the *Melbourne Star*. A couple of tugs with steel helmeted members of their crew alert on their raised Bren guns took the ship in hand to lead her to her berth. Then another ship appeared, this time the *Rochester Castle*, looking more magnificent than her predecessor between the arms of breakwater, to receive the cheering which had not stopped. Her deck was also shattered, but her holds were intact. The *Port Chalmers* came next, with her head still up and steady. The cheering was now choked by tears, and everyone was moved with emotion at seeing the three fine ships which spelled rescue and salvation. There was one man, however, who was the first to lose his smile as he saw the harbour's boom being closed again. Lord Gort looked for the tanker, which was not there.

As the crowds began to disperse, stevedores, labourers and troops were waiting at the berthing places, and as the ships were moored, rushed the decks to start on their work of unloading. There were still some people on the bastions as if to see the operation through, but they soon dispersed when the sirens began wailing. Everyone ran to the shelter, except those who were unloading. They stuck to their job. The gunners, stripped to their waist in the August heat raised their guns. So did the warships inside and outside harbour, while Spitfires roared overhead on their way out to intercept whoever was intruding to harm the hard fought-for ships. But whoever it was, failed to turn up, and the Raiders Passed was soon sounded. The unloading continued without stopping.

Later that evening, while prayers of thanksgiving were being said in churches, and particularly in six of Malta's villages and one in Gozo, where the second day of Triduum in preparation for the feast of Santa Maria being celebrated there on the 15th, something spectacular was happening in Grand Harbour. A spectre had appeared between the arms of breakwater. It was more like some fantastic modern art creation made of torn and blackened steel. But as it limped forward it soon took the form of the ship it had once been. It was the merchantman *Brisbane Star* which had straggled on hugging the Tunisian coast, and now managed to make port. Tugs rushed to her in welcome, and it soon joned the rest. So instead of three, there were now four ships.

But Lord Gort, and those around him were still worried. They had hoped for the tanker which had not arrived. Indeed, they would have had something else to worry about had they known that most of the wheat in the convoy, had been carried in the ships *Santa Eliza* and *Almeria Lykes*. both of which had been sunk. But one could juggle and improvise with four ships, and work out something — except oil and fuel. This could only come from the tanker which had not arrived.

'What are the chances?' asked the ADC to the perturbed Governor, still with the message in his hand that gave him all the story.

Without even lifting his eyes to give the reply, Gort murmured: 'Only a miracle can do it.'

*

I must now digress and return to the early days of this convoy in order to come to an episode which has great significance for my story. When the eight Malta submarines were detailed to their position to intercept the Italian fleet should it attack the convoy, Lieutenant Commander Alastair Mars, the commanding officer of the submarine *Unbroken,* remonstrated with Captain Simpson, the flotilla commanding officer, about the position he was allocated two miles off Cape Milazzo. He thought it unlikely that enemy warships would pass anywhere near it. But Captain Simpson stuck to his orders since they were not of his choosing, but of the Admiralty. So *Unbroken* went to her station as ordered. Whilst there, it was located and attacked and there were no fewer than 70 depth charges dropped on her. When, on the night of 11th August the submarine surfaced in darkness, her commanding officer found himself 15 miles away from Cape Milazzo. The problem he had before he left, now somehow reasserted itself, and something like a sixth sense was telling him to abandon the station he was given and choose another one himself. The lines he was thinking on meant disobeying orders, which would certainly jeopardise his career as well as the mission he was sent on. It was something unheard of in the annals of the British Navy. Yet, after reflection he made his decision to disobey the orders given to him, and to think of a spot where enemy warships were more likely to be hiding from prying submarines, and he could not say how and why he decided on the deep waters between the Lipari Islands, north-west of Messina. He went there, and spent the whole of 12th August there, worrying all the time that he might have made a fool of himself.

As was made obvious in previous paragraphs, the enemy cruisers and destroyers did not make an appearance during the running convoy battle, and it would have only been reasonable to assume that they were sheltering somewhere, avoiding battle with British superior forces, and waiting for something easier to pounce upon.

On 13th August the four convoy ships had reached Malta. But they had not saved the island. There was the question of oil and other fuels which had to be got, if Malta were to be saved. They had not arrived with the four ships, because they were being carried, a whole 11,000 tons of them, in the tanker *Ohio,* which was first torpedoed, then hit five times by bombs, and then again by a crashing blazing Stuka. No one could explain how a tanker full to the brim with aviation spirit and other oils could take all this and live. Yet, the *Ohio* did, and, while the other four ships were approaching Malta, she was still some two hundred miles away in deep trouble, with smashed steering gear, decks awash, and a fire still burning, plodding forward, and as if in answer to

Maltese prayers, willed by the intrepid determination of her
skipper, Captain Mason, and kept afloat by two cables, as if in a
cradle held fast on port and starboard by the destroyers *Penn* and
Bramham. Whilst it was still on the surface, and moving, however
slowly, it still had a chance of making its appointment if left
unmolested. This must have been realised from some message
which somehow reached the wrong ears, offering a chance in a
million to the Italians to pounce on the helpless jewel of the
convoy, and in one stroke bring Malta to her knees. It was an
opportunity not to be missed by any force — like the Italian
cruisers in the Lipari Islands, for example. Because that's where
they were. And it was from there that the four cruisers escorted
by eight destroyers and several Cant anti-submarine seaplanes
emerged at full speed, to proceed south, through the Strait of
Messina, which would bring them to the Malta Channel just in
time to meet the helpless *Ohio*.

There could be no doubt that they would have succeeded in
their scope. There was nothing to stand in their way — except
Unbroken, with her surprised but none the less cool headed
commander who did not bat an eyelid as he fired his torpedoes
at the enemy force, hitting the 10,000 ton *Bolzano* and the 7,000
ton *Muzio Attendolo,* damaging them very seriously. One would
have expected the Italian commander to proceed with his two
remaining cruisers to complete his assignment, and leave some
destroyers to deal with the lurking submarine and protect the
immobile cruisers, but he chose to have his destroyers chase the
submarine for eight hours, dropping 105 depth charges, while the
two healthy cruisers picked up survivors. It was fortunate for
them, that the British submarine had no more torpedoes.

But what concerns my story is that while the Italian ships were
detained, the *Ohio* could proceed on her way, and reach Malta on
the morning of 15th August — the feast of Santa Maria.

It may not seem strange that Lieutenant Commander Mars
should have in the first place objected to the station allocated to
him off Cape Milazzo, but it is indeed incredible that he persisted
in his intention and disobeyed orders at the risk of his career. It is
again incomprehensible how when changing station he picked on
the Lipari Islands, where the Italian squadron which was ordered
to dash and destroy the *Ohio* was sheltering. Had things not
happened as they did, there is no doubt that the Italians would
have reached *Ohio* and destroyed her, which would have meant
the fall of Malta. In one of his books Lieutenant Commander

Alastair Mars writes of his conviction that it was he that saved Malta, and the Maltese agree with him. But, beyond the shores of Malta, no one can explain logically the sequence of events that made it possible for him to do it. He cannot even explain it himself.

It is a Maltese belief that this officer was the instrument of God, and what he did was in answer to Malta's prayers.

So ended the dramatic story of the Santa Maria Convoy, which relieved Malta.

CHAPTER FIFTEEN

Lifting of the Siege

On Sunday, 13th September, all roads in Malta led to Valletta, and the Palace Square had never seen so many people since the beginning of hostilities. The ruined streets of the capital, and the damaged buildings in the square, all bearing the scars of bombardment did not detract from the cheerful looks that were evident all round that morning. It was George Cross day. Lord Gort had finally set the day for the medal's presentation to the people of Malta, and Sir George Borg, the Chief Justice, who was the same one who had administered the oath of allegiance to Gort on his arrival in Malta, was to receive it on the people's behalf. Civilian clothing and black *faldettas* intermingled with the sombre black cassocks, and the spick and span military uniforms, as the crowd pressed closer round the space in the square where an empty dais lay in the centre. The Service Chiefs, Members of the Executive Council and other important people who in one way of another had contributed their share in mèriting the decoration. There were also the two bishops, Dom Maurus Caruana of Malta, and Monsignor Michael Gonzi, bishop of Gozo.

Since Monsignor Gonzi was to play, and had indeed already been playing an important part in Maltese history, he requires special mention. In appearance he was astonishingly diminutive, but with a dignified face that impressed through the benign eyes beneath gold-rimmed spectacles. It was a face clearly cut out for a church dignitary, but hiding an equally clear and exact diplomatic brain, and an equable and philosophical temperament. This is not surprising, since he was a rare person, a clergyman who was also a professional philosopher and a proven political figure. During the 1914-1918 war he had served as a military chaplain as well as a professor of Hebrew at the University. Then in 1921 he contested political elections on the side of Labour, and was elected to the Senate where he served up to 1923. He became bishop of Gozo in 1924 at the age of 39, where he was much loved and respected.

At this time in September 1942, he was already helping the ailing bishop of Malta in his pastoral and administrative duties, and in fact a year later he was appointed his coadjutor with right of succession by Pope Pius XII. When Bishop Caruana died in December 1943, Monsignor Gonzi became Archbishop of Malta, which was considered a contravention as much as a merited appointment since, as Lord Gort had been informed, Monsignor Gonzi was considered anti-British and vetoed for such appointment by the British government. Indeed he had always denied this, and history proved him right. It had to be Lord Gort to bring out the truth on this colourful figure, which might have otherwise remained in the shadows of Maltese history. And it was on George Cross day that he had set out to do it.

'On my appointment as Governor of Malta,' said Lord Gort before presenting the George Cross, "I was entrusted to carry the George Cross to this Island Fortress. By the command of the King I now present to the people of Malta and its Dependencies the Decoration which His Majesty has awarded to them in recognition of the gallant service which they have already rendered to the fight for freedom. How you have withstood for many months the most concentrated bombing attacks in the history of the world has the admiration of all civilised peoples. Your homes and your historic buildings have been destroyed, and only their ruins remain as monuments to the hate of the barbarous foe. The Axis Powers have tried again and again to break your spirit, but your confidence in the final triumph of the United Nations remains undimmed. What Malta has withstood in the past, without flinching, Malta is determined to endure until the day when the second siege is raised. Battle-scarred George Cross Malta, the Sentinel of the Empire in the Mediterranean, meanwhile stands firm, undaunted and undismayed, awaiting the time when we can call: "Pass friend, all is well in the Island Fortress." Now it is my proud duty to hand over the George Cross to the people of Malta for safe keeping.'

But before handing the medal, Lord Gort read the scroll which was written with the King's own hand.

To honour her brave people I award the George Cross to the Island Fortress of Malta to bear witness to a heroism and devotion that will long be famous in history.

It was a brief but significant ceremonial which brought into focus all that Malta had been through for the last twenty six months, and it must have raised many illusions that the difficult times were over. But definitely not with Gort. His was a more comprehensive assessment of the situation, jarred by the miscalculation he had made some days before when to keep a promise he had made to the people he increased the bread ration for males between the age of 16 and 60, without giving due consideration to the wheat which had gone down with two ships of the convoy. But as the crowds were dispersing it was no time for such thoughts, and as he walked to the group of high personages that remained behind he soon became the centre of a talkative noisy group. He greeted them all, exchanging an extra word with the ones he knew best. But all the time he was walking and approaching the short man in the red cassock. Perhaps one of the great pleasures known to man is reunion with some friend after prolonged separation. The man he was approaching now was not what one could call a friend, but more like someone he wanted to know better after a forced separation of twenty-six months. Then he came face to face with him.

'How are you, monsignor?' asked Gort.

'Very well, thank you,' replied the bishop in his modelled voice.

'It was a very nice ceremony. I think you should have a replica in Gozo,' continued the bishop.

'Yes. We'll do that next Sunday.'

They continued talking, and the long shadows of separation seemed to melt away. In their talk about the situation, and the Gozitans' feelings and contribution towards the war there was open and honest exposition of facts which Gort knew to be true, and this took measure of the bishop ... of his heart and spirit, of the thoughts that moved behind his steady eyes. Could he have taken too much for granted after all? As he had done with the wheat that came with the convoy?

While history was being written in Malta on that Sunday, a different but none the less important epic which concerned Malta was being enacted elsewhere. After his flying visit to North Africa on 4th August, Churchill had relieved General Auchinleck, Alexander was put in command, while General Gott was placed in charge of the 8th Army. However, the following day Gott was killed and his place was taken by General Montgomery. The British were then standing firm on the Alam Halfa position, which Montgomery began fortifying in an attempt to contain the expected German attack. This would have probably been launched before had there not been the successful revival of attacks on shipping carrying provisions from Sicily, particularly fuel and ammunition. This was rightly attributed to the RAF in Malta, now given new life by the Santa Maria convoy. The submarines from the island were again going on a spree as if to capitalise on the successes by the 1st Flotilla operating first from Alexandria and now from Beirut which had since May, whilst they were lying dormant and dispersed, sunk about 33,000 tons of enemy shipping. '

Rommel had hoped for a respite but this did not come, and, as Ciano entered in his diary, Italian ships and tankers continued to be preyed upon by British planes and submarines from Malta. It was a desperate move by Rommel when he launched his awaited attack on 31st August, which soon fizzled out when he ran out of petrol, and he began withdrawing three days later. It wasn't the British or Montgomery which made him do this; but the offensive operations from Malta, which four months before Kesselring had stated was neutralised.

It was Malta too which had starved of fuel and petrol the two parachute divisions he got as reinforcements, which had been earmarked for its invasion. The name of Malta became a German and Italian household name. The island was also being blamed for the dysentery epidemic which became rife amongst forces in Africa, attributed to lack of staple food being prevented from reaching them. A casualty of the epidemic was Rommel himself, making it necessary for him to fly to Germany for treatment.

While Rommel went to Germany, Gort went to Gozo for the George Cross ceremonial there. Both had Malta on their mind, the former how to get round it to get his convoys through, the latter how to exploit the new friendship that had suddenly sprung up between him and the bishop for the island's benefit. But leaders must have regretted something from their past — Rommel, his obstinacy about proceeding to Egypt after Tobruk, thus preventing the invasion and possible occupation of the island, Gort thought of the long months of separation from bishop Gonzi, because of what he had been told about him, which he was now doubting. Both of them found a possible solution of their problems, Rommel, before going into hospital at Semmering, received the Führer's assurance that Africa would be given all the support needed —Gort, on the other hand was converted to a new belief in Monsignor Gonzi and felt that he could help him in the serious problem that had beset him. There was a third party however who was now in dead earnest about Malta. General Montgomery, supported by Alexander, had prevailed on Churchill to launch his offensive on 23rd October, for which he wanted absolute air superiority. Sir Arthur Tedder, the Air Commander-in-Chief in the Middle East, could now count on 96 operational squadrons at his disposal, including 13 American, 13 South African, one Rhodesian, 5 Australian, 2 Greek, one French and one Yugoslav, amounting to 1,500 aircraft. Of this, 1,200 based in Egypt and Palestine were to aid the 8th Army's attack. But much more important for the issue of the battle was the indirect and strategic action to strangle the Panzer Armee's sea arteries of supply. This could only be undertaken efficiently by Malta's aircraft and submarines. During the month of September, through Malta's increased intervention nearly a third of the supplies shipped this way were sunk, while many vessels were forced to turn back. This situation was to be maintained, if the offensive was to succeed.

But as we leave the three generals to their own problems, Malta was for the first time since January 1941 taking it easy. With the bread ration increased for men, and a small improvement in Victory Kitchen meals, made possible by the good tomato crop in August, the population sensed that a step in the right direction had been made, which went far to strengthen the prevalent belief that the Santa Maria Convoy had been the turning point in their plight. Given this beginning, the Maltese were soon to take initiative in recuperation. But even in such efforts one could not help but notice the war effort element in their midst. The officers and men of the convoy ships, but now still in Malta, found themselves the mascots of the people and were made the guests of those who could afford it. They were feasted in Gozo, dined in the bombed 'Casino Maltese', the aristocratic club in Valletta, still retaining its Italian name, taken round on tours of what could still be seen. They were also invited to private houses. Each of the convoy ships was adopted by one of the Royal Artillery Regiments of the Light Anti-Aircraft Brigade which arranged sports meetings, concerts and more sight-seeing trips. A small Merchant Navy Entertainment Committee, obviously dormant for a long time, now sprang into action and fixed up boxing tournaments, dances, swimming parties, cricket and ball matches. The 'Raffians', a RAF Concert party put up a special show for the honoured guests, and the venue was the Manoel Theatre in Valletta, which was built in 1731, and miraculously was still standing. Marquis Scicluna, a wealthy philanthropist and owner of many palaces opened his doors to the gallant men, and his Dragonara Palace (now housing the Casino) was host to many of the convoy's seamen.

With the local soldiers now being given a few days of merited leave they could grasp the lost threads of family life. The workers began going more happily to their bleak but still efficient dockyard; the wives again were engrossed with the unceasing scrubbing and polishing, attending to their children, and were only preoccupied with the difficulties of procuring food. It was the first time since March that they could do so.

Fredu Schembri of Vittoriosa, had now resigned himself to never getting his parachutist. He put away his rifle and steel helmet, and began to miss parades. All his time he devoted to his shop, which he opened again, even if to provide him with the place and time to meet people, because he had nothing to sell. Anglu Fenech and Carmelo Vella now had a lot of spare time to be away from their searchlight position, and both of them found a girl, Anglu to have her replace his sister, Carmelo to match his newly found spirit. Belin, the old wine seller now began to have soldiers back in his shop, and having managed to get some looted service rum he mixed it with local wine which gave his clients many hours of gaiety and hangovers. Manwela, the mother of twelve, had two more sons in the service now, but both were stationed in Malta and in touch. However, she still worried about the others who were away. She prayed for them every hour of every day, and trusted in God. After all he had brought the convoy in. The safety of her husband and sons was a small thing, compared to that. John had become a sergeant now, and he had too many things to keep him busy to spare another thought to solving the mystery of Mary, the girl who had disappeared. After all, there would be many girls about when the war was over, and from the look of things it would soon be over.

It was hard for anyone not knowing the Maltese not to think that they had slackened their pace.

With the coming of October attempts were made to reopen schools after what had been too long a holiday, and the churches, where they were still standing, began holding the usual October devotions, now that there was more time for them. Only the RAF and the submarines seemed to have maintained their warlike operations as they did not cease their attacks on enemy shipping, which wrought havoc with Hitler (following his promise to Rommel) and Kesselring's plans.

There seemed to be no better time for Gort to solve the problem that had for the last time been worrying him. The men with the stock lists had juggled well enough to ensure a more balanced diet following the August convoy, but after his rush to increase the bread ration, they had their efforts torpedoed where wheat was concerned. The *Welshman* had done another trip ferrying supplies, and now she was also joined by her sister ship *Manxman*, to run the blockade alone and sometimes escorted by destroyers. But whatever stores they carried, there was never any wheat. So, while other foodstuffs were expected to last till December, wheat would definitely finish well before then. So soon after having obtained relief, Gort had to be talking again of a target date. Lately he had been having some friendly chats with Monsignor Gonzi from which he derived a lot of satisfaction and, in certain cases, even illumination. He could perhaps at their next meeting mention this point.

But this decision had to wait like many others because of Kesselring. Pressed by Hitler and his obligations towards Rommel, and aware of the offensive planned by Montgomery, he turned to Malta again. This time there were no preparations to make. He had the remnants of his II Flieger Korps composed of old hands at the game now with years of operational experience, and putting the unreliable Italians aside, he launched a heavy assault.

It began on the night of Saturday, 10th, October when several German bombers flew over Malta and tried to attack targets by the light of parachute flares. The anti-aircraft guns went immediately into action, and the same old story began all over again, This time however, the three raids that developed were more spectacular with the added light from the flares. In the early dawn of Sunday the 11th, another formation left for Malta. This time it gave the chance to Air Vice Marshal Park to put into operation the new plan of action he had asked his pilots to adopt by going out to meet the raiders before they reached the island. The German formation, composed of a small number of bombers and a strong force of fighters, was surprised by the Spitfires miles away from Malta, which split into two formations, one attacking the bombers and the other tackling the fighters. For the first time ever, one third of the bombers turned back to their base losing one in the process, while the others got mauled by the time some of them reached Malta and dropped their bombs. But in their characteristic determination which we know so well, the Germans continued mounting their attacks by coming back in always increasing formations trying to get to the airfields where there were the bombers which were causing Rommel such havoc with his convoys.

The climax was reached with the last raid at dusk when the

Germans flew over from all directions hoping to confuse the defences. As the sun sunk lower and the day wore to its end the gunners, who had had no time to stretch their limbs, went into action again. They had lost count of the planes they hit that day, and as they fired, more and more planes came over with Spitfires weaving their way amongst them and their pilots risking life and limb from the barrage. As bombs shrieked down, followed by explosions and the rumbling of falling masonry the people in the shelters went back to their days of May. This was definitely something bigger. They cuddled together and prayed, but said nothing more. That was as far as they could go, as they had been stupefied by shock. Had they been outside they would have concluded that there was more an element of vengeance in the attacks than that of tactic. The earth was not torn by the exploding bombs, but dug out by the armour-piercing fuses, then thrown into the air with the explosion and allowed to fall burying everything beneath it. 22 were killed that day, and 47 injured.

The slack feeling induced by the lull had disappeared with the first attack, and any doubts there might have been about the alertness of the defences soon faded. In the first 24 hours of the assault the enemy had lost 15 planes shot down, and 30 so damaged as not likely to have reached their base. In the second 24 hours then, there were 24 shot down, and 41 seriously damaged. British losses were 3 Spitfires. On Monday the 12th, attacks continued in the first light of dawn when 15 Junkers 88, escorted by 50 Messerschmitt 109s approached Malta in two waves. The Spitfires were out to meet them in their new 'Go out and get them' tactic, and before they could reach the coast had shot down 4 Junkers and 1 Messerschmitt, losing one Spitfire in the process. At 8 a.m. then, another attack by 18 Junkers 88, and 50 Messerschmitt 109s with some Macchi 202 were also met miles away from Malta. 3 Junkers, 1 Messerschmitt and 1 Macchi were shot down, while another 12 were seriously damaged. Bombs were dropped and the formation returned back to its base without dropping a single bomb on the intended target. One Spitfire was lost, but now with the new tactic being used, air sea rescue launches began patrolling the sea where battles were taking place and began giving good results in rescuing pilots. At 11 a.m. and again at 1.45 p.m. formations of enemy aircraft were intercepted as far as a few miles south of Sicily, and were again harassed. On that Monday in fact, twelve Junkers 88s, ten Messerschmitt 109s, two Macchis, and one RE 201 were destroyed to the loss of five Spitfires.

The fact that there was no damage to civilian quarters in these raids as much as those of April and May was due to the now bigger force of Spitfires, and Air Vice Marshal Park's new tactic of intercepting the enemy before reaching the island. But there is no doubt that attacks were this time more concentrated with the same target, which was generally an airfield to be incessantly attacked in consecutive raids. This October Blitz was also characterized by the large number of enemy aircraft that were destroyed in such a short time, and this was having a telling effect on Kesselring. In the continued blitz on Tuesday, 13th October, as the island had to submit to another continuous day of attacks, 18 enemy aircraft were shot down, not counting the many others which had to turn back with missing parts or injured or dead crews.

During this day, the 1,000th plane to be shot down on Malta was brought down by a Spitfire. An unofficial source attributed this aircraft to an American pilot flying a Spitfire, Squadron Leader J.J. Lynch of California, but the Air Ministry's official attribution went to Canadian ace fighter pilot, Pilot Officer George Frederick 'Screwball' Beurling, already holding the DFC, and DFM and bar at the age of 21.

On the following day, Wednesday 14th October, out of 12 bombers and 11 fighters shot down, besides another 30 damaged during another persistent blitz, Pilot Officer Beurling shot down 1 bomber and 4 fighters, after which he was shot down himself. But he baled out by parachute, and was picked up by an Air Rescue Launch, none the worse for his ducking.

Although Kesselring later maintained in his papers that he had to stop the attacks after three days, because of the heavy losses that were being incurred by his forces, the blitz continued until Monday 19th October. But on this last day, the enemy and indeed most of the Maltese who had by now been watching the aerial combats which they knew they would never have the chance to see again, had the chance of a lifetime to see at its best an exposition of the coordination infused by Air Vice Marshal Park in his squadrons. The battle began at dusk when the enemy sent in a fighter bomber formation, and a squadron of Spitfires went out as usual to meet it half way. Whilst they were intercepting, three bomber formations were sent over to deliver attacks from the East, West, and North. It was obvious that the enemy was banking on having the Spitfires being engaged until darkness fell when the bombers would reach the island. Another squadron was scrambled to meet the bombers from the west and smashed up the formation with a head on attack, compelling most of them to jettison their bombs in the sea. Then the same squadron rushed back across the island just in time to meet the formation coming from the east and dealing with it just as drastically just as darkness was falling. The formation from the north was then just coming in, safely thinking that they had done it in that the Spitfires would not engage it in darkness, but they soon found a squadron of night fighters which had scrambled to meet them. Only one tenth of the aircraft in the four formations managed to cross the coast, when they were then taken in hand by the anti-aircraft artillery.

This was the end for Kesselring. Although small raids were to continue, mostly by Italians, he was no longer going to send any of his elite Luftwaffe forces against Malta, which, he admitted, had considerably refined its method of defence. It was also a battle in which the Germans used their improved radar apparatus, but Air Vice Marshal Park had a reply even to this by resorting to the dropping of silver paper which interfered with the enemy's radar beams and hampered his tactics for fighter operation and bomber protection.

I was unable to get exact statistics of enemy aircraft which were lost on their way back to base or arrived in a damaged condition, but the official statistics I have in hand speak very clearly. In that week's blitz in October 1942, the enemy had flown 1400 sorties against Malta, during which he lost 114 planes, and at least 200 of his best aircrew. British losses were 25 Spitfires, but 14 of their pilots were safe. It was without a doubt the most hectic time of the Battle of Malta, which until then had given the island 1660 air attacks, and 1386 people killed. The enemy had lost 1069 aircraft.

*

The shrieking and explosions of bombs stopped as suddenly as it had started, but there wasn't the talk and rejoicing that one would have expected. A blanket of silence seemed to have been dropped on everyone who had witnessed and taken part in the melee. Perhaps it had something to do with the way in which the assault had come, surprisingly, after all thoughts of war and air raids had been spent up over weeks of inactivity. Perhaps it had something to do with the assumption or taking for granted that with the August convoy the tide had turned, which was now shattered. But there was no time or occasion to find out the real reason, for one battle had stopped only to draw attention to another one which had been going on simultaneously with the other, and which now monopolized the arena. While the bombings and aerial combats aimed at stopping the demonic attacks by aircraft and submarines on the Axis convoys were going on and keeping everyone on their toes in fear of harm and death, these intruding demons were striking hard at every available target as if flouting the activity that was being generated to stop them. Now that the Germans had retired from the Malta skies never to blot them again, the search-light of attention was focussed on the hefty marauders of the sky and the sleek scorpions of the deep, and their activities. Just when the German's last iota of strength was oozing out on Malta on 18th October, the bombers from Luqa which were their target were out bombing Catania. Torpedo bombers from Hal Far were chasing enemy shipping near Lampedusa. Other aircraft were coordinating efforts with submarines *Safari, Utmost, Unbending, Unbroken* and *United* in attacking a convoy made of a tanker, 4 supply ships and 7 destroyers south of Pantellaria. Wellingtons, Blenheims, Beauforts, Swordfish and Marylands now monopolized the blue skies by day and star spangled darkness of night. Their noises, now sweet to any Maltese ear, filled the people with expectation, and they watched, listened and rejoiced. But they kept silent.

Then late in October, their silence was broken. Not by noise of aircraft or bomb explosion, but by the news of the heavy barrage by one thousand guns, with which Montgomery launched his offensive at El Alamein on 23rd October. As if to celebrate the occasion, Malta submarine *Umbra* met the large 8,670 tons supply ship *Amsterdam*, all festooned with tanks and motor transport being hurried to the Afrika Korps, and torpedoed it with gusto.

Montgomery's offensive broke the silence of indecision and shook the Germans to the core. It also caught Rommel with his pants down while convalescing in Austria, and after his substitute General Stumme died on the first day of the offensive, he had to fly to Africa immediately at Hitler's request to try and stem the British advance. That was the turning point in the Mediterranean, and Malta could now breathe more freely.

This was what Lord Gort told Bishop Gonzi in one of his heart-to-heart talks with him at that time. He had by now been taking him into his confidence, and the time had come to let him know of his wheat problem. So he called the bishop to his palace together with the man who held the stock lists — Mr Ward. In his usual way when he had to say something hot, Gort turned to the bishop and said, 'Your Grace, again I want to divulge something to you which I consider a top secret.'

The bishop did not say anything. He had been accustomed by now to hear those words from the Governor.

'Notwithstanding the good look of the situation, we are short of wheat, and what we've got could not last for more than a few months.'

'I beg your pardon, Sir,' said Ward, 'it's not a question of months, but of days. On paper my stocks made it a month, but I am not sure whether it will last that long.'

'Well, ' said Gort, 'what can we do? We cannot let the Maltese go hungry. We must find a way.'

It was now that the bishop spoke. 'May I say a word?' he said.

'Of course,' said Gort.

'I could find a remedy. In fact I am sure I can get you the wheat you want from Gozo.'

Gort looked at the bishop in amazement. He had all along been hoping he might help, but it had never occurred to him until now.

'Can you really do it?' he asked him.

'Of course,' said the bishop. 'It's the time of the harvest, and if I know the Gozitans they will have enough wheat, which they will not part from for anyone. But for me it will be different.'

The bishop was of course counting on the respect which he enjoyed in Gozo. He knew his people, as they knew him.

'I will do it, Excellency,' he continued, 'but on two conditions.'

'Well, what are they?' asked the Governor.

'The first condition is that this being as you said a top secret, I must be permitted to divulge the state of the situation to the Gozitans, if I am to persuade them.'

'All right,' said Gort, 'tell them what the situation is. Now what is your other condition?'

'You must provide transport, and of course petrol for me to go round. I am only allowed one can of petrol as a bishop, and it will not be enough for the amount of running I'll have to do.'

'You can have all the petrol you want,' Gort told him.

That was that. The following day the bishop returned to Gozo, and began to visit the farmers. They listened to him, and because he was their bishop, contributed some of the wheat they had stored. So that Malta could live. It wasn't much, maybe, but it was all they could spare. It was enough for the target date for wheat to reach that for other foodstuffs, aviation spirit, and ammunition, which was some time during the first week of December. Until then, fresh supplies had to come in. If they did not.......

But thoughts of disaster were quickly put aside with the run of spirit raising events that were happening. Rommel was on the retreat in front of Montgomery's pressure, then on November 8th, Operation Torch, the Allied landings in French North Africa began. The first thought that occurred was that this new front was bound to take priority in Kesselring's list. There it was again, no one could now take the Germans for granted. But even if the Luftwaffe in Sicily was going to be fully occupied with French North Africa and relax in its attention to Malta's blockade, there had to be convoys. As if somebody was thinking that Malta would be forgotten in the tide of new events. But how could it be? If the island had stepped out of the limelight because of the end of air bombardments, it had moved into a new prominent position of now being the attacker instead of the defender. The submarines continued without stop with their attacks on enemy shipping, while Air Vice Marshal Park had by now increased his air force to 200 first line aircraft, half of which were heavy and medium bombers, and the rest Spitfires. The situation had become so demanding, that even Spitfires were now being used on offensive sorties, and rather than leaving all of them waiting for the enemy that would not come.

Park was now fitting the fighters with bombs and spare petrol tanks, and make them go and bomb Sicilian airfields. It was the legend of Mohammed repeating itself; since the enemy did not come, then let them go to him. The airfield accommodation had become too tight for them, and what was to follow. It was because of this need that a new airfield at Qrendi was constructed, and it was ceremoniously opened on 10th November by Lord Gort, with Air Vice Marshal Park landing the first aircraft in it.

There were bold tear-jerking speeches given on that day, both by Gort and Park. The latter finished his speech by saying that Malta had shown the world how a brave population could take heavy bombing. It was now going to show the enemy how hard it could hit back. Little did the audience listening to him think, that behind the smile on Park's face there were depressing thoughts about the supply aviation spirit available for his air force; there was only a four-week supply. That was his problem, and Gort had a similar one, with his target date for foodstuffs running out being 7th December.

Did they perhaps know there would be relief by then? Maybe they did. Or maybe not. Even if they did, who can foresee what can happen in war? Most of Kesselring's aircraft had been taken to Corsica to be nearer to the new front in French North Africa. His torpedo bombers were still in Sardinia. From both islands his planes could attack any convoy for Malta, as they had always done.

But Park's smile must have meant something else. From the 11th his aircraft taking it in turn began a round the clock offensive against the enemy. One after the other, Sicilian airfields, aircraft, ships and military offensive installations, were hammered. Once, twice or even three times in a day. News reached Malta every day of aircraft being intercepted and shot down, or burned in their airfields. Squadrons of Spitfires flew out every day to patrol the Sicilian channel, and returned only to be relieved by others. There was no let-up until 23rd November. On that day every available aircraft must have flown out on one sortie or more. A round the clock pounding was given to Sicilian airfields, with the last raid taking place during the night. When a wing of Spitfires went out for its last watch at dusk, it returned forming an umbrella to four merchantmen which entered harbour. The long expected convoy had arrived. Safe and intact, and what's more — unmolested.

On that day there had only been thirteen days of supplies of foodstuffs, ammunition and aviation spirit. But now, it was all being replenished. More important than this was the evident fact that the blockade was over. The Siege of Malta was lifted.

CHAPTER SIXTEEN

The Nightmare is Over

The nightmare was over. At last one would be able to go about his life as one's self, without having to worry whether the next bomb might have one's number on it, or where one's next meal was coming from. Although there was no noise in the rejoicing, it could be seen in every look, word or action. The message was delivered. Malta had won through, and the toast was Air Vice Marshal Sir Keith Park. He was awarded the KBE on 23rd November, and there had never been a more welcome decoration. It was most of all a time for reflection which momentarily placed every other thing aside. It had even put out of the limelight the trial of Carmelo Borg Pisani, the Italian spy that had landed in Malta five months back. His trial came to an end on 18th November and he was sentenced to death for espionage. He was hanged ten days later.

As one might have expected, the biggest impact of the lifting of the siege was on the food situation. Malta was still at war, and could still expect air attacks. Her soldiers and gunners retained their places, and so did the Passive Defence personnel. Indeed alerts were still prevalent, but most of them did not materialise. When they did, they were only by single or a few aircraft which did not worry anybody. But there was never a single moment when the island's alertness was relaxed. The food front, however was a different thing. The population had suffered and it was only right that it should expect early relief. Lord Gort must have been in two minds. He could increase rations, hoping the four ships would be followed by more and that they would not be just a flash in the pan. Or he could stick to the strict rationing a little longer. He chose a middle way. A slightly increased scale of rations was made, but graduated to take full effect by January 1943, by which time he hoped the situation would be better. He had apparently learned the lesson of the August convoy. As things were, he needed not have worried. The lifting of the siege was no fluke, and within the next month nine further merchantmen with provisions and aviation spirit reached Malta. They came as a confirmation of the now open routes from both Gibraltar and

Alexandria, and more than this of the fact that Britain, particularly the person the Maltese called 'The Brain' who had to decide what and how much supplies had to be sent to Malta, had the island's welfare at the top in their priority lists. Lord Gort did not waste time in having this reflected in Malta by increasing further the bread ration for men from ½ ratal for five days of the week to 5/8 ratal (17½ ounces) daily. Other increases were made in sugar, fats, and cheese as from December, while a much appreciated special issue of sugar, flour, beans and dried fruit was made for the approaching Christmas. Victory Kitchens now became optional, and anyone could opt to have his full rations and fend for himself, rather than having to queue up and take the national menu. Before Christmas the RAF was strengthened with the latest type of Mosquito aircraft which was destined to take an integral part in the offensive action that had began and was never to stop from Malta's airfields.

In January 1943 it seemed that with the battles won on both the air and the food fronts the situation was well in hand and that Malta could now look for better times. But arguing in this way would not be taking into consideration the years of famine and hardships the population had been labouring under. The lack of food, hygienic facilities and other factors required for a normal living must have taken its toll on the Maltese population seeing the birth of the new year. The disease of scabies which had made an appearance months back, was now still rife, and no amount of sulphur would placate it. Everywhere one looked in those days, was bound to see a scratching dance, with people unknowingly scratching all parts of their body, sometimes with humorous albeit desperate motions. And they would scratch until they break the skin and bring blood out of their system, without ever managing to get to the source of it all, getting lifelong body marks for all their trouble. But that was the most one could get. Unlike the case of Acute Poliomyelitis, or Infantile Paralysis as it is called in layman's language, that began to stalk the population in the first weeks after the lifting of the siege. This disease was a killer, and where death was avoided the sufferer was more likely than not maimed for life. This was a new terror that was suddenly facing Malta in that January of 1943. It was worse than the most devilish of enemy aircraft because there were no guns or planes to check it, deadlier than bombs as no shelter could be provided against it. Because it came in silence and hidden, it was a coward killer, and most of its victims were the young. It might have been a malevolent coincidence, but no one could help attributing it to the malnutrition or other conditions the people had to live under which produced or harboured the responsible virus. No one could say it wasn't so, because nothing was known of the disease. So, while cinemas and places of entertainment which were open throughout the blitz were now being closed to discourage crowds being together under one ceiling, the disease was rampant, and those who one or two years before had survived the shaking in their mother's womb by the exploding life around them, were now to face death or maiming for life by this new merciless terror.

Today, there are the blind, the dead, the legless, the handless or those who are similar reminders of the terrible days of the battle of Malta. There are also the cripples who are a living monument of those days, when, even though young of age and mind, they were also required to give their limbs in a sacrifice to the fight Malta was going through.

Even this suffering the Maltese took with their now character-istic courage and forebearance, and as Britain and the rest of the free but stricken world continued to shower praise and admiration on small Malta, they began to realise more than ever before the sense of service, of participation and endeavour which would be so deeply needed in the new life they were trying to make. They were now discovering that it was not only Malta that needed them, but they who needed her. They needed Maltese simplicity and courage; their trust and determination. Above all, they needed the consciousness it had given them of a God believing world deeper and more real than that which had been theirs, and had made Malta emerge victoriously from two deadly sieges in a lifetime. But this last siege, which had wrought havoc to the island, made ruins of its churches, palaces and beautiful buildings, killed 1597 of its people and seriously injured 1818, some of them maimed for life, with another 1889 lightly injured, had not taken her to the end. Unlike the Great Siege of 1565, this modern epic had given Malta strength, and rather than falling down exhausted from the ordeal, she had thrown everything into the battle that was still to be won. The non-stop onslaught was now going the opposite way, and the blows were being delivered, every day and every night throughout the weeks that were now running fast. When Tripoli fell to the Eighth Army on 23rd January 1943, it marked a milestone in the fierce battle in which Malta was at the front.

The Regia Aeronautica delivered its last air raids on Malta on 26th February 1943, with one plane approaching the island before daybreak without crossing the coast, and a few fighters in the evening which flew away fast without giving chance to the anti-aircraft batteries to engage them. Humorous till the end Italian bulletins stated on the following day that the harbour of Valletta had been bombed, but indeed this was the last Italian breath in trying to put out the glowing embers of two years nine months back which had now fanned into an inferno. Nicola Malizia, the Italian historian of the Italian war on Malta, however, concludes his history here, by saying that Malta had definitely won the war.

One might have expected that with the stopping of Italian raids Maltese efforts would slacken. But they did not. There was more to be attained, to which the Maltese now channelled their endeavours and prayers. And this unbelievable fire which rather than being spent was raging brighter and fiercer drew more the admiration of the world. It seemed that people had to see to believe and there was a flow of visitors to the island as if to see for themselves that the legendary story they had been hearing was in fact true. Admirals Cunningham and Harwood, Archbishop Spellman of New York, and Air Marshal Lord Trenchard were the torch bearers to King George VI who followed on 20th June.

The sun rose in a fiery splendour on that day on a busy ant-like community. From the early hours shopkeepers were folding their shutters back, and women carrying out their shopping so that they could hurry to find a place of vantage on the bastions at the harbour. It was now no longer an empty harbour as it had been for many months, and the many pinnaces fleeting from ships to shore brought back the nostalgic look of the old days. When the hour was close there was not a single empty space on the bastions and the jetties, and as the first destroyers entered harbour there was the murmuring of the thousands, which broke out into mighty continuous cheering as the cruiser *Aurora* slowly swung in towards the harbour entrance with the white-dressed figure of the King standing on the bridge, which everybody could see, saluting and acknowledging the welcome by the island to which a year back he had awarded the George Cross.

The place of honour at the landing place was justly given to the Royal Malta Artillery, the regiment to whom the King had graciously accorded his Colonelcy in Chief, and it provided the salute. At a signal from the bell of Fort St Angelo then, a general salute broke forth, not by the conventional guns, but by the church bells of Vittoriosa, Cospicua, Senglea and Valletta, the four beleaguered cities round the harbour, as if to show that

notwithstanding the beating they had taken they were still alive
and kicking. The harbour resounded to the cheering from the
people on the bastions, the men on the warships, and the hundreds
who had filled the harbour in their coloured *dghajsas*. At the
Governor's Palace the King then carried out his first duty and
presented Lord Gort with his Field Marshal's Baton. The most
spectacular presentation made by Lord Gort on that day was
doubtlessly that of Monsignor Gonzi, the Bishop of Gozo.

'He has in his own time saved Malta, Your Majesty,' said Lord
Gort to the King. Then he told him about the collection and
supply of wheat when it was most needed. The misconception
about the bishop's loyalty was also clarified, and as became known
later the King rectified matters with Britain which removed the
objections from the Vatican and brought Monsignor Gonzi the
merited appointment of Archbishop of Malta, after the death of
Dom Maurus Caruana, and later the honorary rank of Major
General in the British Army.

In going round Malta the King met and spoke to the people, and
everywhere he was met with tears of joy which also brought tears
to his eyes. The places he visited moved him, and he had an
understanding smile as he went through 'Petticoat Lane',
'Lambeth Walk' and other nostalgically called underground
tunnels at the dockyard where men had toiled and laboured under
continuous bombardment, as well as a moving tear when he was
greeted by the people of Senglea emerging out of their shelters and
shambles that were once their homes. He met the airmen at their
airfields, and the gunners at their batteries, where they were still
standing to, because as one of them said when asked, there was
still a battle to be won, and the enemy was not yet destroyed. The
King also showed interest in the shrines and chapels in the
batteries, and where these did not exist, in the open air altars
where mass and holy services were held for the gunners, with or
without air attacks.

And the King saw all and knew that never before had a
decoration been so justified as the George Cross he had awarded
to Malta.

*

With the King's departure, Malta turned back to her business of
war. The Germans and Italians had now been defeated in North
Africa which was occupied by the Allies. The RAF in Malta could

therefore concentrate its attacks on Sicily and Italy. There began to be daily tolls of enemy aircraft being shot down as in the days of the Malta Blitz, like 34 in a day, or 104 in four. But this time the war was being taken in the enemy's air, and his aircraft were being shot down in his country. Spitfires, Beaufighters and Mosquitos from Malta flew numerous sorties every day. The occasional alert that Malta had, could hardly be called a response to this. Indeed now everyone was feeling that the next step should be an attack on Europe, and although small movements before the King's visit could be interpreted as being in preparation for this, real and hurried preparations began after the King had left. An airfield which was being constructed in Gozo was ready in June, and an American anti-aircraft unit was posted to Gozo, where equipped with Bofors guns it was given the responsibility to defend the airfield. Planes began to be added to the RAF in Malta, which had now some 600 front line aircraft. Then, when convoy ships began to arrive the Maltese were surprised to see that they did not contain the usual provisions they had known them to carry. Instead they brought trucks, tanks, landrovers, amphibian vehicles, field guns and an assorted list of war materials which were certainly not needed for Malta. Warships began coming to Grand Harbour to stay, but besides the usual cruisers and destroyers there were now the new types of landing barges. They came in various sizes, small pontoon like to take a platoon, and the bigger ones taking a battalion, there were tank carrying craft, and others capable of taking a whole regiment.

Malta had never seen such a concentration of armour, but the people understood what it all meant. When the island's countryside became all covered with vehicles and armament dumps, and the harbours blocked with hundreds of small vessels and barges, then in the beginning of July, the men began to arrive. The prime regiments were from the British 8th Army which had defeated Rommel, but there were also regiments from the American 7th Army; the 51st Highland Division, battalions from West Africa and other colonial troops; Syrians, Mauritians, Basutos and Palestinians. It began to appear as if there were more of these soldiers than local people in the towns and villages.

After the men, came their leaders. General Dwight Eisenhower, General Harold Alexander, General Bernard Montgomery, and Admiral Andrew Cunningham. The air cover for the invasion was to be the responsibility of the Air Officer Commanding, Malta, Sir Keith Park.

During the few days that these forces were assembling and mixing with the Maltese in dances and other forms of entertainment, the dark clouds of war seemed to depart. But the skies were constantly patrolled by Spitfires while the anti-aircraft batteries were on a 24 hour watch. Spitfires and Beaufighters also flew out to sea on patrol where other convoys for the invasion armada had to assemble. To the east of Malta was coming the Eastern British Task Force under Vice-Admiral Sir Bertram Ramsay, comprising 795 vessels with 715 landing craft, together with ships carrying the 5th and 50th Divisions, all coming from Suez, Alexandria and Haifa. To the west the Western Naval Task Force was coming under Vice Admiral H. Kent Hewitt, comprising 580 vessels with 1,124 landing craft and two convoys carrying the 45th Infantry Division, the 1st Infantry and 2nd Infantry Division and 2nd Armoured Division. There was also another convoy bringing in the 1st Canadian Division.

The passages and assembly of this armada were achieved without any serious interference, and only 4 ships and 2 LSTs were lost to submarine attack. More commented upon was the fact that there was no intervention from enemy aircraft, due, without a doubt, to the continuous attacks carried out by Malta aircraft on enemy airfields.

The convoys assembled east and west of Malta on 9th July. On that same day the forces in Malta began to board their vessels and landing craft. The villages and outlying districts emptied themselves of troops, while columns of men and vehicles began moving along roads leading to the harbour. In the afternoon, the wind rose sharply, and by night the sea became rough posing a difficult decision to be taken by Admiral Cunningham and General Eisenhower. It raised doubts and misgivings also in the Maltese who were all watching these preparations going on, and feeling that this was going to be the last stage of Malta's fight, wanted it so much to go on with success. When the storm continued on the 10th, which was the date for the forces to leave, everything seemed still in the balance, and everybody watched the hours fly as night approached, since the force had to leave that night.

Admiral Cunningham remarked that the unfavourable weather conditions would probably send the Italians to their beds thinking that no invasion force would venture in that weather. But at zero hour, notwithstanding the rough sea and whistling wind, General Eisenhower gave the word. Go. And the mighty armada swooped on Sicily.

As destiny would have it, the invasion date of 10th July, 1943, was exactly a year after the other date of 10th July 1942, which had been the German date for Malta's invasion. But coincidence does not stop there.

When Sicily was invaded, General Student, the German Paratroop specialist who had won Crete, and who was also earmarked for Malta, proposed to launch a counter attack with his two paratroop divisions from where they were standing in Nimes. This was refused, but one of his divisions, the 1st Parachute Division was moved and dropped in Sicily where it took control of a bridge leading into the plain of Catania. When the British forces came up, by coincidence the German paratroopers had to face the 231st Brigade from Malta. They were the same troops that had awaited the Germans in the island a year back, when they never came. Now, they were keeping the appointment in Sicily, themselves.

*

As the Allied armies rolled on in Sicily, maps were checked, and airfields which were until some time before the hornets' nests from where the enemy had hit Malta, were crossed out as they fell. Each move and each day was pushing farther away the threat the island had been living with, and bringing closer the day of reckoning. It was a very hot summer, and many found a way through rusty barbed wire to reach the beaches for a swim. Because invasion was an impossibility, people were allowed through, as they were also allowed to move where until some weeks back they would have been trespassing. With a theatre of operations so close, naval ships were very often in the harbours, bringing back some of the nostalgic life of before, to boatmen and barmaids. The American gunners, now stationed in Malta, and airmen on furlough from the Gozo airfield brought what could be termed a boom to the reopened bars in Valletta's Strait Street, where women made up for lost time and money. As if in silent agreement to this state of relaxation the authorities themselves were also allowing the use of lights when unloading ships during the night.

Even with this general return to normality, there still seemed to hover over the people and their ruined cities an air of suspense as if confirming their feeling that the battle was not over yet. The inescapable logic of dwindling enemy potential was not deluding them into any hasty assumptions. After all, three years of war and siege had driven their lessons home.

If there was any justification needed for this sombre attitude, it came on 19th July, when against all expectations German aircraft delivered a night attack, causing damage and casualties. For the one and only time American anti-aircraft gunners went into action in defence of the airfield at Gozo. This was followed by a heavier one two days later, and after months of idleness anti-aircraft guns and night fighters went into action again, sharing between them the destruction of 6 enemy planes. This contre-temps however, did not affect the people and their attitude, and the new tension crackling in the air came only from the authorities as they harangued the population for taking things for granted. It was pointed out that most of the casualties during the surprise raids were due to shrapnel from anti aircraft shells, hitting those who failed to take cover. But now, no one seemed to be in mood for reasoning. It suddenly occurred to the authorities that they were now dealing with different people, who after all that they had been through, were now mesmerized into seeing their battle to its conclusion in the way they believed in. But rather than hope, theirs was now a conviction.

They might have been proved right when Mussolini resigned, and the more balanced General Badoglio took over Italian reins. But even this, although a step in the right direction, was not what they wanted. As they went about their somewhat easier daily life they kept pressing for the end, and this could be seen in their praying, while the grim look of determination never left their faces. It was with them at home, in the streets, and in their churches or shelter chapels. It was even with them as they followed their priests and monks in the processions that were now being held along streets full of ruins, to celebrate the feasts that fell during the weeks of August. Dust rose round them, in filthy enveloping clouds, and the dark robes of the clerical became white with dust, and uncomfortably hot with the sun's rays slamming down against them with the weight and ferocity of an August heat wave. But even this, did not keep anyone back. It was a sacrifice borne with the fortitude that now belonged to a new nation.

The memorable day of 15th August passed by with its memories of the convoy a year back, and all Maltese attention was now focussed on the next popular feast of 8th September, dedicated to the Lady of Victories which had signified the end of another siege by the Turks in 1565. But what was most significant was the fact that this was also the titular feast of Senglea, the most heavily bombed city. A good omen was spelt when Allied forces, having occupied all Sicily, crossed over to the Italian mainland on 3rd September, and as fate would have it, this coincided with the day when the RAF decided on its heart-warming gesture of presenting to the people of Malta the aircraft *Faith,* the sole survivor of the heroic Gladiator trio *Faith, Hope* and *Charity,* with which the Italian onslaught had been faced. It was a momentous ceremony, with Air Vice-Marshal Sir Keith Park reading the citation to a huge crowd with eyes all focussed on the sole naked plane lying on the spot of honour in Valletta, where a year back the George Cross had lain. The Chief Justice Sir George Borg received the aircraft on behalf of the people of Malta, and appropriately concluded his speech by saying that *Faith* would always remind the Maltese of the gratitude they owe to the Royal Air Force. In the few seconds of silence that preceded the clamorous applause in confirmation of those words, the people could only think of the 547 British aircraft that were lost in battle in the Malta skies, and the hundreds of brave pilots that died with them, apart from the other 160 aircraft destroyed on the ground. It was true that the enemy had paid for this with 1252 of his aircraft destroyed, and another 1051 probables. But this was not considered as just payment. Satisfaction would only be forthcoming with the successful conclusion of battle, which was being felt more than ever before, to be near.

All roads in Malta seemed to lead to Senglea on 8th September, and the city welcomed them with 80% of its buildings demolished and still lying along its hardly passable streets, and the other 20% of damaged and uninhabitable houses. The welcoming parties emerged from tunnels and caves beneath the rubble, or the shelters dug in the bastions. But this made no difference, and hosts and visitors joined ranks in the evening to follow the statue of the Our Lady of Victories in procession. With the procession past the once beautiful church built by the Knights of St John, now lying in ruins by German bombs, the statue was turned round to face the ruins. The minutes of silence that followed were significant in the message they seemed to convey.

When the procession and statue reached the church of St Philip, which was substituting as the parish church for the occasion, the multitude followed inside, and the church was soon crammed to its seams with humanity delirious with joy. Those who could not get in, stayed outside to join in the ceremony in spirit if not in body. As if at a signal, the murmuring crowd became silent, and for what appeared to be long moments there was not a sound or word to break the strangely silence-charged air. On the sea of faces lifted towards the statue there appeared a significant look, more of hope than determination, for that something which had after all not happened even though hearts had hoped till that very last moment. As the minutes ran out, they became a test for the people's fortitude and belief.

Then suddenly there was a slight commotion, and a ripple of a thousand voices. The parish priest, dressed up in his vestments was seen walking quickly, half running, to mount the pulpit. And all could see the light from the candles glistening on the tears that were flowing from his eyes. He was a staunch priest who had not wept in face of the desolation and death amongst his people; he had not wept when he had taken the King around his desolate city, and his conduct throughout the siege had been of great heroism which earned him an MBE. It must have been something heavy which made him weep that evening; and the congregation was hushed into silence, waiting to learn what it was.

Looking at the congregation from the pulpit, he could not utter his first words. His throat seemed to have been suddenly blocked with the tension that could be seen all over him. Then mastering himself he did it. 'My brethren,' he shouted. 'Rejoice. I've just had the news. Italy has surrendered.'

It took only one second for the message to drive in. Then the people inside and outside the church exploded into a roar of shouting. They were shouting with joy for a minute or two, then they all stopped, and everybody was weeping. I wept too, because I was there as well.

The bells of Senglea began to ring at that moment, and all the bells of Malta followed them as a sign of rejoicing and thanksgiving. Their sound became like sweet music, and its echoes from the devastation around brought feelings of pride and defiance.

Even in the scarce lights inside and outside the church, smiles could be seen on every face, replacing the grim looks of determination which disappeared for ever.

The Battle of Malta was over. To see for themselves, and seal the occasion for posterity, two days later people rushed to the bastions as they had always done to see and cheer convoys in. This time however, their eyes stood fixed on 28 warships of all types, lying at anchor off the island, silent and subdued. This time there were neither tears nor cheering, but only a deep sense of gratitude for those who lead them, and of pride in themselves, for having made this possible.

When after a week, the number of warships grew to 65, under the ever watchful eyes of Admiral Sir Andrew Cunningham, it was time to conclude, as the Admiral did with his message to the Admiralty that made history:

'Pleased to inform their Lordships that the Italian battle fleet now lies at anchor under the guns of the fortress of Malta.'

Bibliography

British Submarines at War 1939-1945, Alastair Mars; William Kimber & Co. London.

History of the Second World War, Basil H. Liddell Hart; Cassell & Co. London.

Inferno su Malta, Nicola Malizia; Ugo Mursia, Editore, Milan, Italy 1976.

La Decima Flottiglia Mas, Valerio J. Borghese; Aldo Garzanti Editore, Milan, Italy. Permission granted by Avv. Pierluigi Manfredonia, Rome, Italy on behalf of the heirs of the author.

Last Bastion, Eric Brockman; Darton, Longman & Todd Ltd. London.

Luftwaffe War Diaries, Cajus Bekker; Macdonald & Co. (Publishers) Ltd. London.

Malta, Sir Harry Luke (Edition 1963); George G. Harrap & Co. Ltd. London.

Memoirs of Field Marshal Kesselring; William Kimber & Co. London.

Ministry of Defence (Naval Historical Branch), London.

Rommel, Desmond Young; Wm. Collins & Sons, London.

Storja 78, edited by Dr Henry Frendo LL.D; Review by Department of History, University of Malta, Malta.

Times of Malta, 1939/43 Allied Malta Newspapers, Valletta, Malta.

Articles:

In Malta's Defence and *Invasion of Malta* by Capt. Joseph Wismayer. Published in *Sunday Times of Malia* of 19/11/78 and 17/12/78 respectively.

Index

Also in Hamlyn Paperbacks

Nigel Hamilton
MONTY
The making of a general 1887-1942

Alex Henshaw
THE FLIGHT OF THE MEW GULL
To Cape Town and back – a record-breaking feat of solo aviation

Alex Henshaw
SIGH FOR A MERLIN
The testing of the Spitfire

Alexander McKee
THE COAL-SCUTTLE BRIGADE
The heroic true story of the Channel convoys

Marvin Tokayer and Mary Swartz
THE FUGU PLAN
The astonishing untold story of the Jews in wartime Japan

Shelford Bidwell
WORLD WAR 3
A terrifying military projection founded on today's facts

Glenn B. Infield
HITLER'S SECRET LIFE
The scandalous reality of the Fuhrer's private world

Rupert Butler
THE BLACK ANGELS
The story of the Waffen-SS

REFERENCE

NON-FICTION

GENERAL
☐ The Chinese Mafia — Fenton Bresler — £1.50
☐ The Piracy Business — Barbara Conway — £1.50
☐ Strange Deaths — John Dunning — £1.35
☐ Shocktrauma — John Franklin & Alan Doelp — £1.50
☐ The War Machine — James Avery Joyce — £1.50

BIOGRAPHY/AUTOBIOGRAPHY
☐ All You Needed Was Love — John Blake — £1.50
☐ Clues to the Unknown — Robert Cracknell — £1.50
☐ William Wordsworth — Hunter Davies — £1.95
☐ The Family Story — Lord Denning — £1.95
☐ The Borgias — Harry Edgington — £1.50
☐ Rachman — Shirley Green — £1.50
☐ Nancy Astor — John Grigg — £2.95
☐ Monty:The Making of a General 1887-1942 — Nigel Hamilton — £4.95
☐ The Windsors in Exile — Michael Pye — £1.50
☐ 50 Years with Mountbatten — Charles Smith — £1.25
☐ Maria Callas — Arianna Stassinopoulos — £1.75
☐ Swanson on Swanson — Gloria Swanson — £2.50

HEALTH/SELF-HELP
☐ The Hamlyn Family First Aid Book — Dr Robert Andrew — £1.50
☐ Girl! — Brandenburger & Curry — £1.25
☐ The Good Health Guide for Women — Cooke & Dworkin — £2.95
☐ The Babysitter Book — Curry & Cunningham — £1.25
☐ Living Together — Dyer & Berlins — £1.50
☑ The Pick of Woman's Own Diets — Jo Foley — 95p
☐ Coping With Redundancy — Fred Kemp — £1.50
☐ Cystitis: A Complete Self-help Guide — Angela Kilmartin — £1.00
☐ Fit for Life — Donald Norfolk — £1.35
☐ The Stress Factor — Donald Norfolk — £1.25
☐ Fat is a Feminist Issue — Susie Orbach — £1.25
☐ Fat is a Feminist Issue II — Susie Orbach — £3.50
☐ Living With Your New Baby — Rakowitz & Rubin — £1.50
☐ Related to Sex — Claire Rayner — £1.50
☐ Natural Sex — Mary Shivanandan — £1.25
☐ Woman's Own Birth Control — Dr Michael Smith — £1.25
☐ Overcoming Depression — Dr Andrew Stanway — £1.50
☐ Health Shock — Martin Weitz — £1.75

POCKET HEALTH GUIDES
☐ Depression and Anxiety — Dr Arthur Graham — 85p
☐ Diabetes — Dr Alex D. G. Gunn — 85p
☐ Heart Trouble — Dr Simon Joseph — 85p
☐ High Blood Pressure — Dr James Knapton — 85p
☐ The Menopause — Studd & Thom — 85p
☐ Children's Illnesses — Dr Luke Zander — 85p

TRAVEL
☐ The Complete Traveller — Joan Bakewell — £1.95
☐ Time Out London Shopping Guide — Lindsey Bareham — £1.50
☐ A Walk Around the Lakes — Hunter Davies — £1.75
☐ Britain By Train — Patrick Goldring — £1.75
☐ England By Bus — Elizabeth Gundrey — £1.25
☐ Staying Off the Beaten Track — Elizabeth Gundrey — £2.95
☐ Britain at Your Feet — Wickers & Pedersen — £1.75

HUMOUR
☐ Don't Quote Me — Atyeo & Green — £1.00
☐ Ireland Strikes Back! — Seamus B. Gorrah — 85p
☐ Pun Fun — Paul Jennings — 95p
☐ 1001 Logical Laws — John Peers — 95p
☐ The Devil's Bedside Book — Leonard Rossiter — 85p

FICTION

GENERAL

☐ Chains	Justin Adams	£1.25
☐ Secrets	F. Lee Bailey	£1.25
☐ Skyship	John Brosnan	£1.65
☐ The Free Fishers	John Buchan	£1.50
☐ Huntingtower	John Buchan	£1.50
☐ Midwinter	John Buchan	£1.25
☐ A Prince of the Captivity	John Buchan	£1.25
☐ The Eve of St Venus	Anthony Burgess	£1.10
☐ Nothing Like the Sun	Anthony Burgess	£1.50
☐ The Memoirs of Maria Brown	John Cleland	£1.25
☐ The Last Liberator	John Clive	£1.25
☐ Wyndward Fury	Norman Daniels	£1.50
☐ Ladies in Waiting	Gwen Davis	£1.50
☐ The Money Wolves	Paul Erikson	£1.50
☐ Rich Little Poor Girl	Terence Feely	£1.50
☐ Fever Pitch	Betty Ferm	£1.50
☐ The Bride of Lowther Fell	Margaret Forster	£1.75
☐ Forced Feedings	Maxine Herman	£1.50
☐ Savannah Blue	William Harrison	£1.50
☐ Duncton Wood	William Horwood	£1.95
☐ Dingley Falls	Michael Malone	£1.95
☐ Gossip	Marc Olden	£1.25
☐ Buccaneer	Dudley Pope	£1.50
☐ An Inch of Fortune	Simon Raven	£1.25
☐ The Dream Makers	John Sherlock	£1.50
☐ The Reichling Affair	Jack Stoneley	£1.75
☐ Eclipse	Margaret Tabor	£1.35
☐ Pillars of the Establishment	Alexander Thynn	£1.50
☐ Cat Stories	Stella Whitelaw	£1.10

WESTERN — BLADE SERIES by Matt Chisholm

☐ No. 5 The Colorado Virgins	85p
☐ No. 6 The Mexican Proposition	85p
☐ No. 7 The Arizona Climax	85p
☐ No. 8 The Nevada Mustang	85p
☐ No. 9 The Montana Deadlock	95p
☐ No. 10 The Cheyenne Trap	95p
☐ No. 11 The Navaho Trail	95p
☐ No. 12 The Last Act	95p

NAME ....

ADDRESS ....

....

Write to Hamlyn Paperbacks Cash Sales, PO Box 11, Falmouth, Cornwall TR10 9EN.

Please indicate order and enclose remittance to the value of the cover price plus:

U.K.: Please allow 45p for the first book plus 20p for the second book and 14p for each additional book ordered, to a maximum charge of £1.63.

B.F.P.O. & EIRE: Please allow 45p for the first book plus 20p for the second book and 14p per copy for the next 7 books, thereafter 8p per book.

OVERSEAS: Please allow 75p for the first book and 21p per copy for each additional book.

Whilst every effort is made to keep prices low it is sometimes necessary to increase cover prices and also postage and packing rates at short notice. Hamlyn Paperbacks reserve the right to show new retail prices on covers which may differ from those previously advertised in the text or elsewhere.